Miss Kobayashi's DRAGON MAID

7

story & art by
Coolkyousinnjya

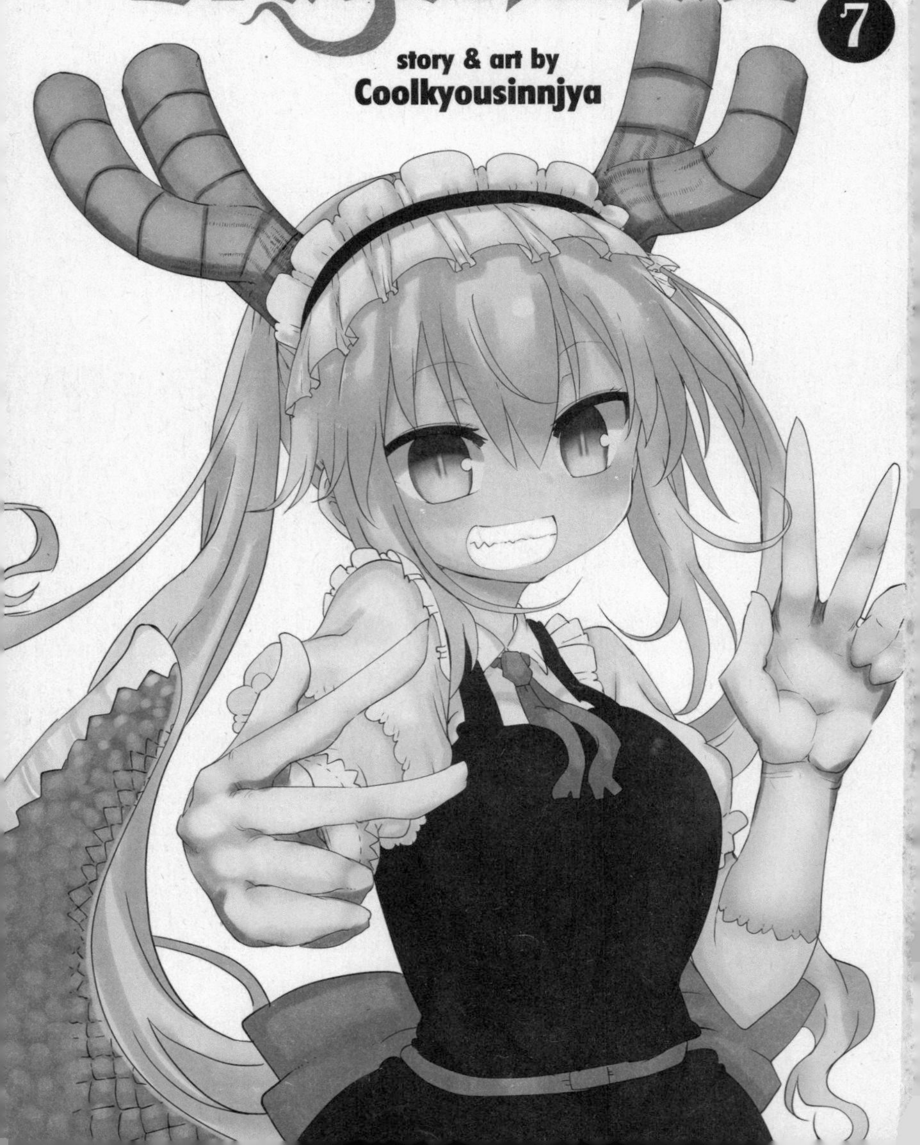

Miss Kobayashi's
Dragon Maid

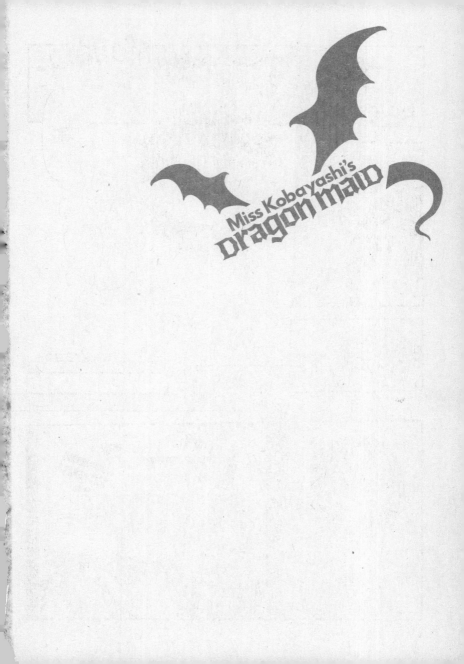

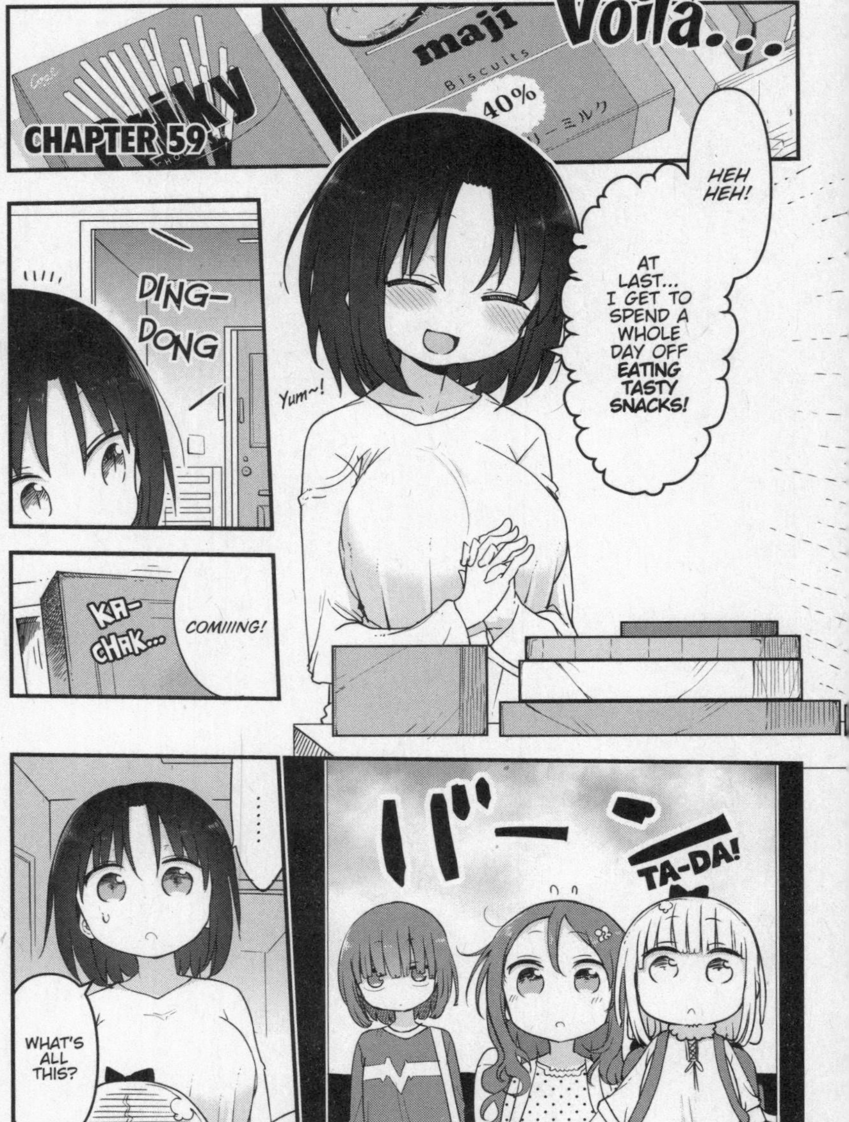
Voilà...
CHAPTER 59
maji
Biscuits
40%
HEH HEH!
AT LAST... I GET TO SPEND A WHOLE DAY OFF EATING TASTY SNACKS!
Yum~!
DING-DONG
COMIIING!
KA-CHAK...
TA-DA!
......
WHAT'S ALL THIS?

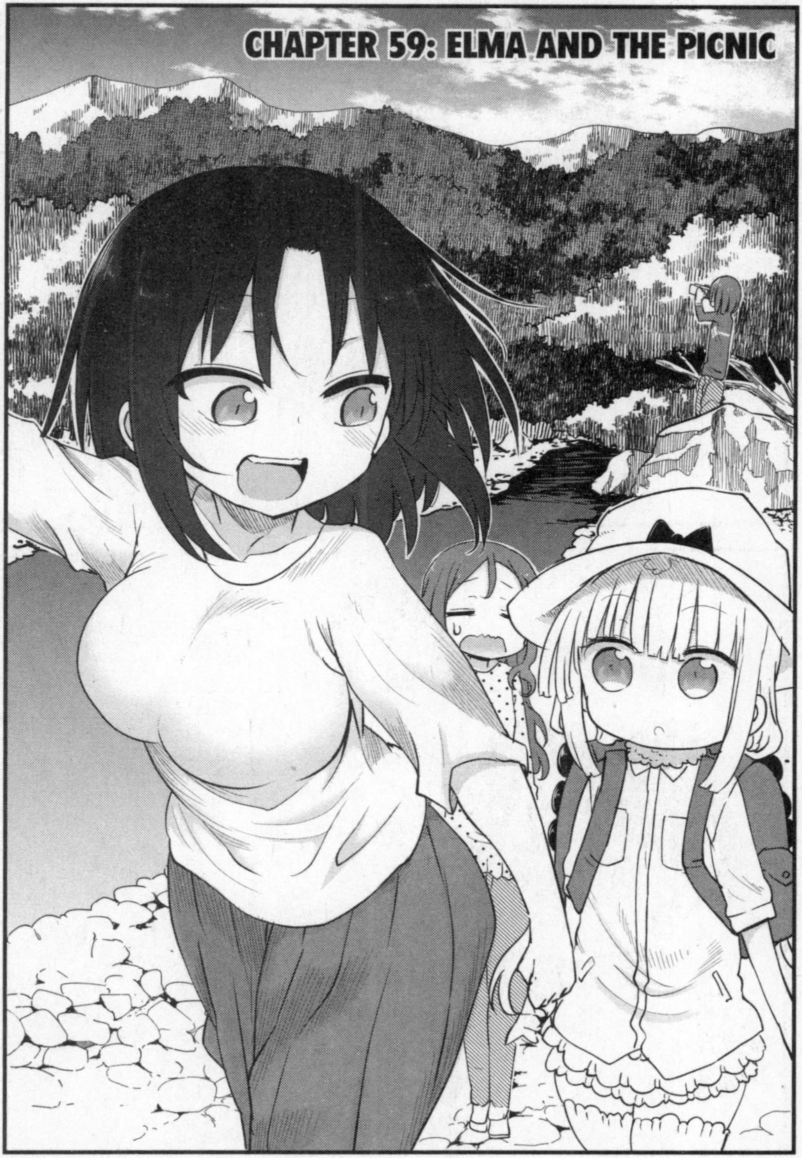
CHAPTER 59: ELMA AND THE PICNIC

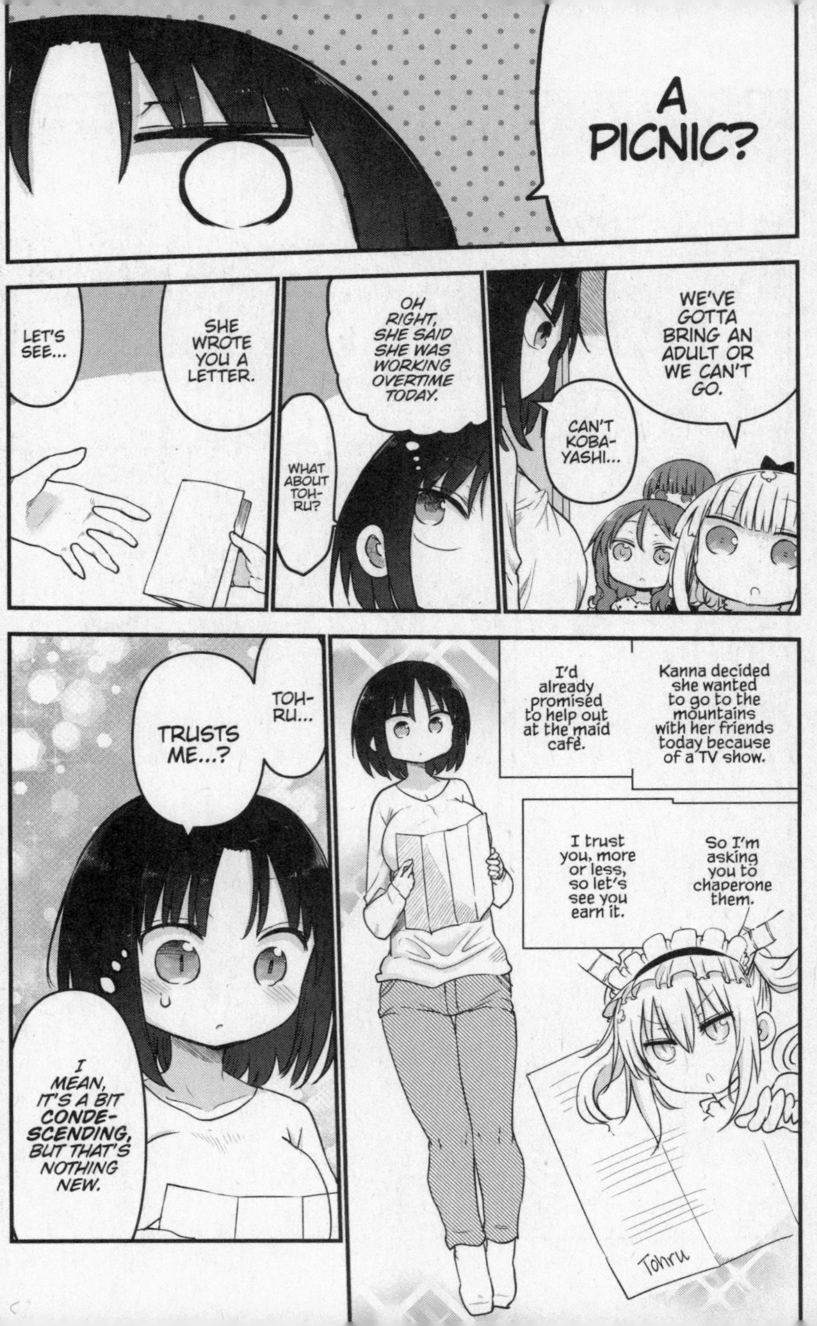
A PICNIC?
WE'VE GOTTA BRING AN ADULT OR WE CAN'T GO.
CAN'T KOBA-YASHI...
OH RIGHT, SHE SAID SHE WAS WORKING OVERTIME TODAY.
WHAT ABOUT TOH-RU?
SHE WROTE YOU A LETTER.
LET'S SEE...
Kanna decided she wanted to go to the mountains with her friends today because of a TV show.
I'd already promised to help out at the maid café.
So I'm asking you to chaperone them.
I trust you, more or less, so let's see you earn it.
Tohru
TOH-RU...
TRUSTS ME...?
I MEAN, IT'S A BIT CONDE-SCENDING, BUT THAT'S NOTHING NEW.

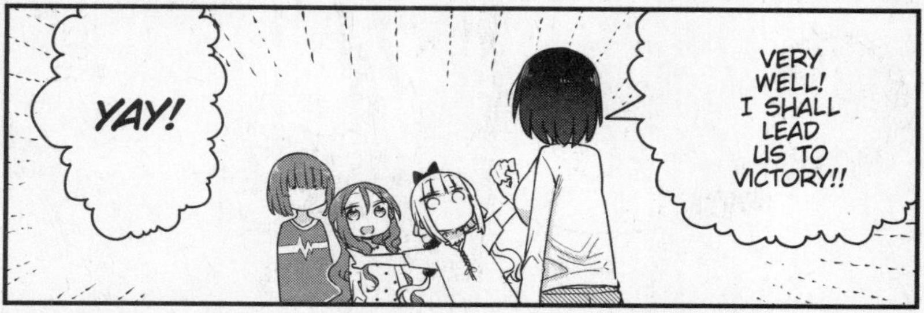
VERY WELL! I SHALL LEAD US TO VICTORY!!
YAY!
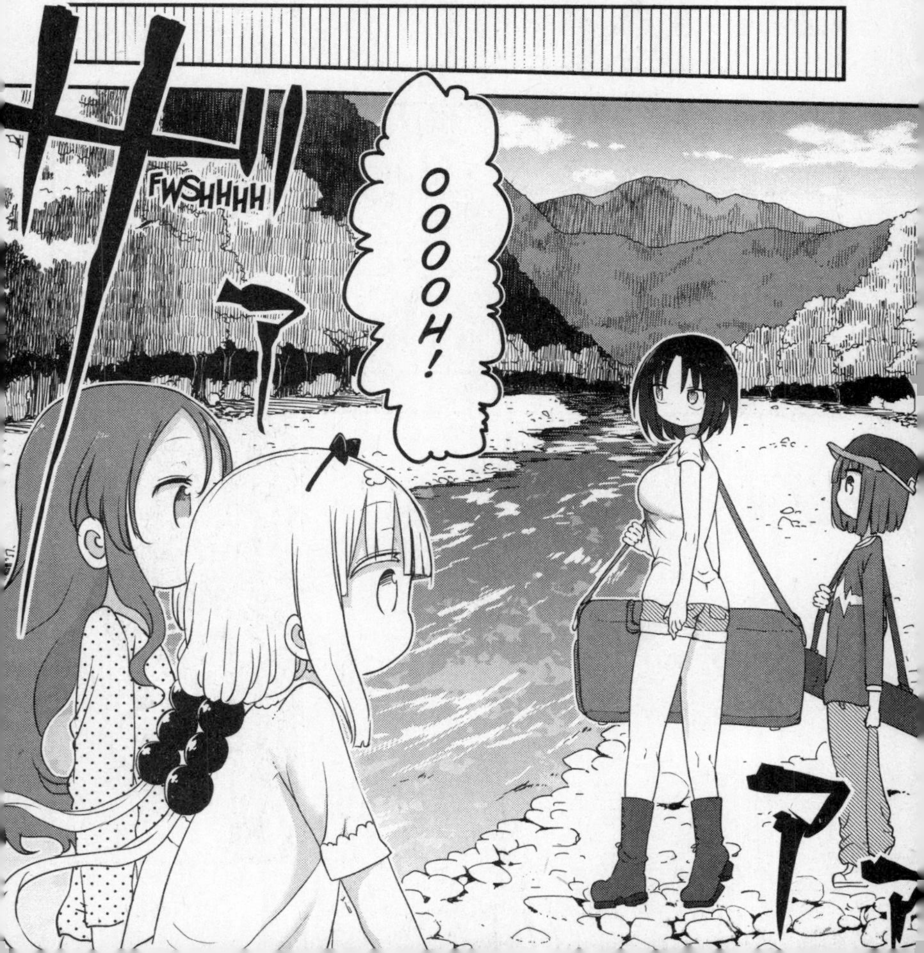
OOOOOH!
FWSHHHH

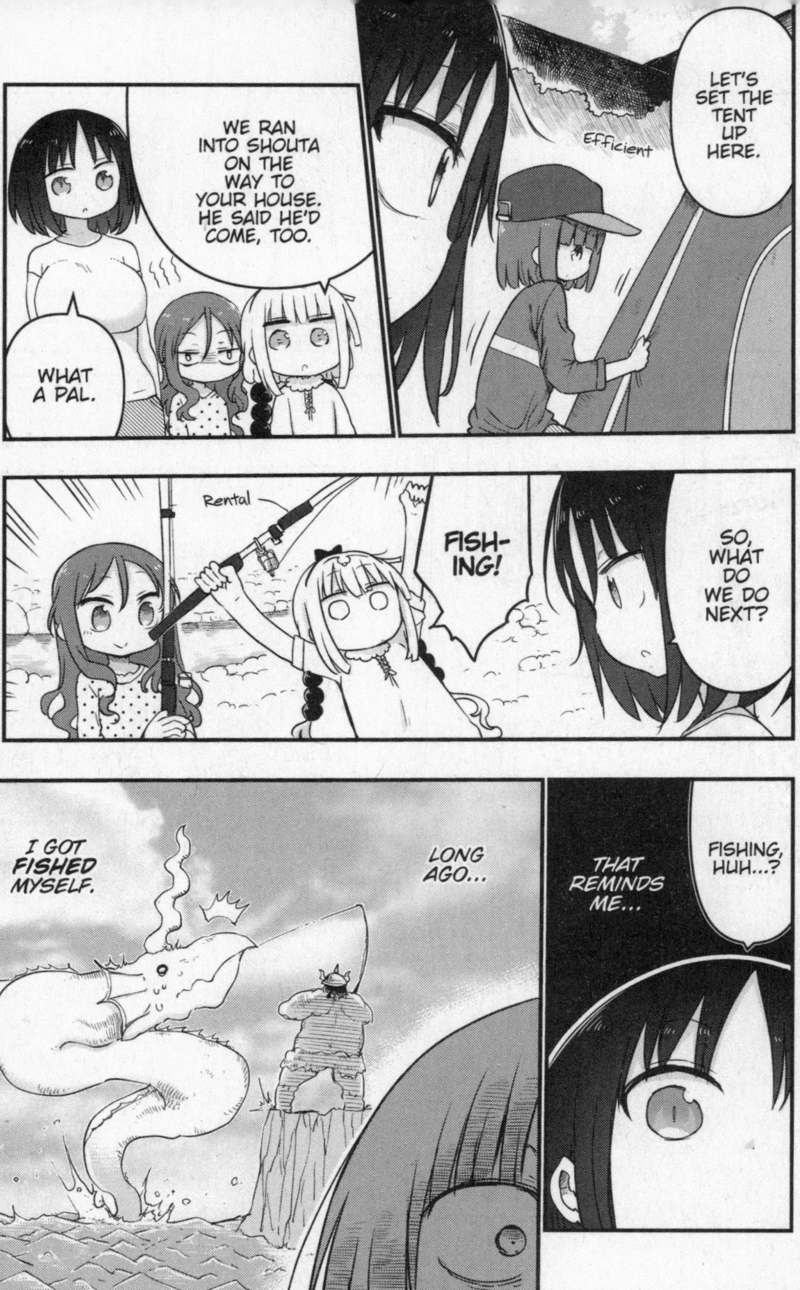

LET'S SET THE TENT UP HERE.
Efficient
WE RAN INTO SHOUTA ON THE WAY TO YOUR HOUSE. HE SAID HE'D COME, TOO.
WHAT A PAL.
SO, WHAT DO WE DO NEXT?
FISHING!
Rental
FISHING, HUH...?
THAT REMINDS ME...
LONG AGO...
I GOT FISHED MYSELF.

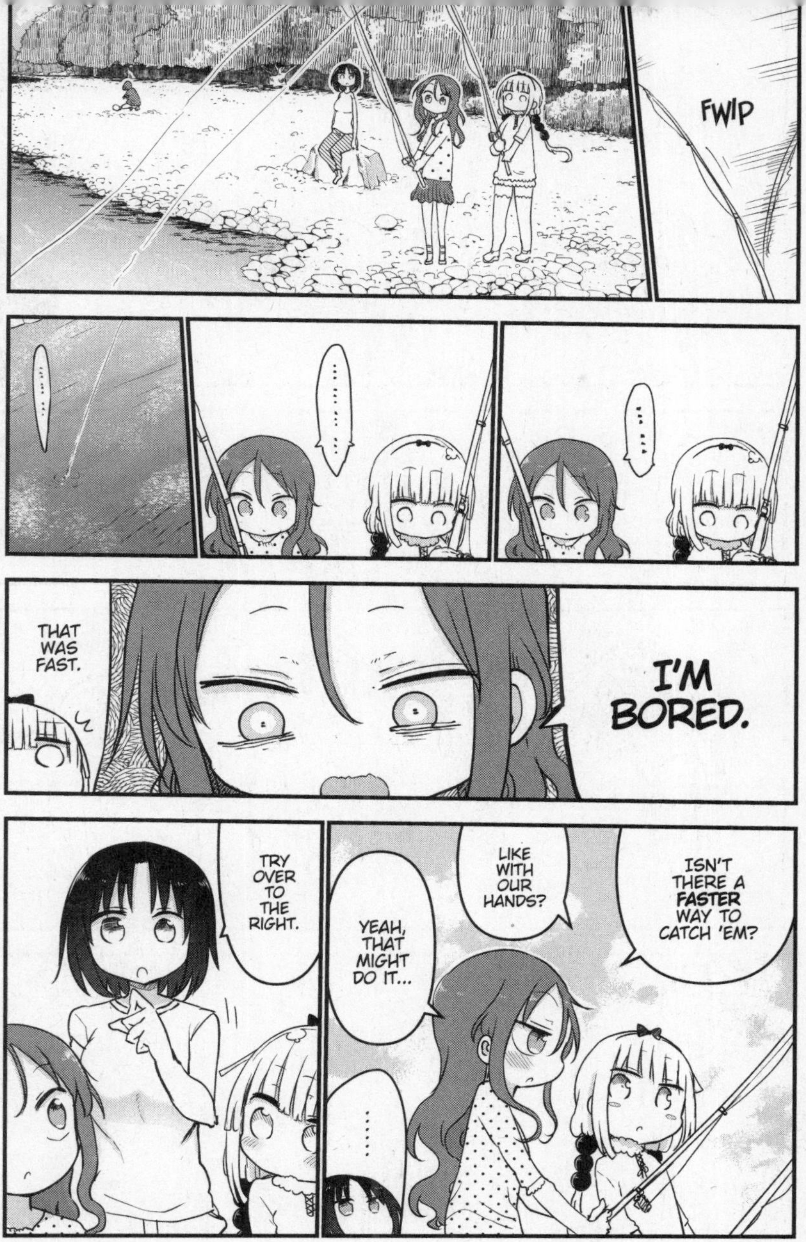

FWIP
...
......
......
I'M BORED.
THAT WAS FAST.
ISN'T THERE A FASTER WAY TO CATCH 'EM?
LIKE WITH OUR HANDS?
YEAH, THAT MIGHT DO IT...
......
TRY OVER TO THE RIGHT.

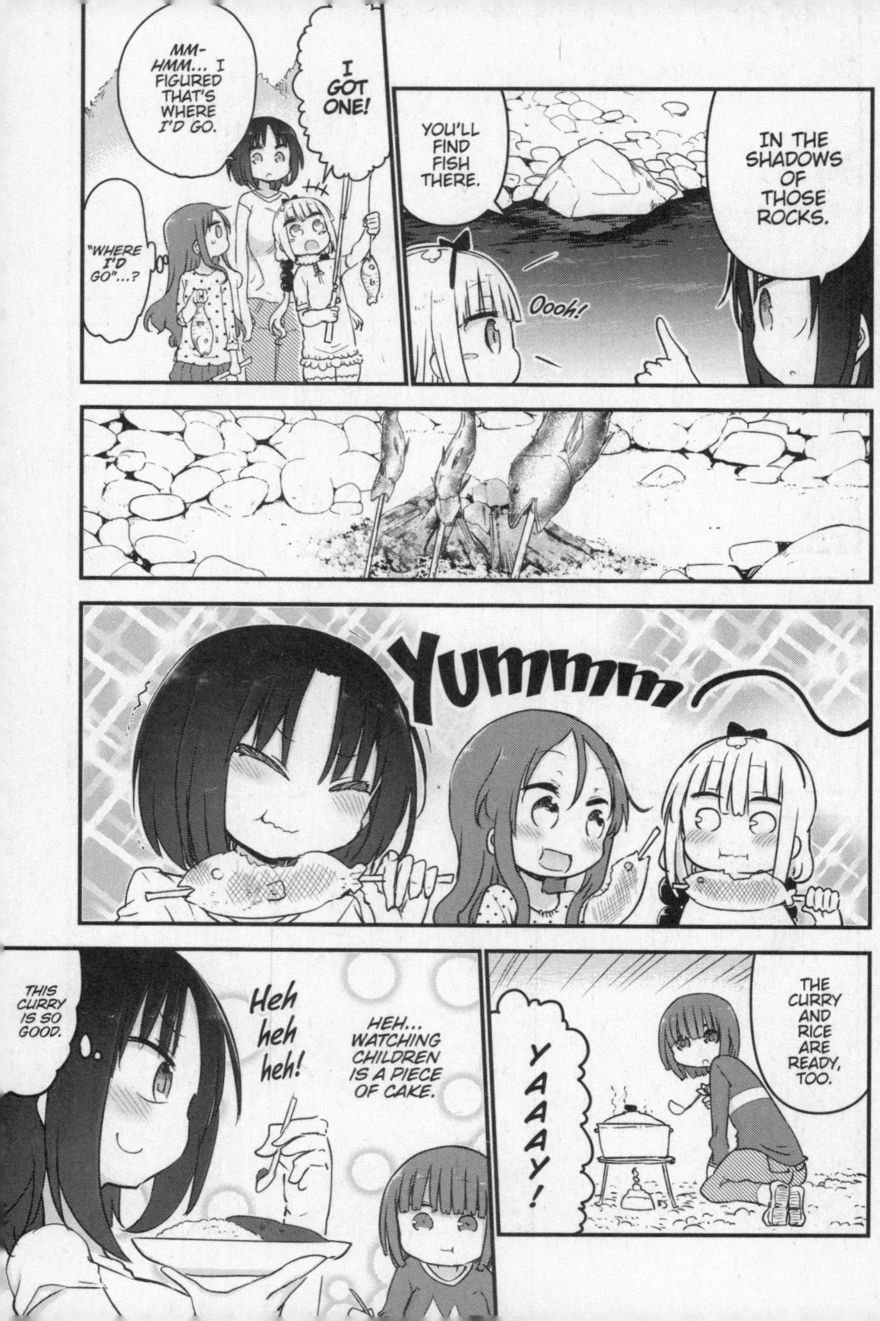
IN THE SHADOWS OF THOSE ROCKS.
YOU'LL FIND FISH THERE.
Oooh!
I GOT ONE!
MM-HMM... I FIGURED THAT'S WHERE I'D GO.
"WHERE I'D GO"...?
Yummmm
THE CURRY AND RICE ARE READY, TOO.
YAAAAY!
HEH... WATCHING CHILDREN IS A PIECE OF CAKE.
Heh heh heh!
THIS CURRY IS SO GOOD.

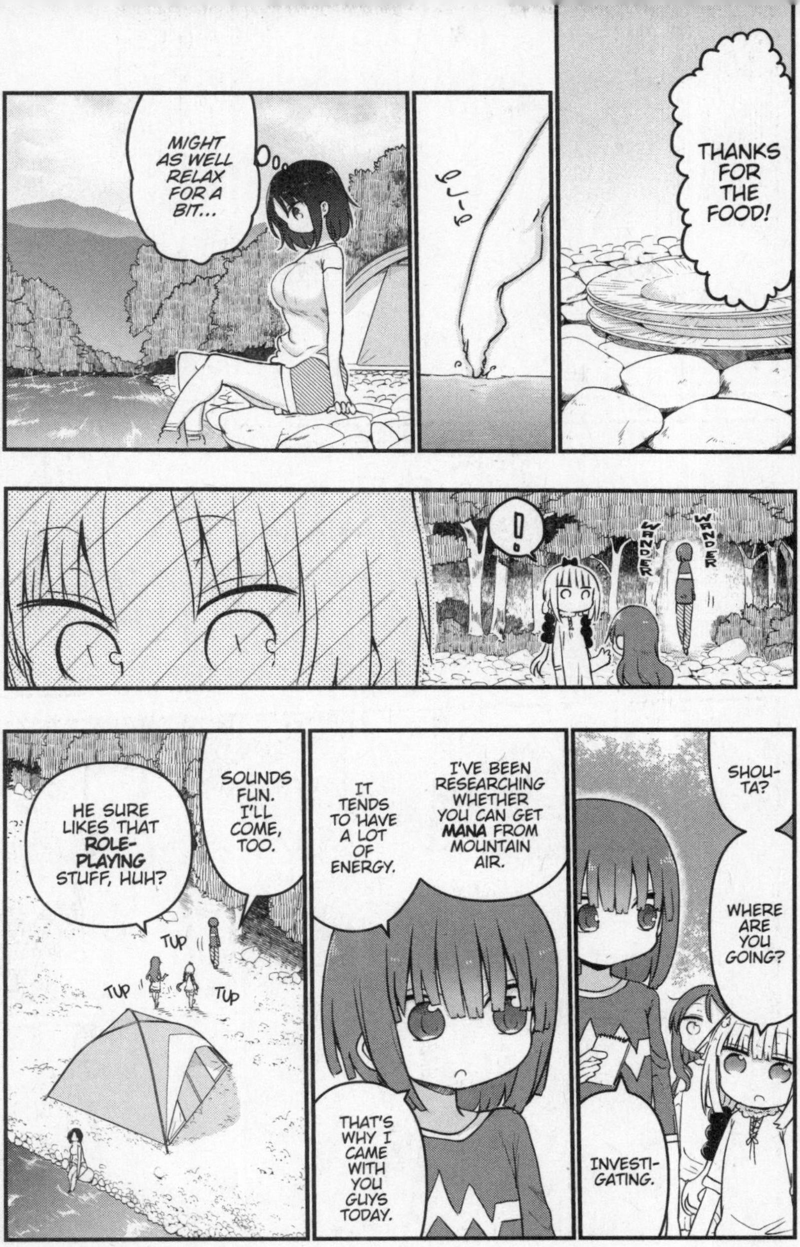
THANKS FOR THE FOOD!
MIGHT AS WELL RELAX FOR A BIT...
!
WANDER
WANDER
SHOUTA? WHERE ARE YOU GOING?
INVESTIGATING.
I'VE BEEN RESEARCHING WHETHER YOU CAN GET MANA FROM MOUNTAIN AIR.
IT TENDS TO HAVE A LOT OF ENERGY.
THAT'S WHY I CAME WITH YOU GUYS TODAY.
SOUNDS FUN. I'LL COME, TOO.
HE SURE LIKES THAT ROLE-PLAYING STUFF, HUH?
TUP
TUP
TUP

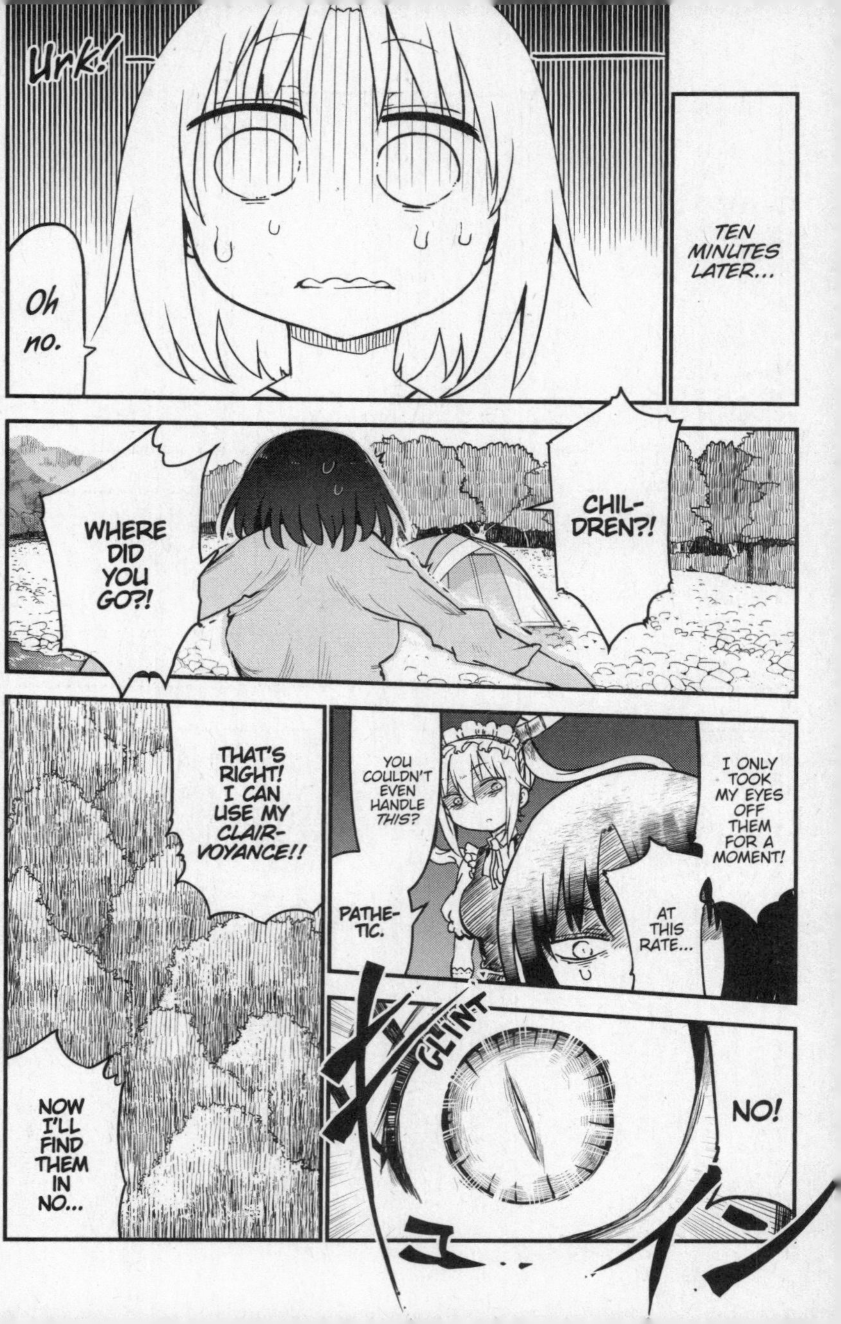
TEN MINUTES LATER...
Urk!
Oh no.
CHIL- DREN?!
WHERE DID YOU GO?!
I ONLY TOOK MY EYES OFF THEM FOR A MOMENT!
AT THIS RATE...
YOU COULDN'T EVEN HANDLE *THIS*?
PATHE- TIC.
NO!
CLINT
THAT'S RIGHT! I CAN USE MY CLAIR- VOYANCE!!
NOW I'LL FIND THEM IN NO...

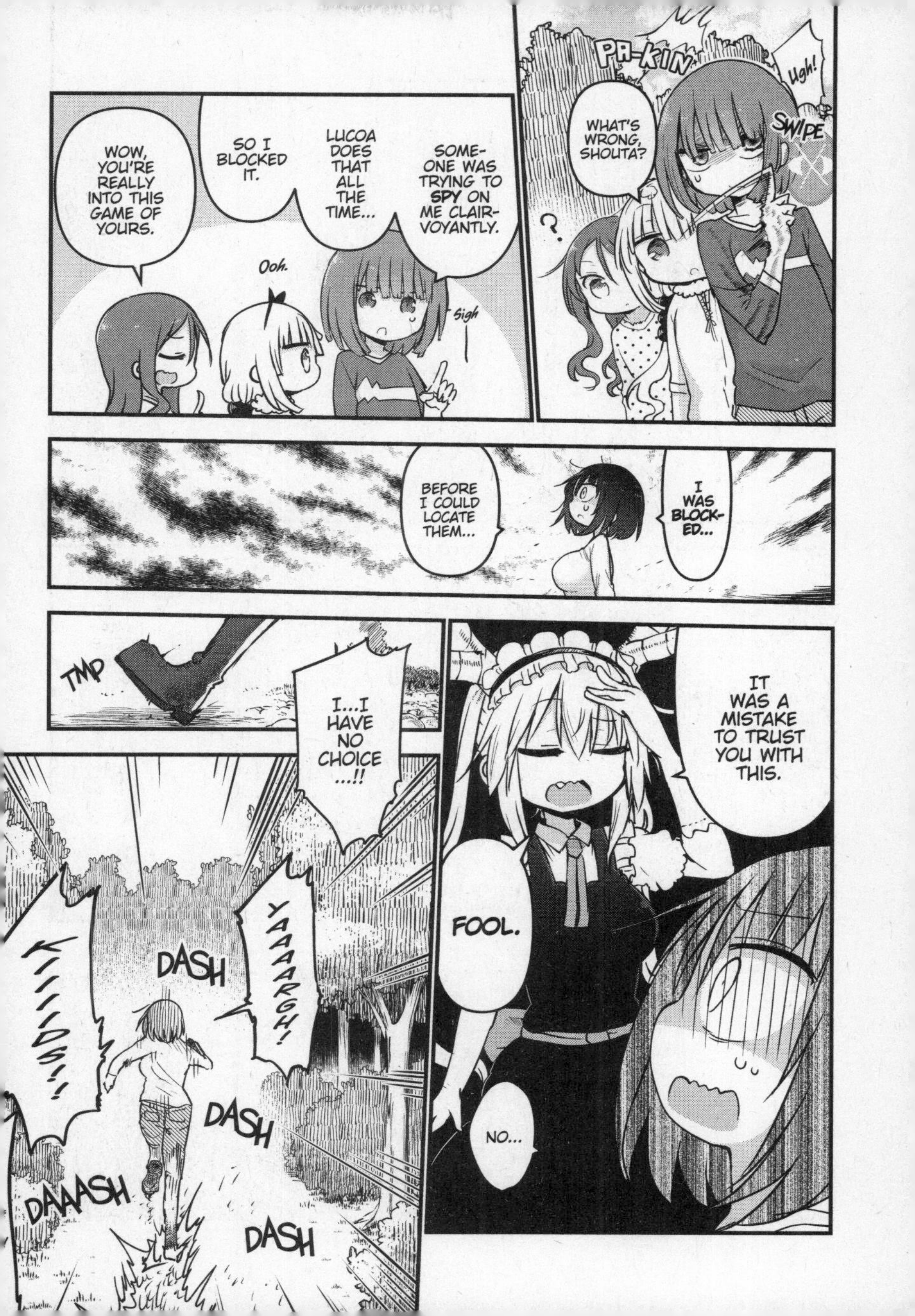
PA-KIN
Ugh!
SWIPE
WHAT'S WRONG, SHOUTA?
?
SOME-ONE WAS TRYING TO SPY ON ME CLAIR-VOYANTLY.
LUCOA DOES THAT ALL THE TIME...
SO I BLOCKED IT.
Sigh
Ooh.
WOW, YOU'RE REALLY INTO THIS GAME OF YOURS.
I WAS BLOCK-ED...
BEFORE I COULD LOCATE THEM...
IT WAS A MISTAKE TO TRUST YOU WITH THIS.
FOOL.
NO...
TMP
I...I HAVE NO CHOICE ...!!
YAAAARGH!
KIIIIDS!!
DASH
DASH
DAAASH
DASH

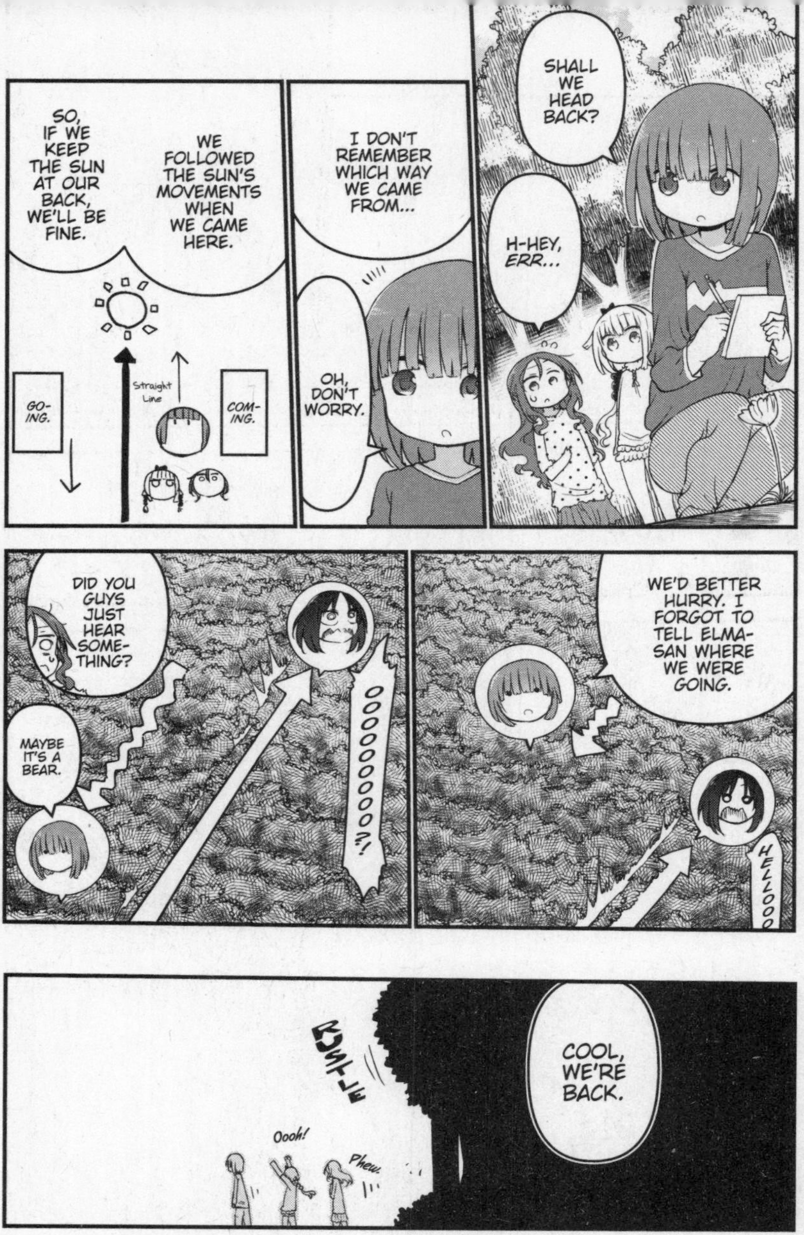
SHALL WE HEAD BACK?
H-HEY, ERR...
I DON'T REMEMBER WHICH WAY WE CAME FROM...
OH, DON'T WORRY.
WE FOLLOWED THE SUN'S MOVEMENTS WHEN WE CAME HERE.
SO, IF WE KEEP THE SUN AT OUR BACK, WE'LL BE FINE.
COMING.
Straight Line
GOING.
WE'D BETTER HURRY. I FORGOT TO TELL ELMA-SAN WHERE WE WERE GOING.
HELLOOO
OOOOOOOOOOO?!
DID YOU GUYS JUST HEAR SOMETHING?
MAYBE IT'S A BEAR.
COOL, WE'RE BACK.
RUSTLE
Oooh!
Phew.

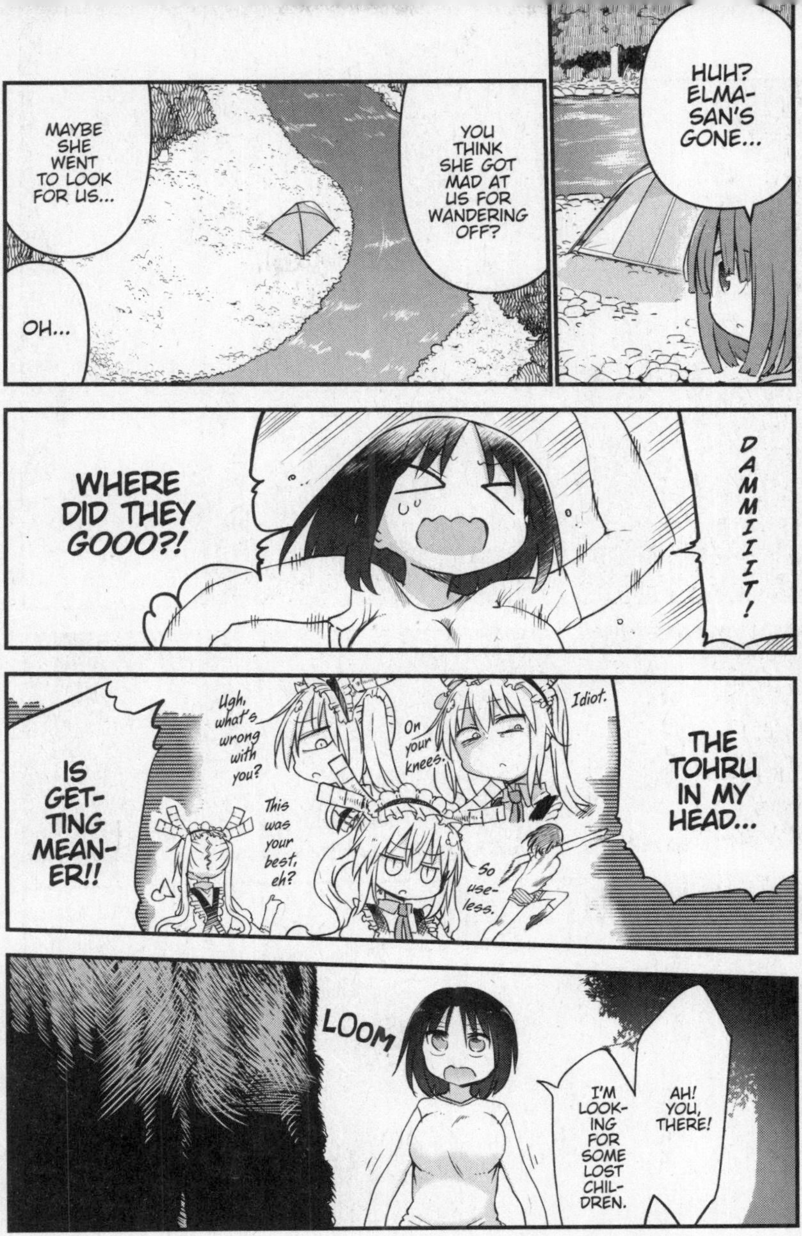
HUH? ELMA-SAN'S GONE...
YOU THINK SHE GOT MAD AT US FOR WANDERING OFF?
MAYBE SHE WENT TO LOOK FOR US...
OH...
DAMMIIIT!
WHERE DID THEY GOOO?!
THE TOHRU IN MY HEAD...
Idiot.
On your knees.
Ugh, what's wrong with you?
So useless.
This was your best, eh?
IS GETTING MEANER!!
AH! YOU, THERE!
I'M LOOKING FOR SOME LOST CHILDREN.
LOOM

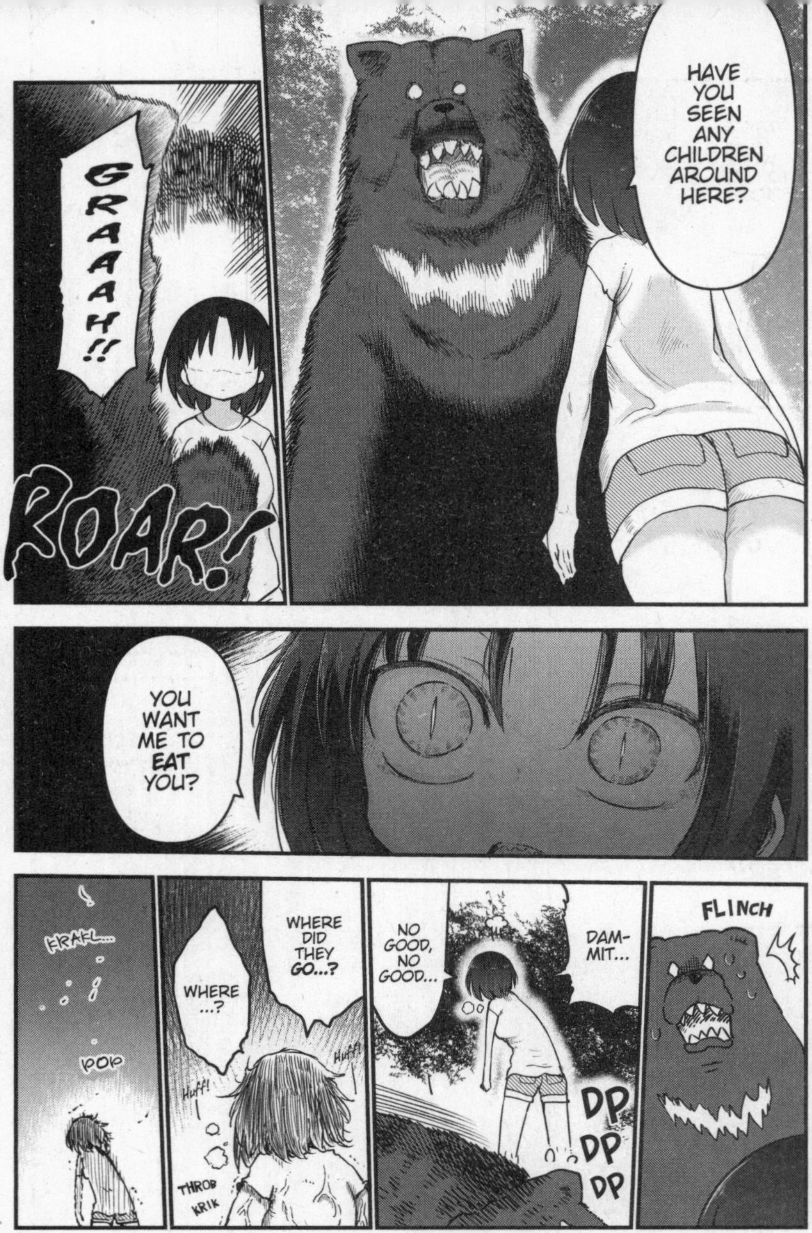
HAVE YOU SEEN ANY CHILDREN AROUND HERE?
GRAAAH!!
ROAR!
YOU WANT ME TO EAT YOU?
FLINCH
DAM-MIT...
NO GOOD, NO GOOD...
DP DP DP
WHERE DID THEY GO...?
WHERE ...?
Huff!
Huff!
THROB
KRIK
KRAKL...
POP

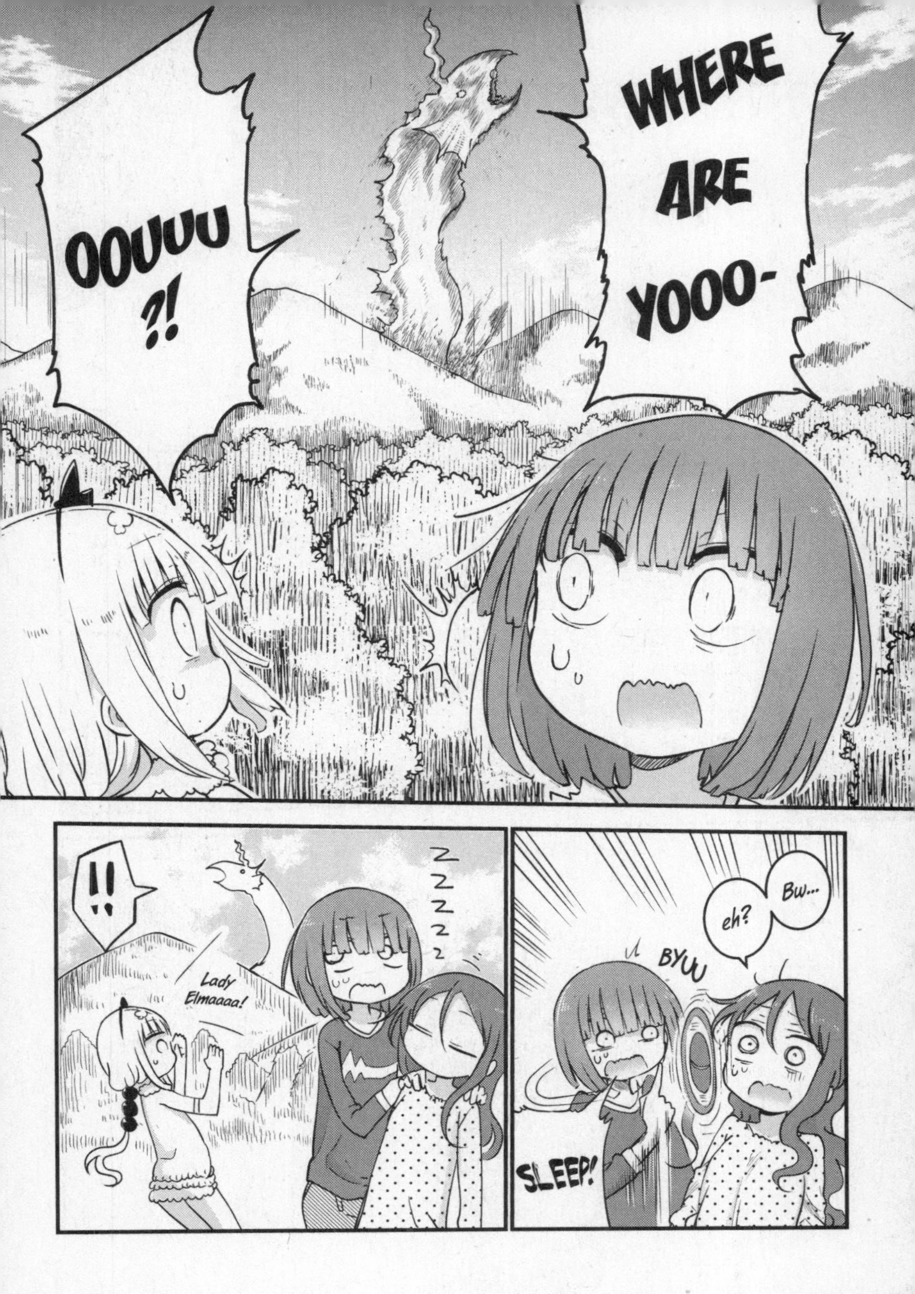
WHERE ARE YOOO-
OOUUU ?!
Bw...
eh?
BYUU
SLEEP!
ZZZZZ
!!
Lady Elmaaaa!

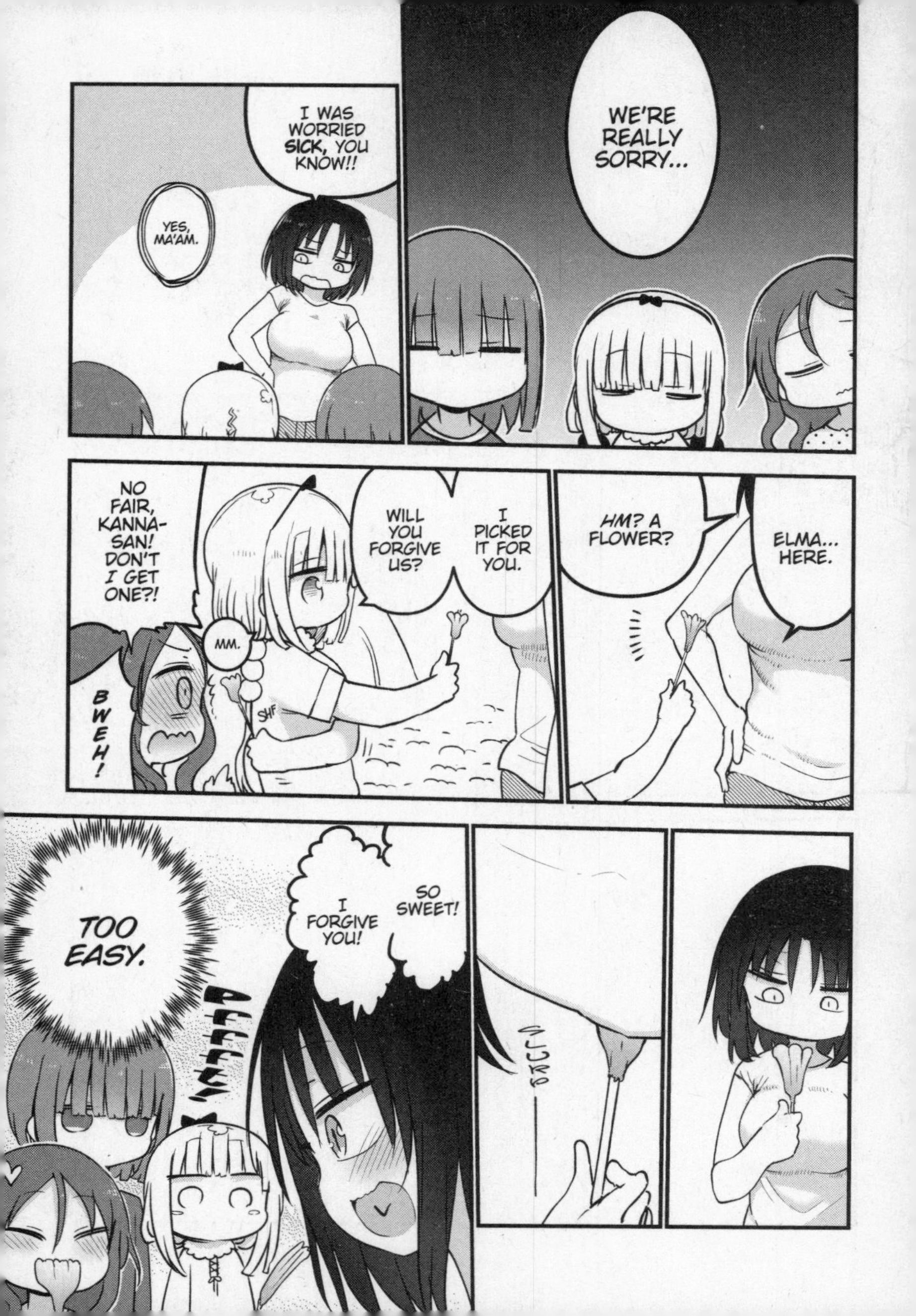
WE'RE REALLY SORRY...
I WAS WORRIED SICK, YOU KNOW!!
YES, MA'AM.
ELMA... HERE.
HM? A FLOWER?
I PICKED IT FOR YOU.
WILL YOU FORGIVE US?
MM.
SHF
NO FAIR, KANNA-SAN! DON'T I GET ONE?!
BWEH!
SO SWEET!
I FORGIVE YOU!
TOO EASY.

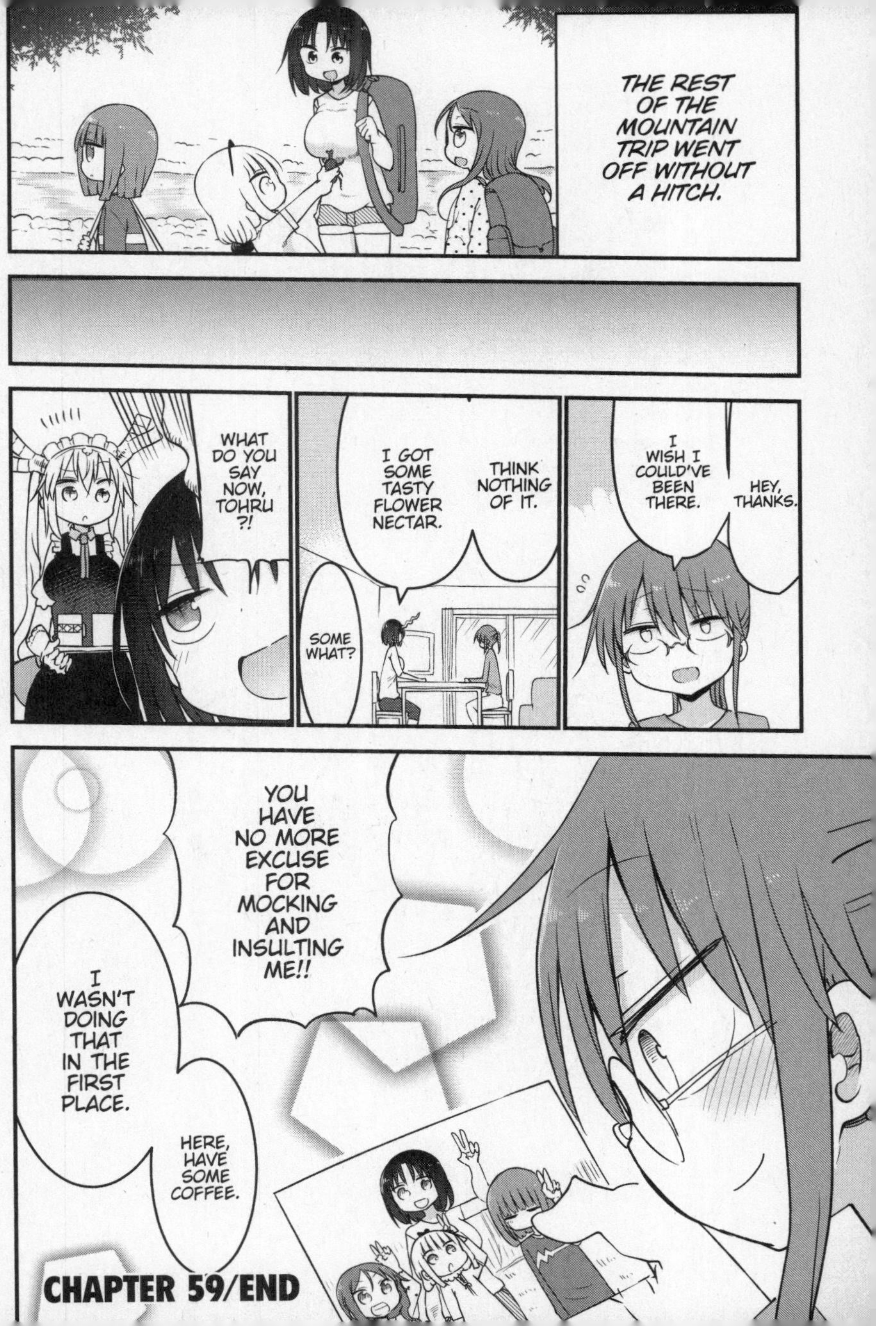
THE REST OF THE MOUNTAIN TRIP WENT OFF WITHOUT A HITCH.
HEY, THANKS.
I WISH I COULD'VE BEEN THERE.
THINK NOTHING OF IT.
I GOT SOME TASTY FLOWER NECTAR.
SOME WHAT?
WHAT DO YOU SAY NOW, TOHRU?!
YOU HAVE NO MORE EXCUSE FOR MOCKING AND INSULTING ME!!
I WASN'T DOING THAT IN THE FIRST PLACE.
HERE, HAVE SOME COFFEE.

CHAPTER 59/END

A witness reported seeing a dragon in the mountains yesterday. Our analysts suggest the illusion was most likely an effect of atmospheric pressure or an advertising stunt.

A Dragon in the Mountains?!

What the hell was she thinking...?

Miss Kobayashi's
DRAGON MAID

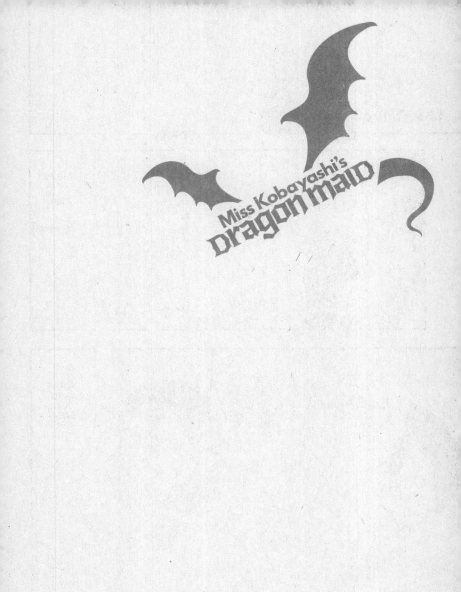

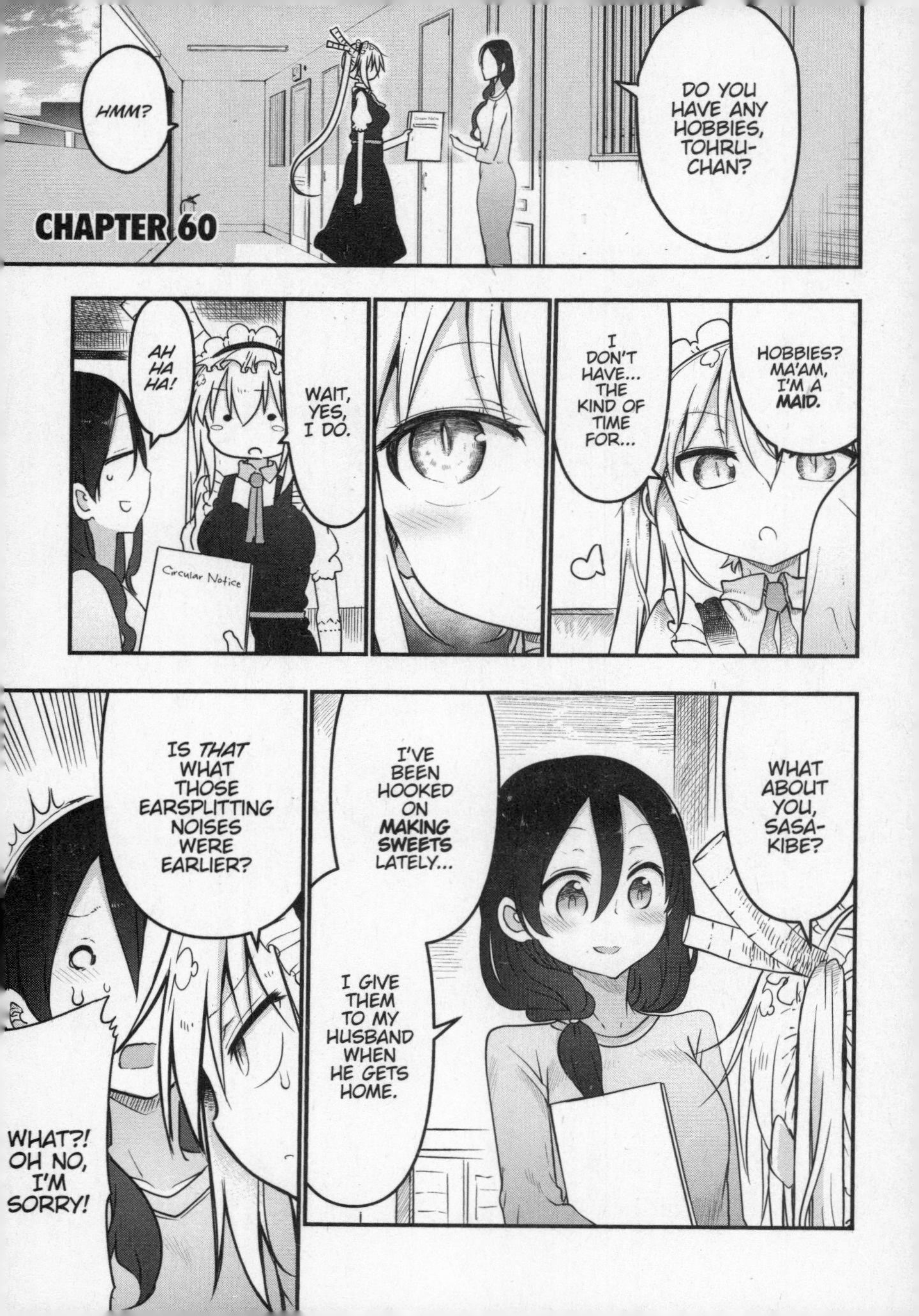
CHAPTER 60
DO YOU HAVE ANY HOBBIES, TOHRU-CHAN?
HMM?
HOBBIES? MA'AM, I'M A MAID.
I DON'T HAVE... THE KIND OF TIME FOR...
WAIT, YES, I DO.
AH HA HA!
Circular Notice
WHAT ABOUT YOU, SASA-KIBE?
I'VE BEEN HOOKED ON MAKING SWEETS LATELY...
I GIVE THEM TO MY HUSBAND WHEN HE GETS HOME.
IS THAT WHAT THOSE EARSPLITTING NOISES WERE EARLIER?
WHAT?! OH NO, I'M SORRY!

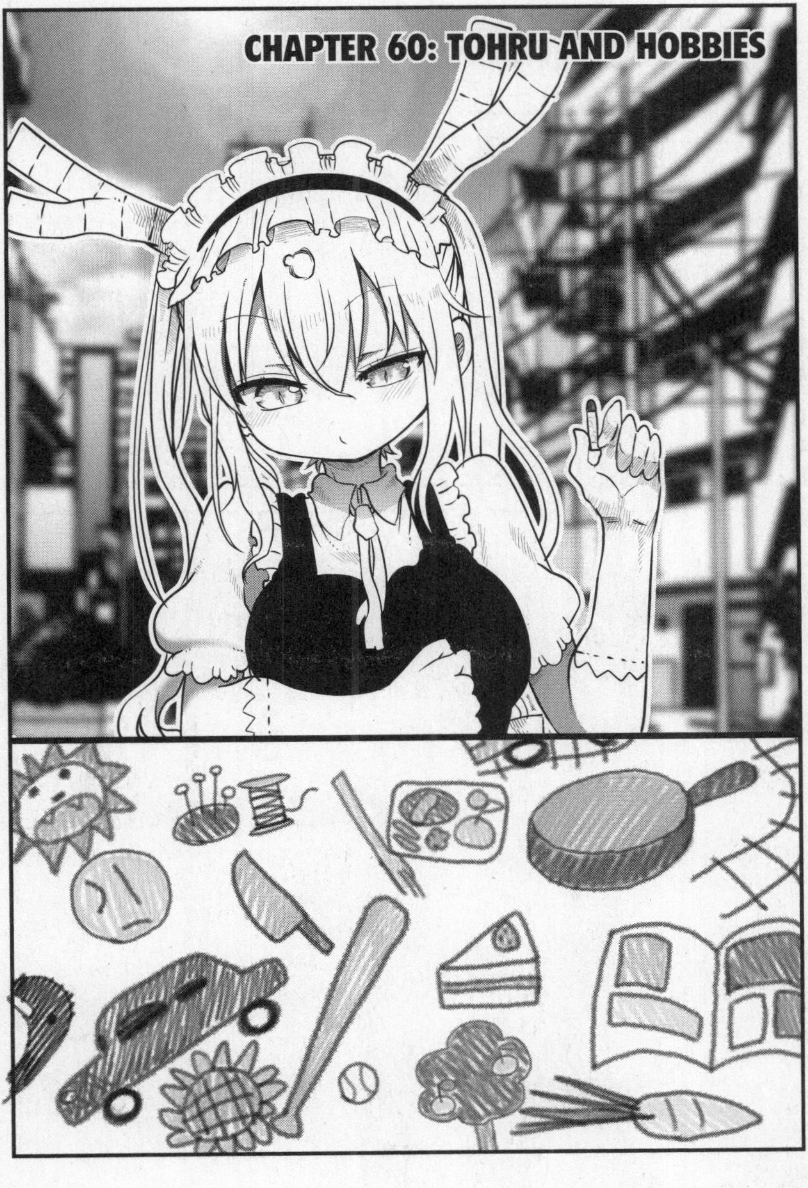
CHAPTER 60: TOHRU AND HOBBIES

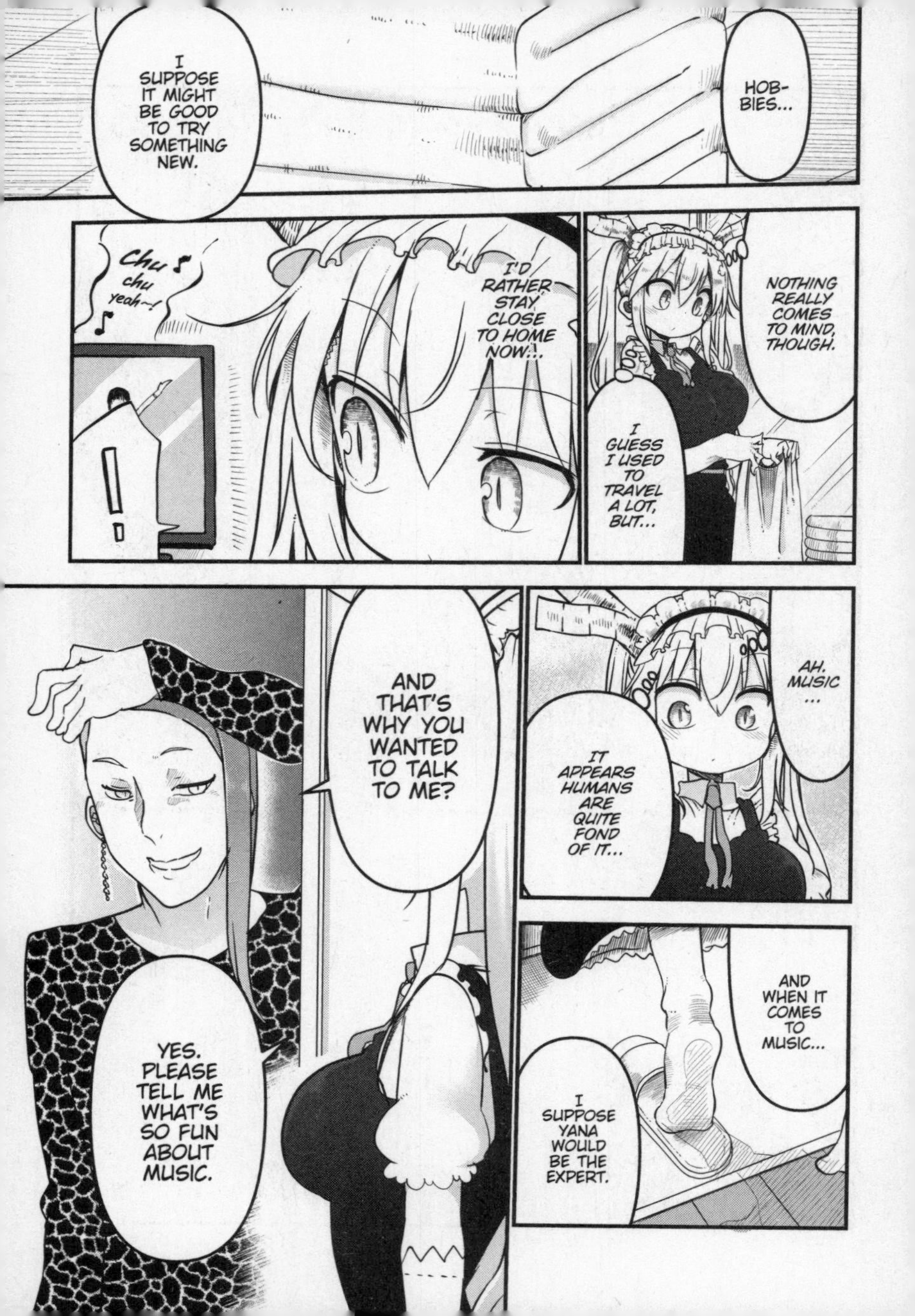
HOB-BIES...
I SUPPOSE IT MIGHT BE GOOD TO TRY SOMETHING NEW.
NOTHING REALLY COMES TO MIND, THOUGH.
I GUESS I USED TO TRAVEL A LOT, BUT...
I'D RATHER STAY CLOSE TO HOME NOW...
Chu ♪ chu yeah~!
AH. MUSIC ...
IT APPEARS HUMANS ARE QUITE FOND OF IT...
AND WHEN IT COMES TO MUSIC...
I SUPPOSE YANA WOULD BE THE EXPERT.
AND THAT'S WHY YOU WANTED TO TALK TO ME?
YES. PLEASE TELL ME WHAT'S SO FUN ABOUT MUSIC.

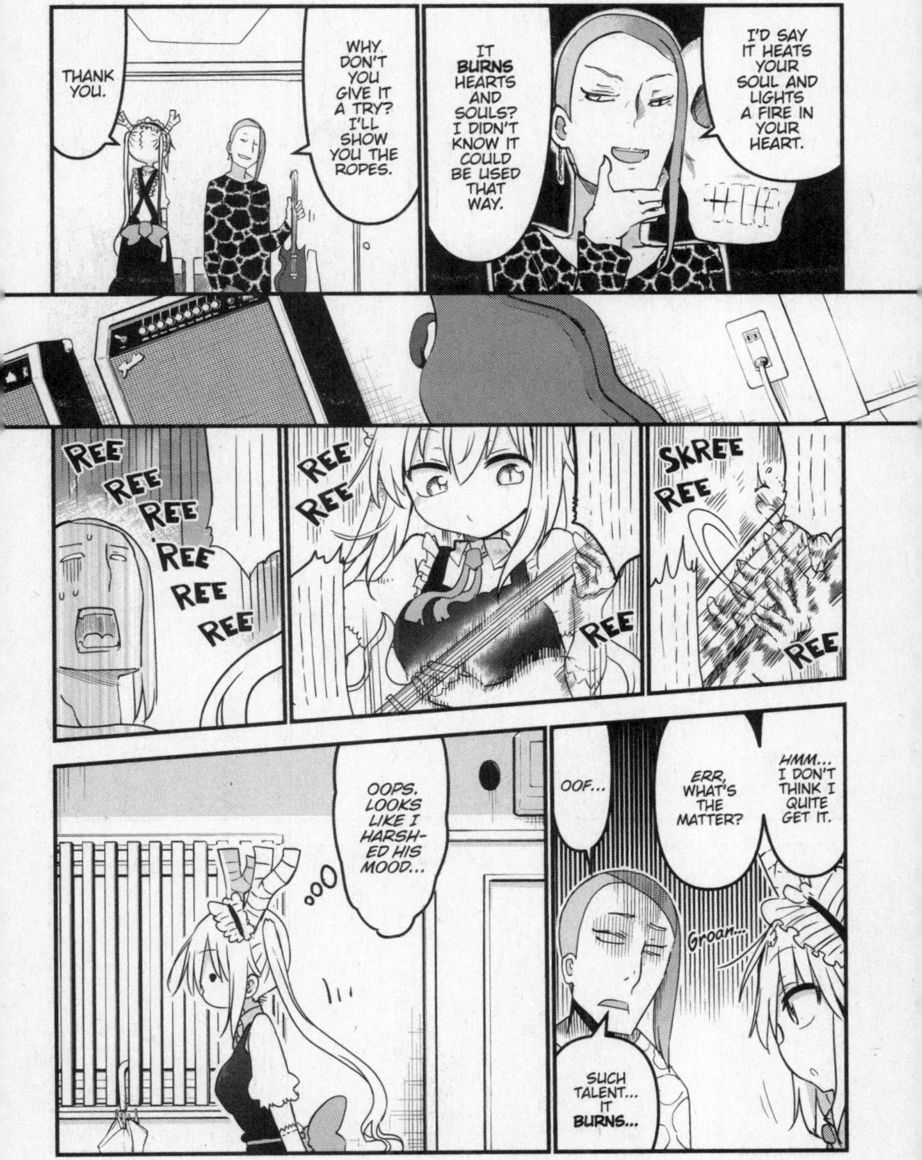
I'D SAY IT HEATS YOUR SOUL AND LIGHTS A FIRE IN YOUR HEART.
IT **BURNS** HEARTS AND SOULS? I DIDN'T KNOW IT COULD BE USED THAT WAY.
WHY. DON'T YOU GIVE IT A TRY? I'LL SHOW YOU THE ROPES.
THANK YOU.
SKREE
REE
REE
REE
REE
REE
REE
REE
REE
REE
REE
REE
HMM... I DON'T THINK I QUITE GET IT.
ERR, WHAT'S THE MATTER?
OOF...
Groan...
SUCH TALENT... IT **BURNS**...
OOPS. LOOKS LIKE I HARSHED HIS MOOD...

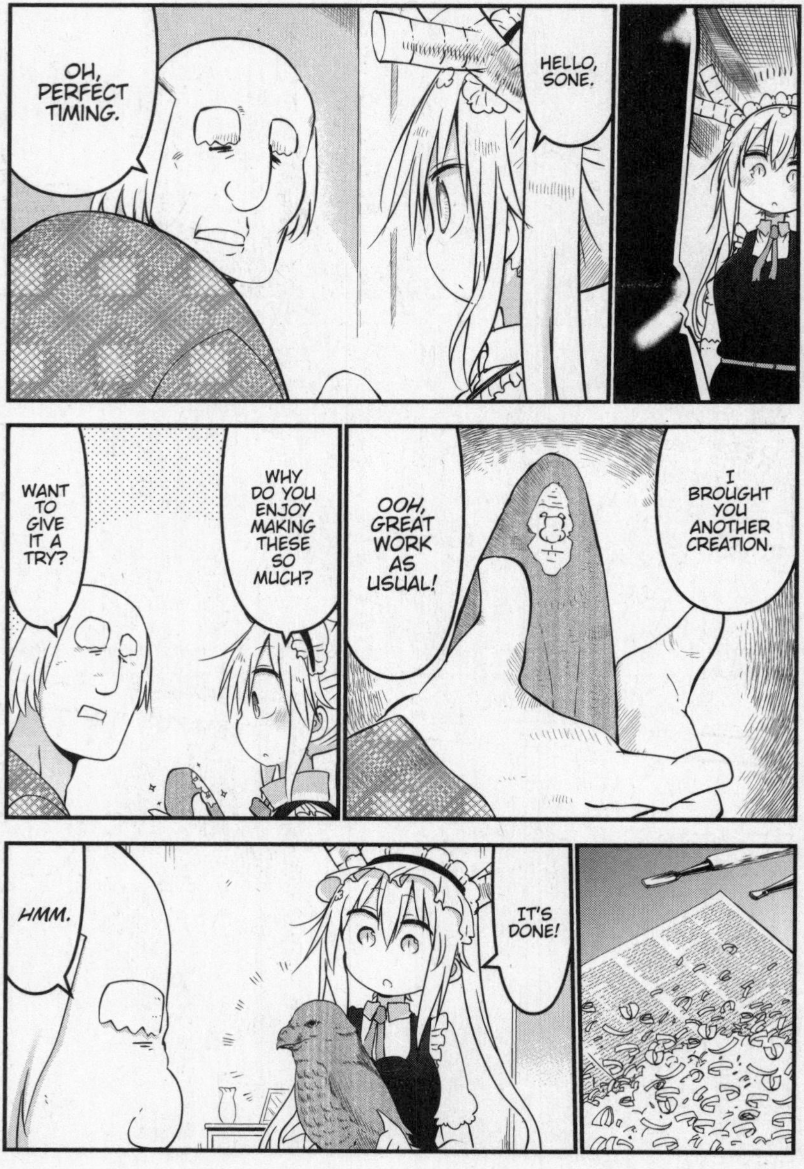
HELLO, SONE.
OH, PERFECT TIMING.
I BROUGHT YOU ANOTHER CREATION.
OOH, GREAT WORK AS USUAL!
WHY DO YOU ENJOY MAKING THESE SO MUCH?
WANT TO GIVE IT A TRY?
IT'S DONE!
HMM.

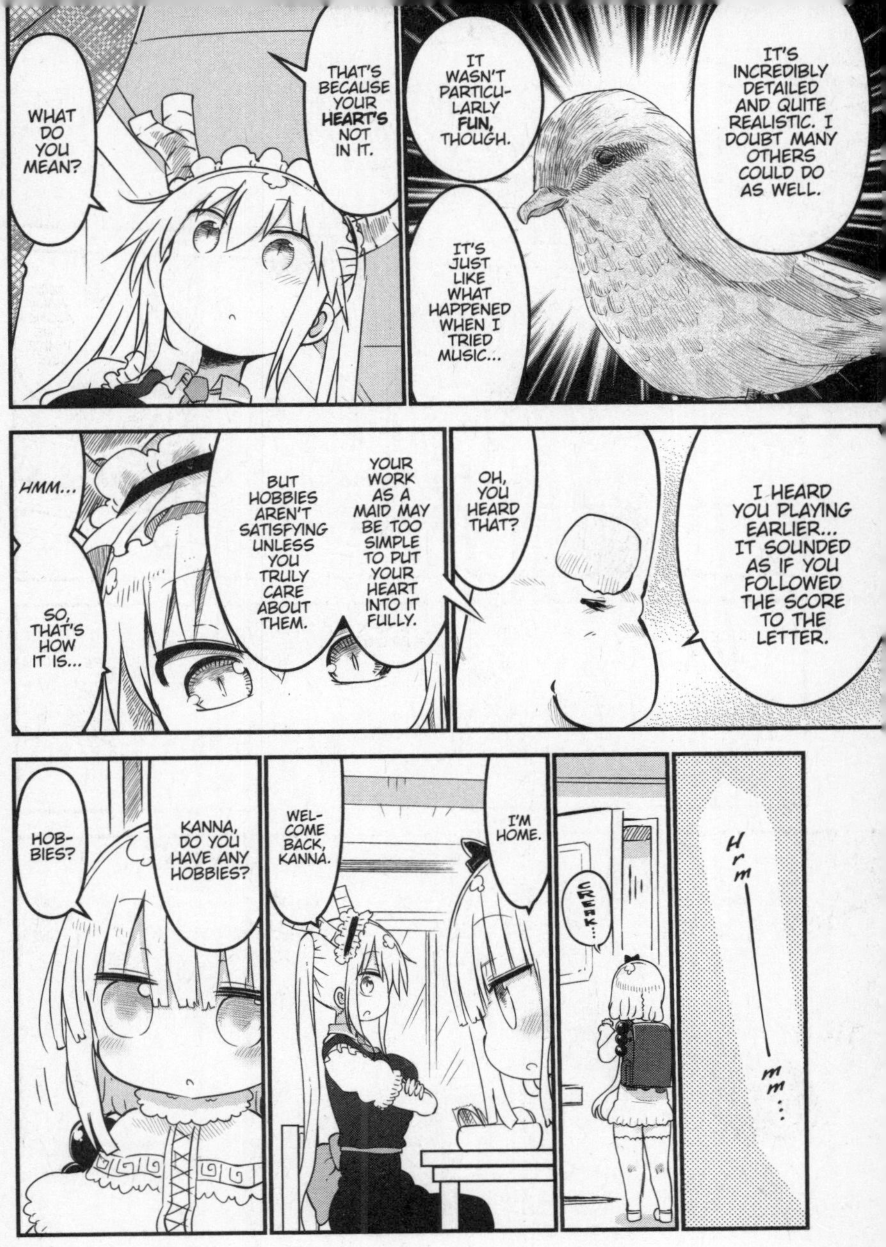
IT'S INCREDIBLY DETAILED AND QUITE REALISTIC. I DOUBT MANY OTHERS COULD DO AS WELL.
IT WASN'T PARTICU-LARLY **FUN,** THOUGH.
IT'S JUST LIKE WHAT HAPPENED WHEN I TRIED MUSIC...
THAT'S BECAUSE YOUR **HEART'S** NOT IN IT.
WHAT DO YOU MEAN?
I HEARD YOU PLAYING EARLIER... IT SOUNDED AS IF YOU FOLLOWED THE SCORE TO THE LETTER.
OH, YOU HEARD THAT?
YOUR WORK AS A MAID MAY BE TOO SIMPLE TO PUT YOUR HEART INTO IT FULLY.
BUT HOBBIES AREN'T SATISFYING UNLESS YOU TRULY CARE ABOUT THEM.
HMM...
SO, THAT'S HOW IT IS...
Hrm——mm...
CREAK...
I'M HOME.
WEL-COME BACK, KANNA.
KANNA, DO YOU HAVE ANY HOBBIES?
HOB-BIES?

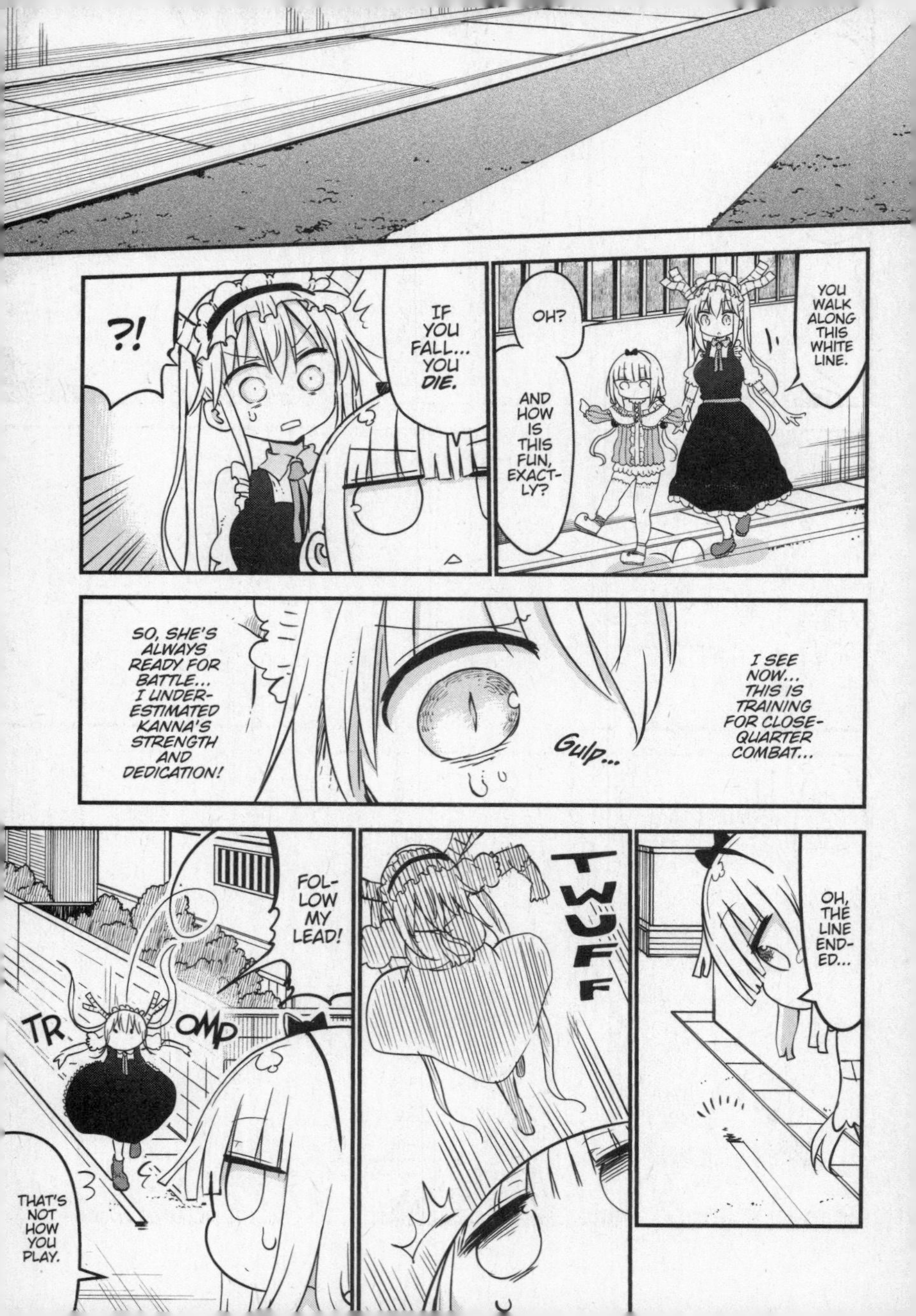
YOU WALK ALONG THIS WHITE LINE.
OH?
AND HOW IS THIS FUN, EXACTLY?
IF YOU FALL... YOU *DIE.*
?!
I SEE NOW... THIS IS TRAINING FOR CLOSE-QUARTER COMBAT...
Gulp...
SO, SHE'S ALWAYS READY FOR BATTLE... I UNDERESTIMATED KANNA'S STRENGTH AND DEDICATION!
OH, THE LINE ENDED...
TWUFF
FOLLOW MY LEAD!
TROMP
THAT'S NOT HOW YOU PLAY.

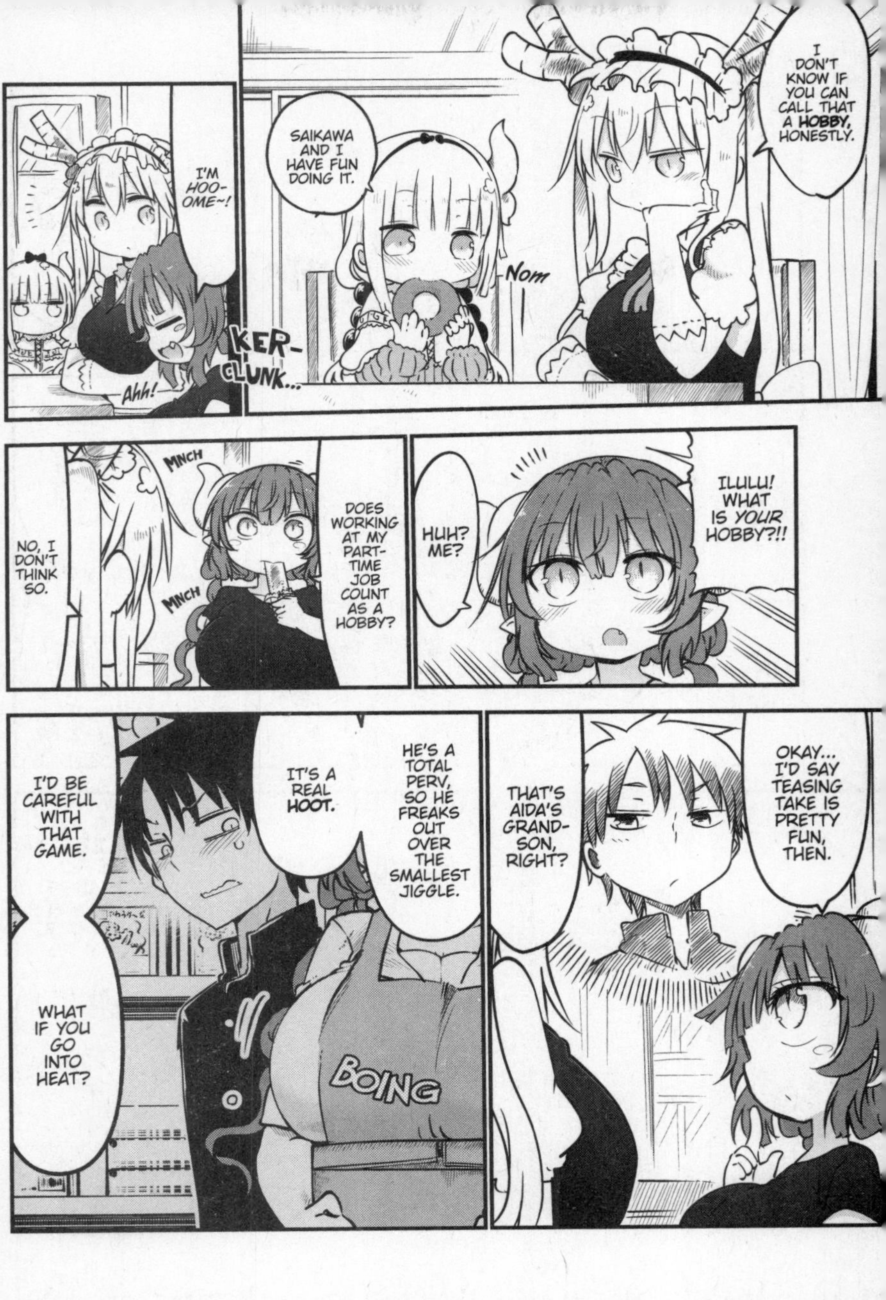
I DON'T KNOW IF YOU CAN CALL THAT A HOBBY, HONESTLY.
SAIKAWA AND I HAVE FUN DOING IT.
Nom
I'M HOO-OME~!
KER-CLUNK...
Ahh!
ILULU! WHAT IS YOUR HOBBY?!!
HUH? ME?
DOES WORKING AT MY PART-TIME JOB COUNT AS A HOBBY?
MNCH
MNCH
NO, I DON'T THINK SO.
OKAY... I'D SAY TEASING TAKE IS PRETTY FUN, THEN.
THAT'S AIDA'S GRAND-SON, RIGHT?
HE'S A TOTAL PERV, SO HE FREAKS OUT OVER THE SMALLEST JIGGLE.
IT'S A REAL HOOT.
BOING
I'D BE CAREFUL WITH THAT GAME.
WHAT IF YOU GO INTO HEAT?

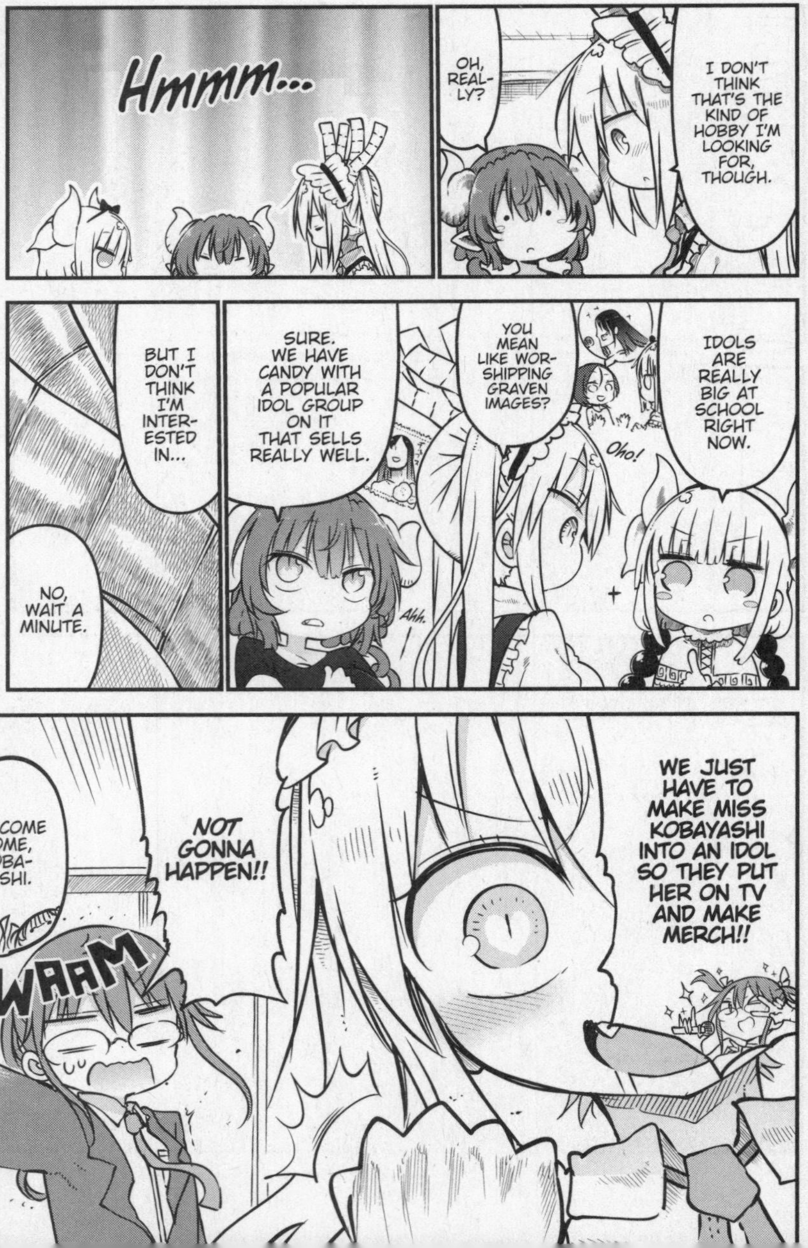
I DON'T THINK THAT'S THE KIND OF HOBBY I'M LOOKING FOR, THOUGH.
OH, REALLY?
Hmmm...
IDOLS ARE REALLY BIG AT SCHOOL RIGHT NOW.
YOU MEAN LIKE WOR-SHIPPING GRAVEN IMAGES?
Oho!
SURE. WE HAVE CANDY WITH A POPULAR IDOL GROUP ON IT THAT SELLS REALLY WELL.
Ahh.
BUT I DON'T THINK I'M INTER-ESTED IN...
NO, WAIT A MINUTE.
WE JUST HAVE TO MAKE MISS KOBAYASHI INTO AN IDOL SO THEY PUT HER ON TV AND MAKE MERCH!!
NOT GONNA HAPPEN!!
WELCOME HOME, KOBA-YASHI.
BWAAM

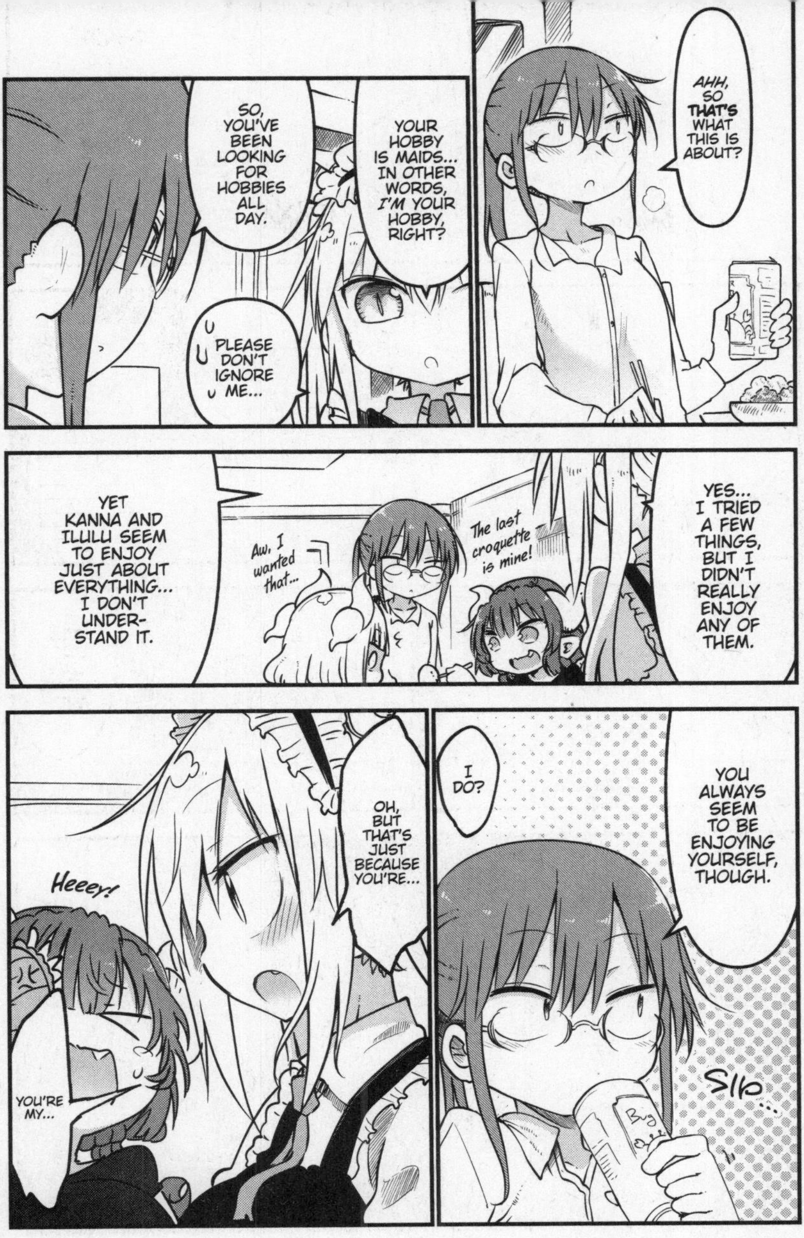

AHH, SO THAT'S WHAT THIS IS ABOUT?
YOUR HOBBY IS MAIDS... IN OTHER WORDS, I'M YOUR HOBBY, RIGHT?
SO, YOU'VE BEEN LOOKING FOR HOBBIES ALL DAY.
PLEASE DON'T IGNORE ME...
YES... I TRIED A FEW THINGS, BUT I DIDN'T REALLY ENJOY ANY OF THEM.
The last croquette is mine!
Aw, I wanted that...
YET KANNA AND ILULU SEEM TO ENJOY JUST ABOUT EVERYTHING... I DON'T UNDERSTAND IT.
YOU ALWAYS SEEM TO BE ENJOYING YOURSELF, THOUGH.
Slp...
I DO?
OH, BUT THAT'S JUST BECAUSE YOU'RE...
Heeey!
YOU'RE MY...

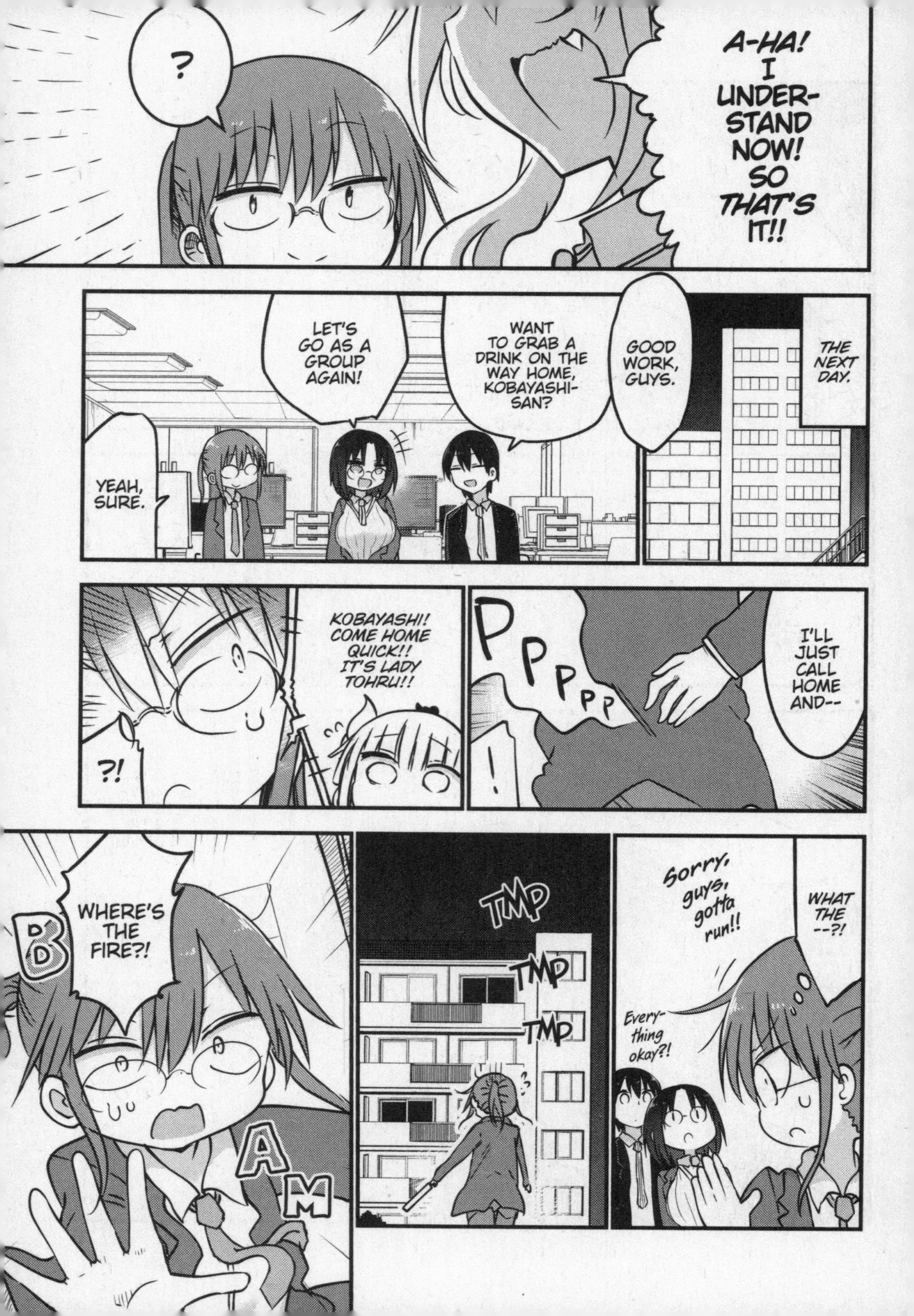
A-HA! I UNDER-STAND NOW! SO THAT'S IT!!
?
THE NEXT DAY.
GOOD WORK, GUYS.
WANT TO GRAB A DRINK ON THE WAY HOME, KOBAYASHI-SAN?
LET'S GO AS A GROUP AGAIN!
YEAH, SURE.
I'LL JUST CALL HOME AND--
PPPPP
!
KOBAYASHI! COME HOME QUICK!! IT'S LADY TOHRU!!
?!
WHAT THE --?!
Sorry, guys, gotta run!!
Every-thing okay?!
TMP
TMP
TMP
WHERE'S THE FIRE?!
BAM

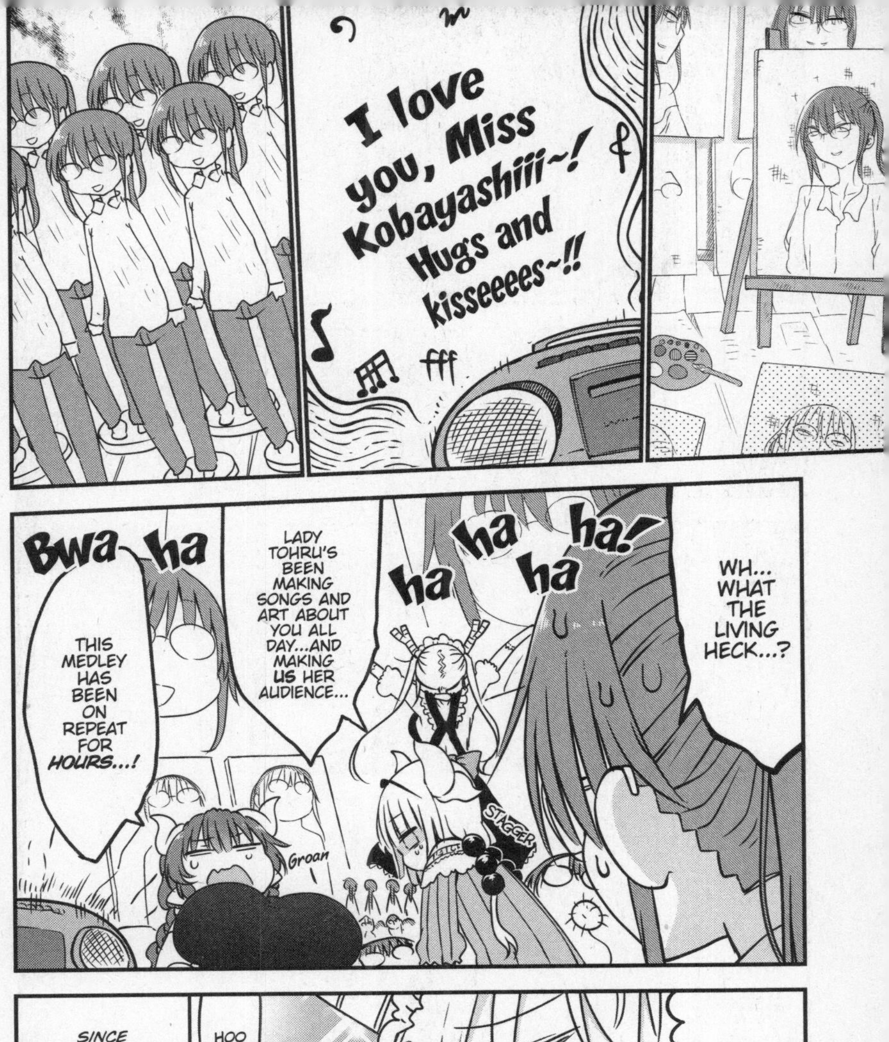
I love you, Miss Kobayashiii~! Hugs and kisseeeees~!!
fff
WH... WHAT THE LIVING HECK...?
ha ha ha ha!
LADY TOHRU'S BEEN MAKING SONGS AND ART ABOUT YOU ALL DAY...AND MAKING US HER AUDIENCE...
Bwa-ha
THIS MEDLEY HAS BEEN ON REPEAT FOR HOURS...!
STAGGER
Groan
MISS KOBA-YASHI IS MY PERFECT HOBBY!!
HOO BOY...
SINCE SHE CAN GET LIKE THIS HERSELF WHEN SHE'S DRUNK, KOBAYASHI HAD A HARD TIME TELLING TOHRU OFF.

CHAPTER 60/END

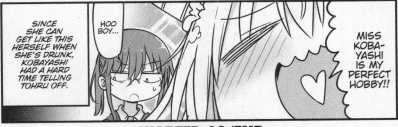

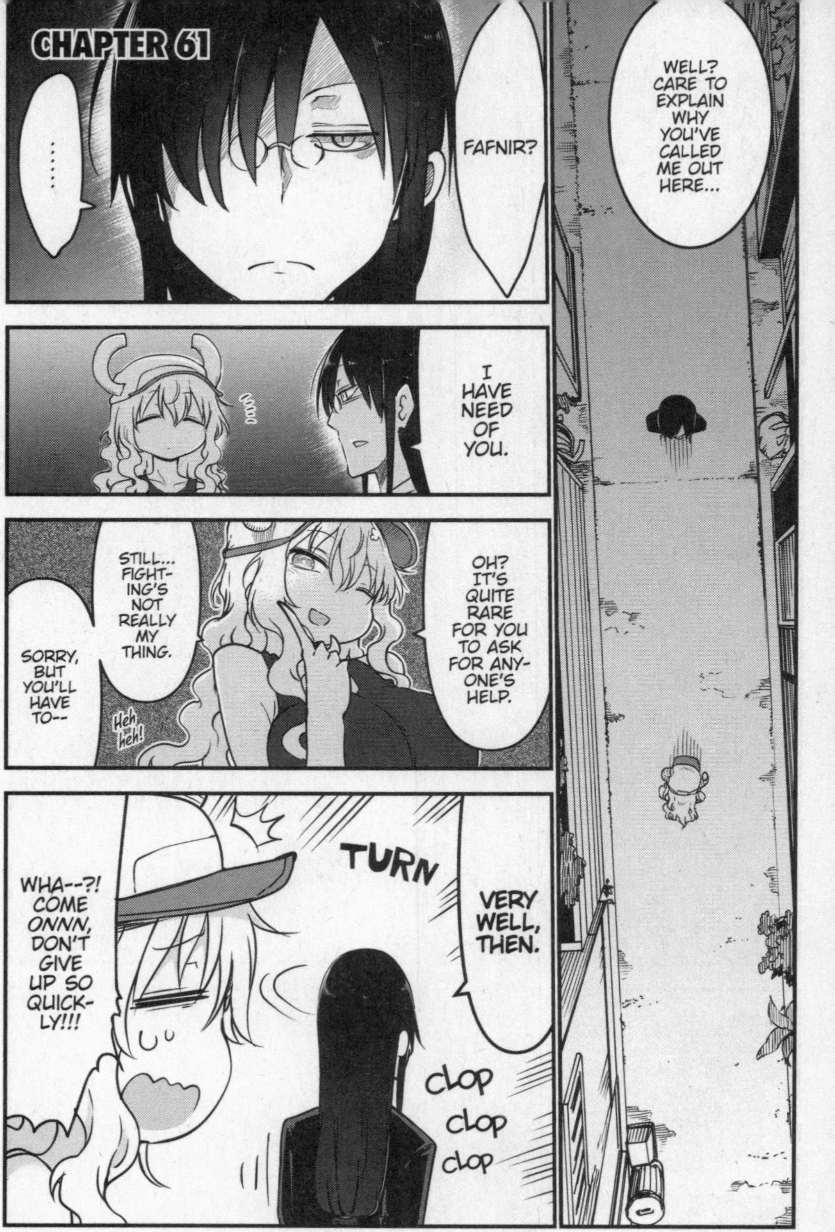
WELL? CARE TO EXPLAIN WHY YOU'VE CALLED ME OUT HERE...
CHAPTER 61
FAFNIR?
......
I HAVE NEED OF YOU.
OH? IT'S QUITE RARE FOR YOU TO ASK FOR ANYONE'S HELP.
STILL... FIGHTING'S NOT REALLY MY THING.
Heh heh!
SORRY, BUT YOU'LL HAVE TO--
TURN
VERY WELL, THEN.
CLOP
CLOP
CLOP
WHA--?! COME ONNN, DON'T GIVE UP SO QUICKLY!!!

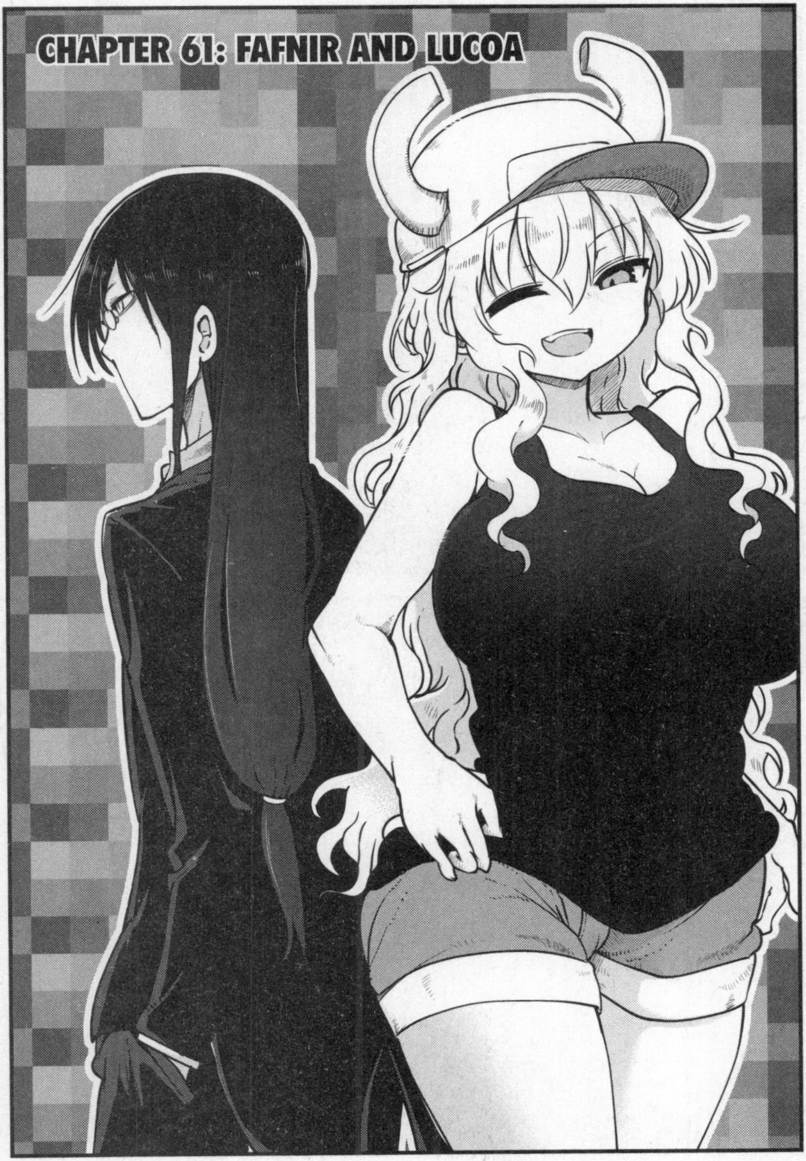
CHAPTER 61: FAFNIR AND LUCOA

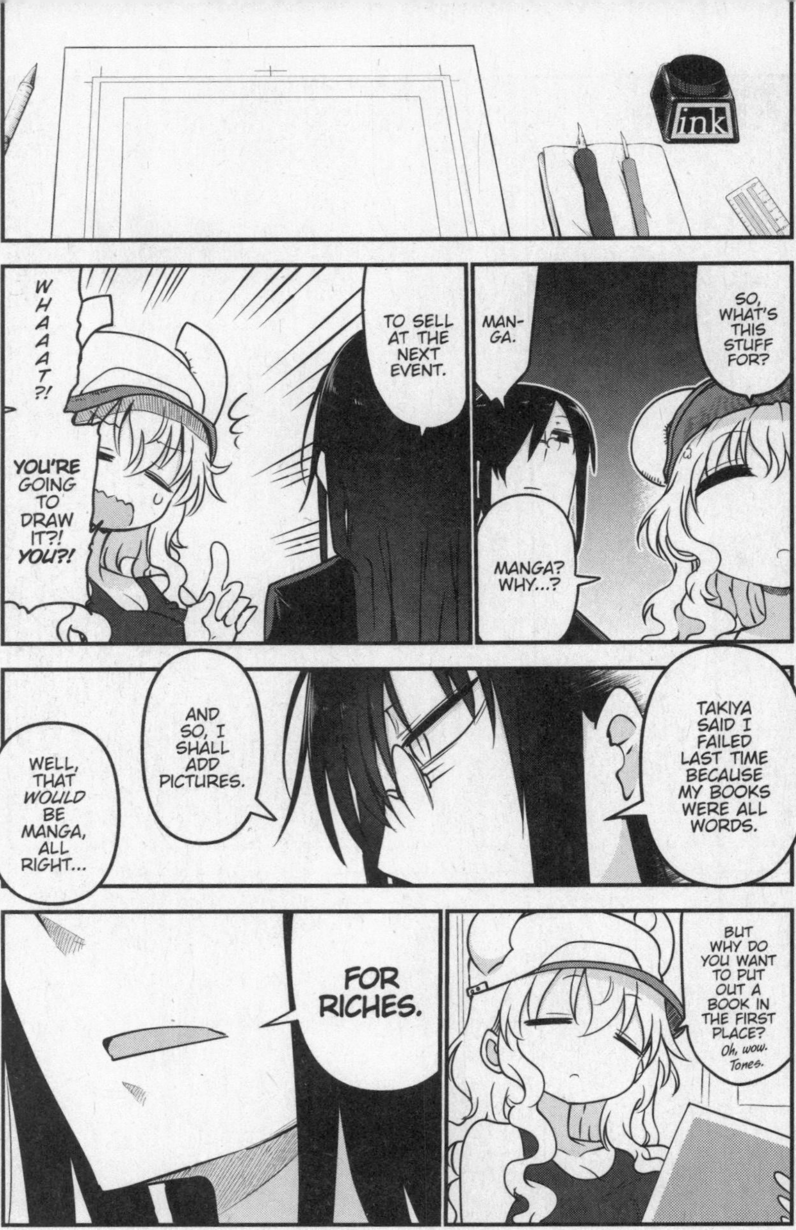
ink
SO, WHAT'S THIS STUFF FOR?
MANGA.
MANGA? WHY...?
TO SELL AT THE NEXT EVENT.
WHAAAAT?!
YOU'RE GOING TO DRAW IT?! YOU?!
TAKIYA SAID I FAILED LAST TIME BECAUSE MY BOOKS WERE ALL WORDS.
AND SO, I SHALL ADD PICTURES.
WELL, THAT WOULD BE MANGA, ALL RIGHT...
BUT WHY DO YOU WANT TO PUT OUT A BOOK IN THE FIRST PLACE?
Oh, wow. Tones.
FOR RICHES.

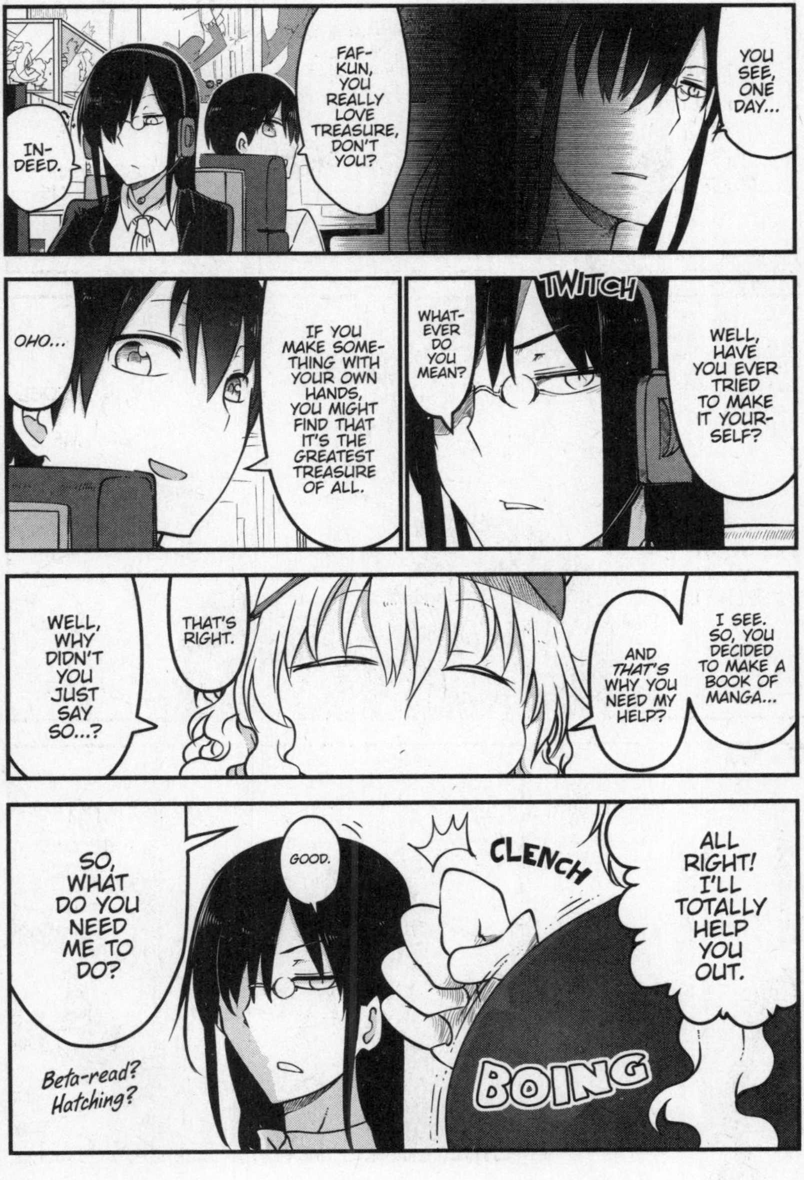
YOU SEE, ONE DAY...
FAF-KUN, YOU REALLY LOVE TREASURE, DON'T YOU?
IN-DEED.
TWITCH
WELL, HAVE YOU EVER TRIED TO MAKE IT YOUR-SELF?
WHAT-EVER DO YOU MEAN?
IF YOU MAKE SOME-THING WITH YOUR OWN HANDS, YOU MIGHT FIND THAT IT'S THE GREATEST TREASURE OF ALL.
OHO...
I SEE. SO, YOU DECIDED TO MAKE A BOOK OF MANGA...
AND *THAT'S* WHY YOU NEED MY HELP?
THAT'S RIGHT.
WELL, WHY DIDN'T YOU JUST SAY SO...?
ALL RIGHT! I'LL TOTALLY HELP YOU OUT.
CLENCH
GOOD.
BOING
SO, WHAT DO YOU NEED ME TO DO?
Beta-read? Hatching?

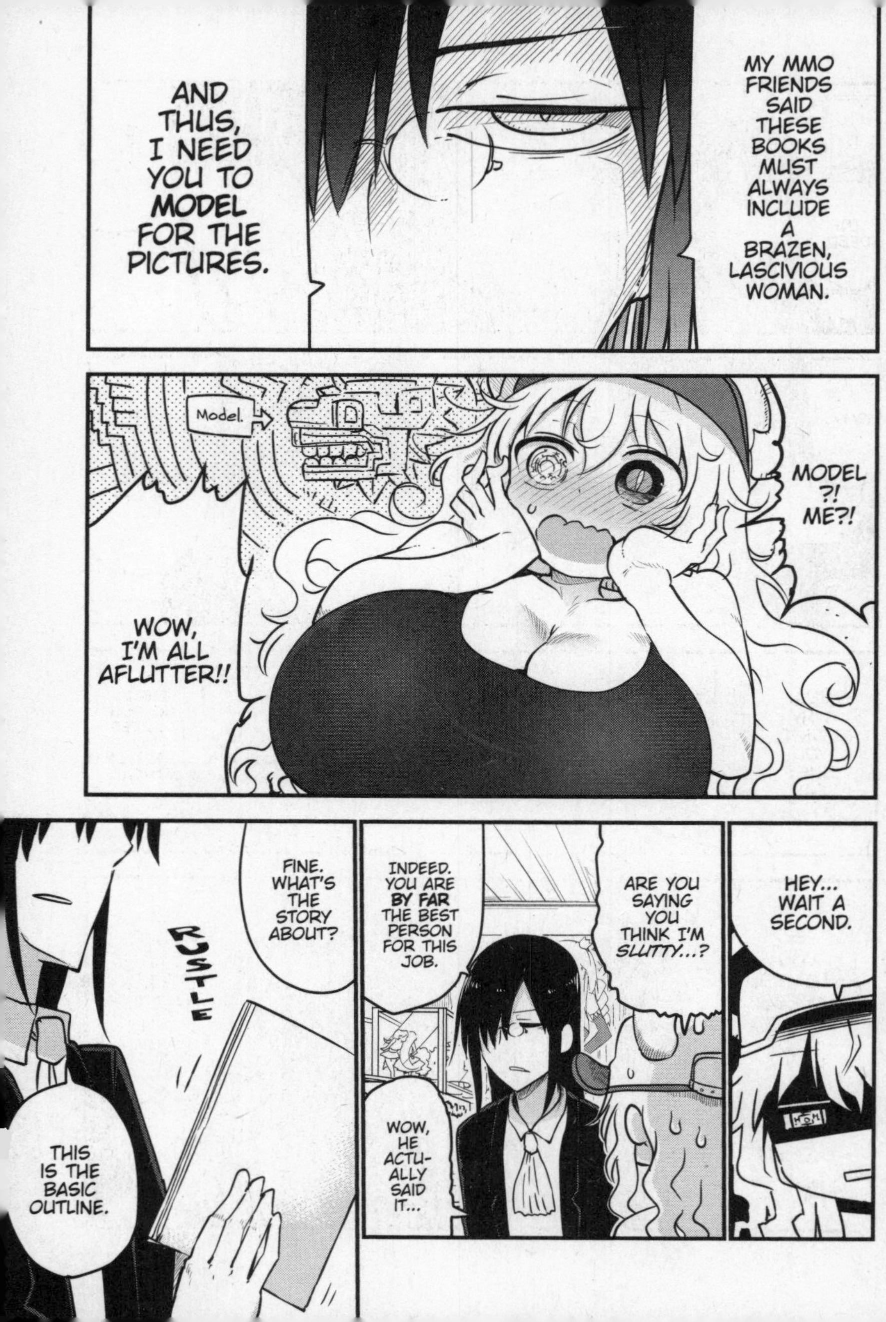
MY MMO FRIENDS SAID THESE BOOKS MUST ALWAYS INCLUDE A BRAZEN, LASCIVIOUS WOMAN.
AND THUS, I NEED YOU TO MODEL FOR THE PICTURES.
MODEL ?! ME?!
Model.
WOW, I'M ALL AFLUTTER!!
HEY... WAIT A SECOND.
ARE YOU SAYING YOU THINK I'M *SLUTTY...?*
INDEED. YOU ARE **BY FAR** THE BEST PERSON FOR THIS JOB.
WOW, HE ACTU-ALLY SAID IT...
FINE. WHAT'S THE STORY ABOUT?
RUSTLE
THIS IS THE BASIC OUTLINE.

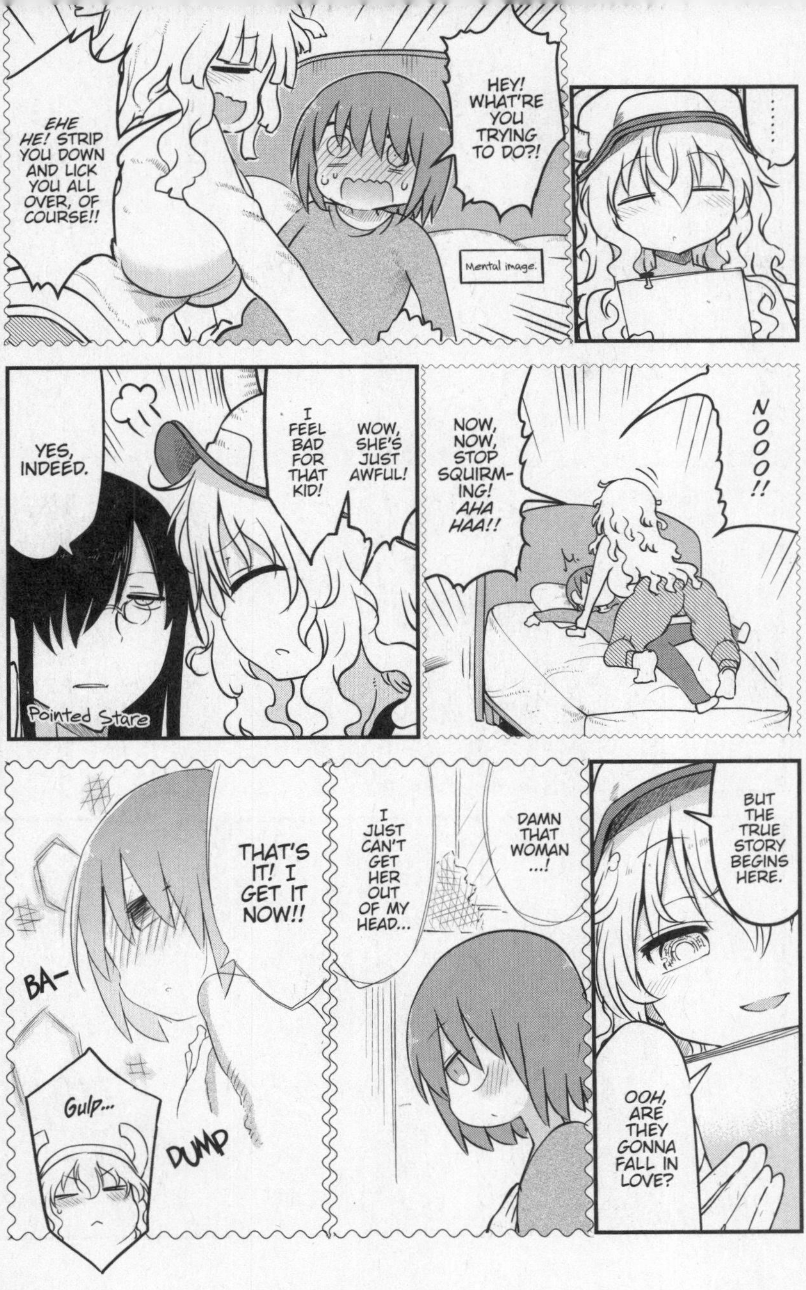
......
HEY! WHAT'RE YOU TRYING TO DO?!
EHE HE! STRIP YOU DOWN AND LICK YOU ALL OVER, OF COURSE!!
Mental image.
NOOOO!!
NOW, NOW, STOP SQUIRMING! AHA HAA!!
WOW, SHE'S JUST AWFUL!
I FEEL BAD FOR THAT KID!
YES, INDEED.
Pointed Stare
BUT THE TRUE STORY BEGINS HERE.
OOH, ARE THEY GONNA FALL IN LOVE?
DAMN THAT WOMAN ...!
I JUST CAN'T GET HER OUT OF MY HEAD...
THAT'S IT! I GET IT NOW!!
BA-
DUMP
Gulp...

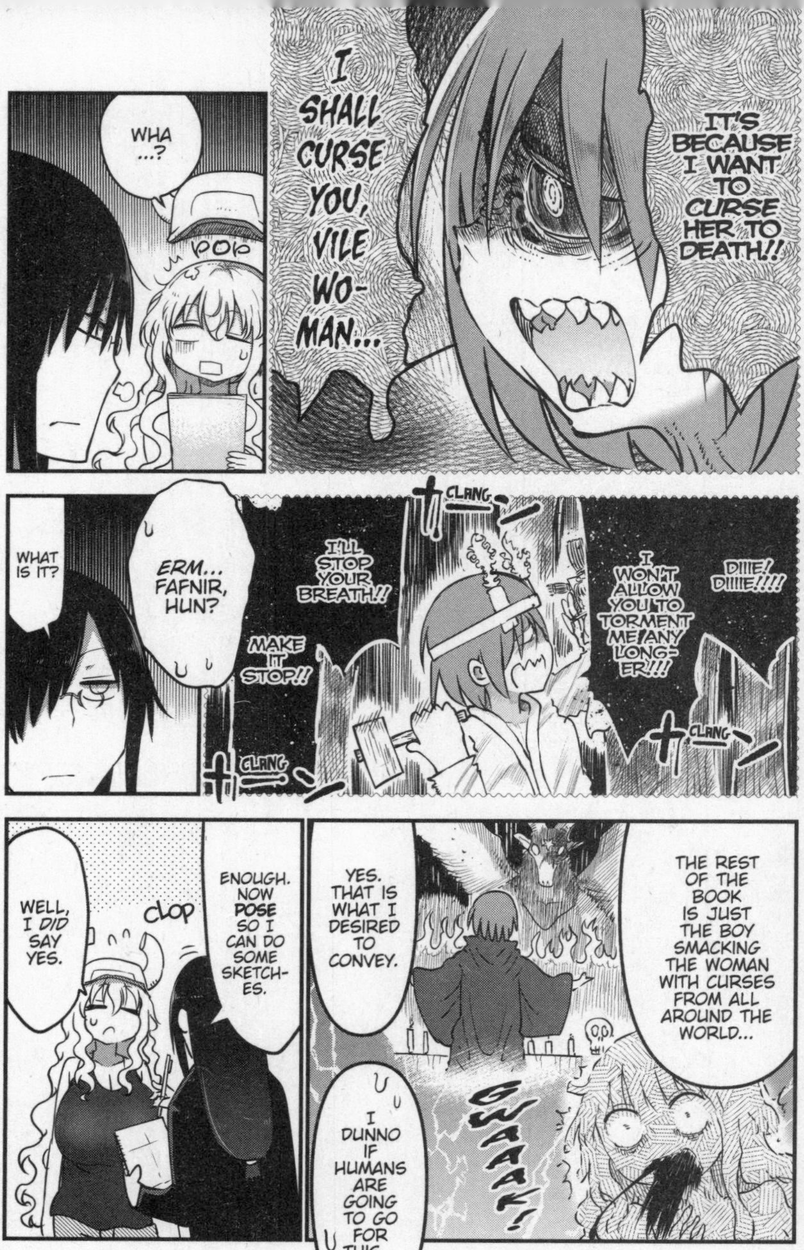
IT'S BECAUSE I WANT TO CURSE HER TO DEATH!!
I SHALL CURSE YOU, VILE WO-MAN...
WHA ...?
POP
CLANG
DIIIE! DIIIE!!!!
I WON'T ALLOW YOU TO TORMENT ME ANY LONGER!!!
CLANG
I'LL STOP YOUR BREATH!!
MAKE IT STOP!!
CLANG
ERM... FAFNIR, HUN?
WHAT IS IT?
THE REST OF THE BOOK IS JUST THE BOY SMACKING THE WOMAN WITH CURSES FROM ALL AROUND THE WORLD...
GWAAAK!
I DUNNO IF HUMANS ARE GOING TO GO FOR THIS...
YES. THAT IS WHAT I DESIRED TO CONVEY.
ENOUGH. NOW POSE SO I CAN DO SOME SKETCHES.
CLOP
WELL, I DID SAY YES.

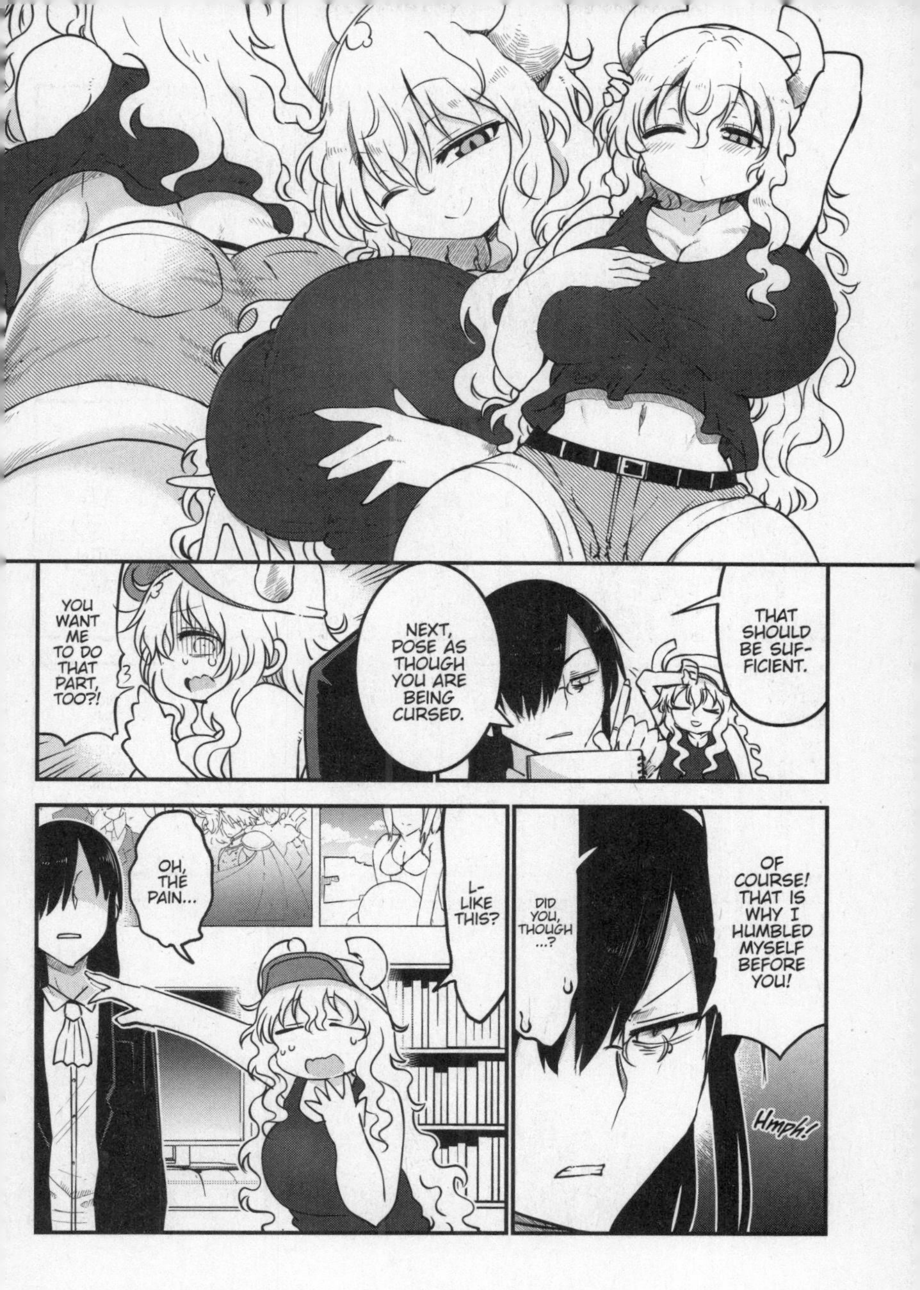
THAT SHOULD BE SUF- FICIENT.
NEXT, POSE AS THOUGH YOU ARE BEING CURSED.
YOU WANT ME TO DO THAT PART, TOO?!
OF COURSE! THAT IS WHY I HUMBLED MYSELF BEFORE YOU!
DID YOU, THOUGH ...?
Hmph!
L- LIKE THIS?
OH, THE PAIN...

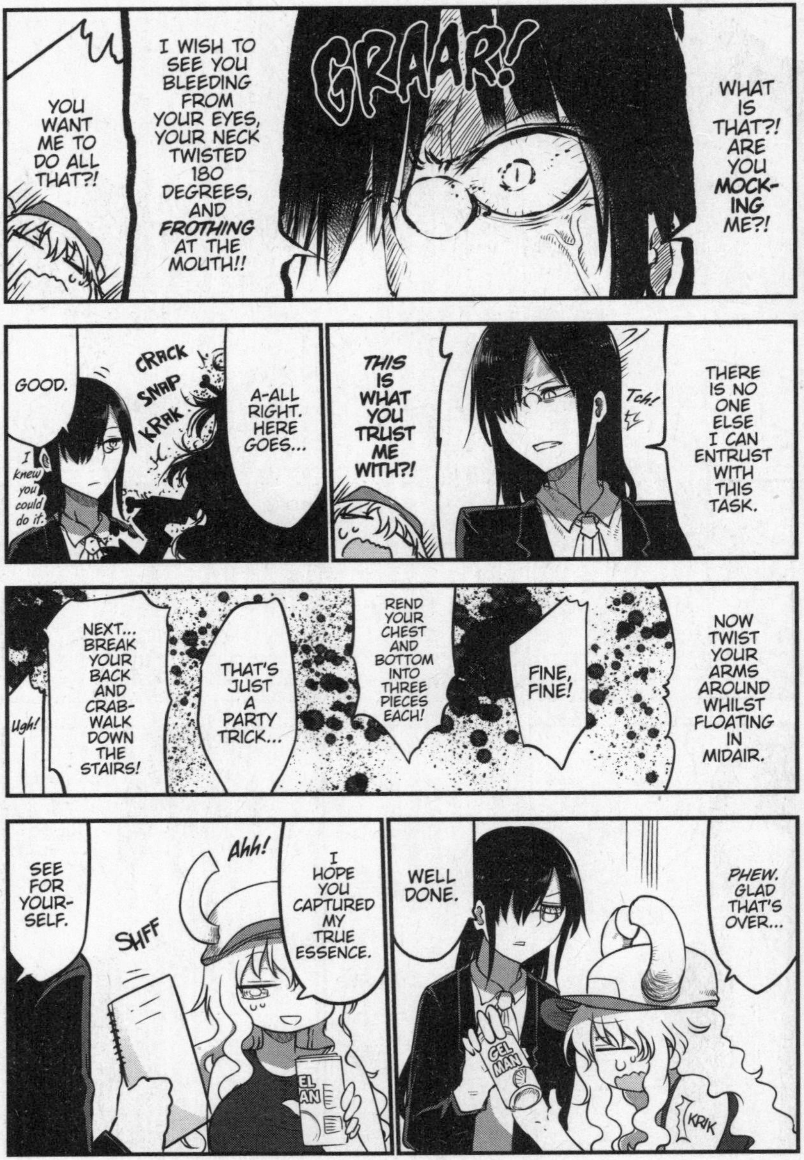
WHAT IS THAT?! ARE YOU MOCKING ME?!
GRAAR!
I WISH TO SEE YOU BLEEDING FROM YOUR EYES, YOUR NECK TWISTED 180 DEGREES, AND FROTHING AT THE MOUTH!!
YOU WANT ME TO DO ALL THAT?!
THERE IS NO ONE ELSE I CAN ENTRUST WITH THIS TASK.
Tch!
THIS IS WHAT YOU TRUST ME WITH?!
A-ALL RIGHT. HERE GOES...
CRACK
SNAP
KRAK
GOOD.
I knew you could do it.
NOW TWIST YOUR ARMS AROUND WHILST FLOATING IN MIDAIR.
FINE, FINE!
REND YOUR CHEST AND BOTTOM INTO THREE PIECES EACH!
THAT'S JUST A PARTY TRICK...
NEXT... BREAK YOUR BACK AND CRAB-WALK DOWN THE STAIRS!
Ugh!
PHEW. GLAD THAT'S OVER...
WELL DONE.
GEL MAN
KRIK
I HOPE YOU CAPTURED MY TRUE ESSENCE.
Ahh!
SEE FOR YOURSELF.
SHFF

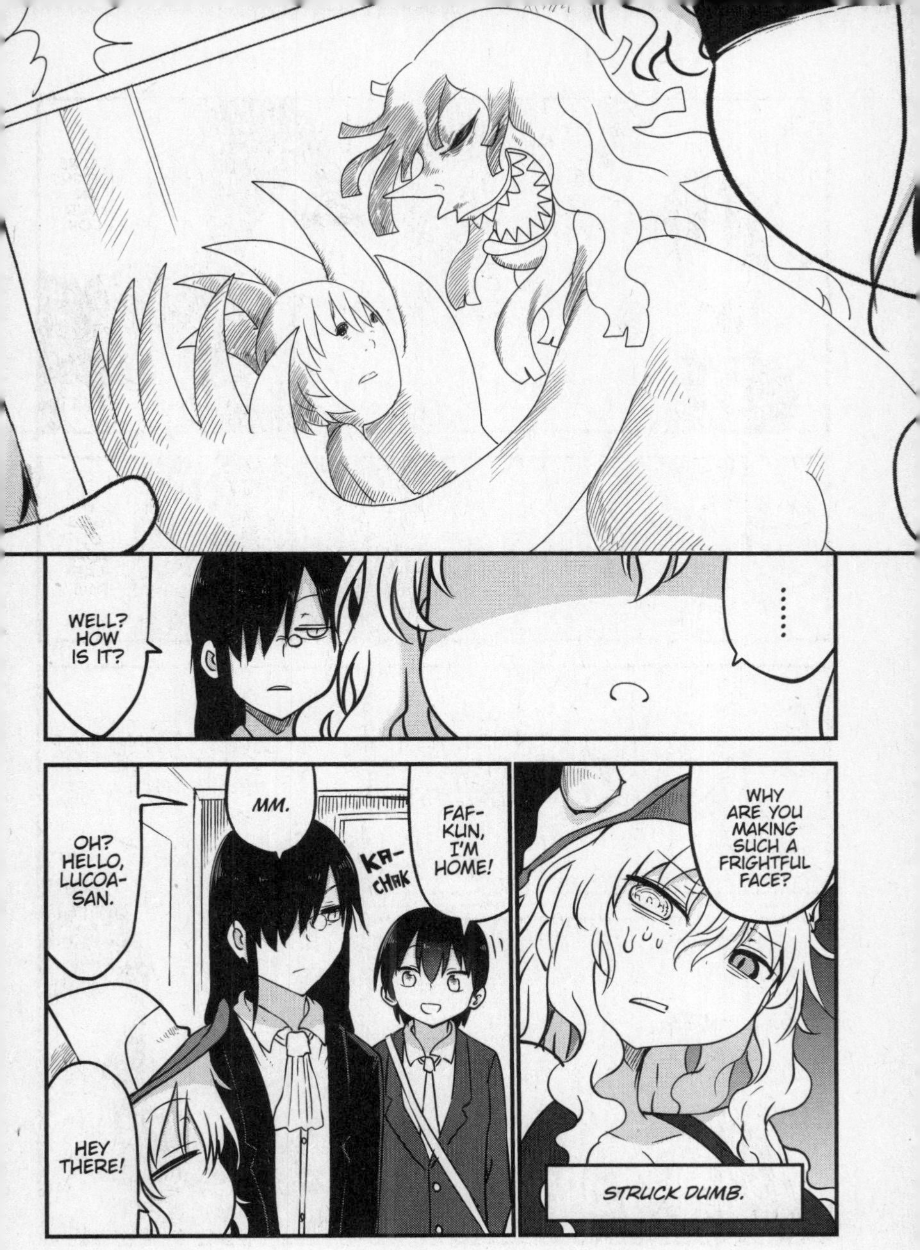
......
WELL? HOW IS IT?
WHY ARE YOU MAKING SUCH A FRIGHTFUL FACE?
STRUCK DUMB.
FAF-KUN, I'M HOME!
KA-CHAK
MM.
OH? HELLO, LUCOA-SAN.
HEY THERE!

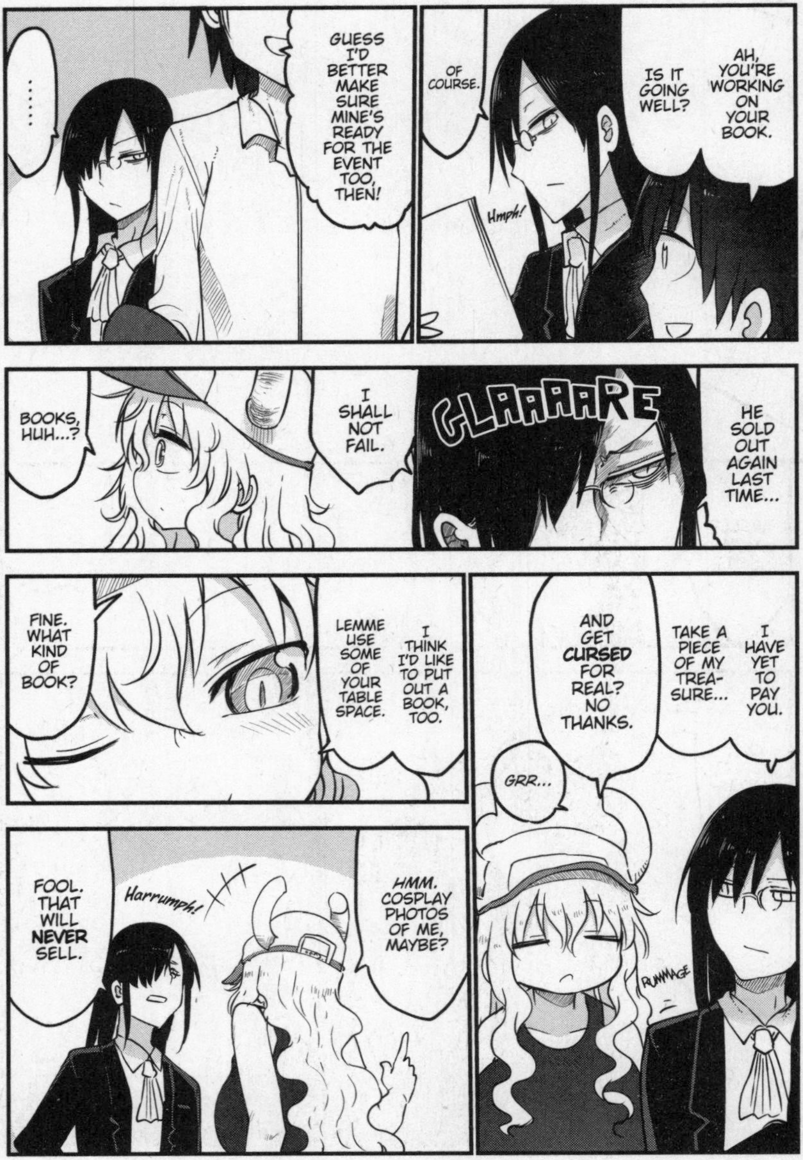
AH, YOU'RE WORKING ON YOUR BOOK.
IS IT GOING WELL?
OF COURSE.
Hmph!
GUESS I'D BETTER MAKE SURE MINE'S READY FOR THE EVENT TOO, THEN!
......
HE SOLD OUT AGAIN LAST TIME...
GLAAAARE
I SHALL NOT FAIL.
BOOKS, HUH...?
I HAVE YET TO PAY YOU.
TAKE A PIECE OF MY TREA-SURE...
AND GET **CURSED** FOR REAL? NO THANKS.
GRR...
RUMMAGE
I THINK I'D LIKE TO PUT OUT A BOOK, TOO.
LEMME USE SOME OF YOUR TABLE SPACE.
FINE. WHAT KIND OF BOOK?
HMM. COSPLAY PHOTOS OF ME, MAYBE?
Harrumph!
FOOL. THAT WILL **NEVER** SELL.

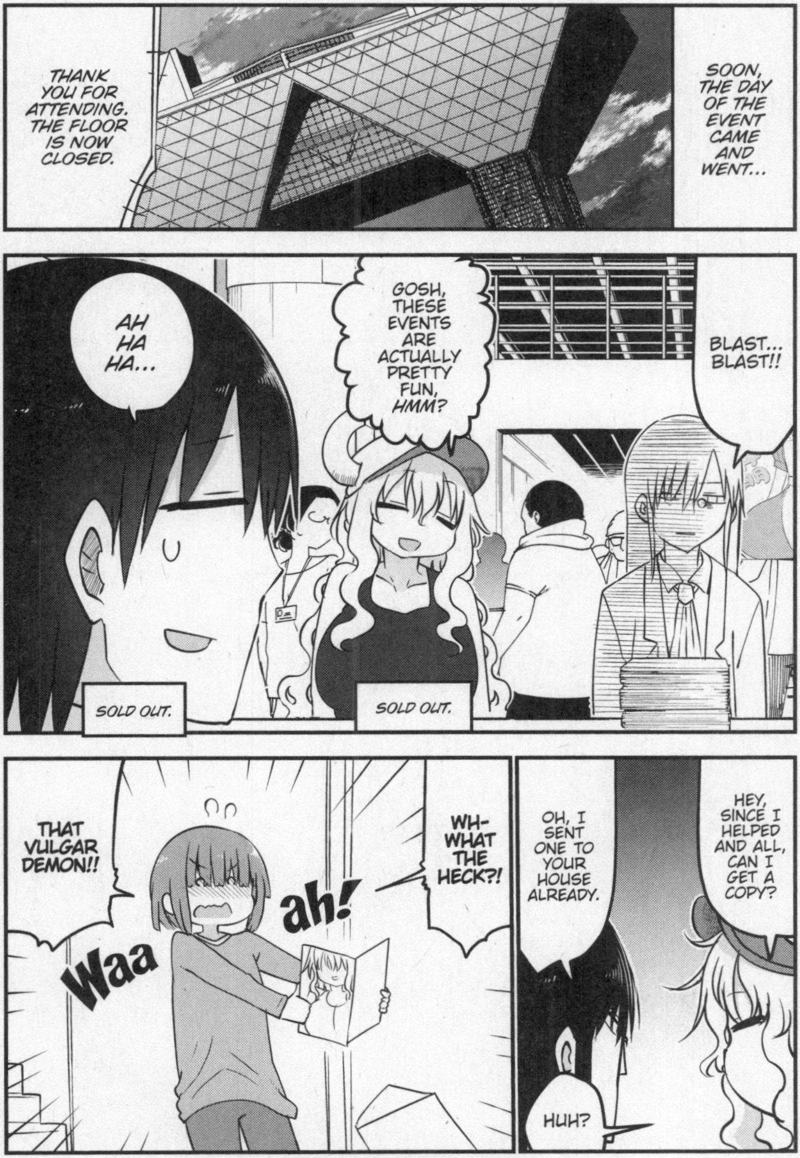
SOON, THE DAY OF THE EVENT CAME AND WENT...
THANK YOU FOR ATTENDING. THE FLOOR IS NOW CLOSED.
BLAST... BLAST!!
GOSH, THESE EVENTS ARE ACTUALLY PRETTY FUN, HMM?
AH HA HA...
SOLD OUT.
SOLD OUT.
HEY, SINCE I HELPED AND ALL, CAN I GET A COPY?
OH, I SENT ONE TO YOUR HOUSE ALREADY.
HUH?
WH- WHAT THE HECK?!
ah!
Waa
THAT VULGAR DEMON!!

CHAPTER 61/END

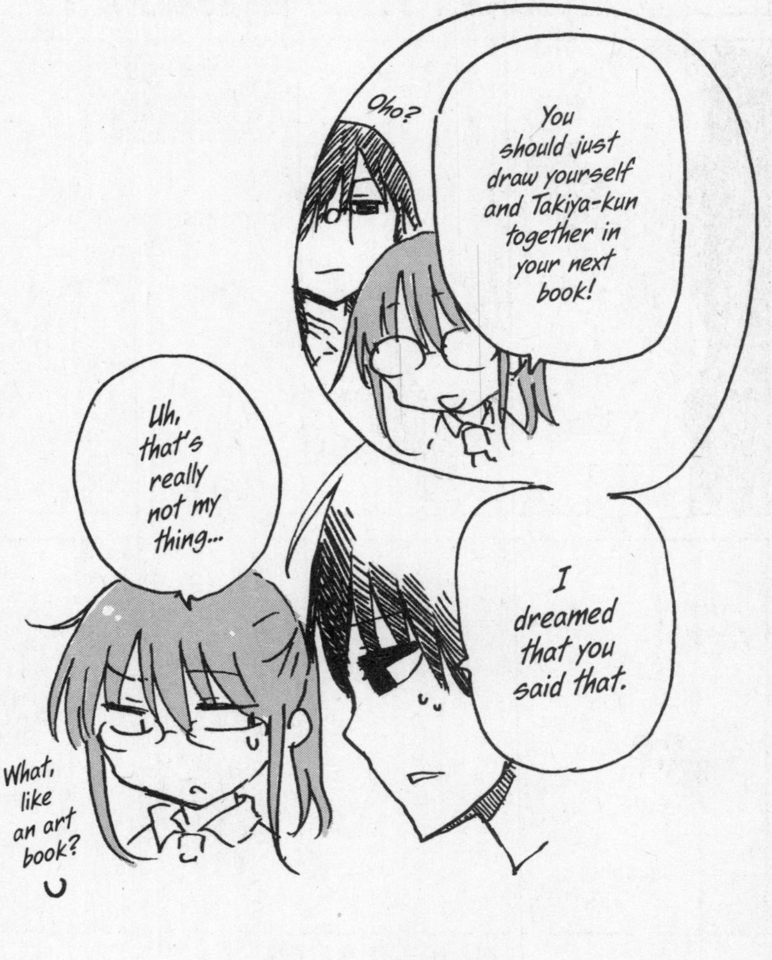
Oho?
You should just draw yourself and Takiya-kun together in your next book!
Uh, that's really not my thing...
I dreamed that you said that.
What, like an art book?

Miss Kobayashi's Dragon Maid

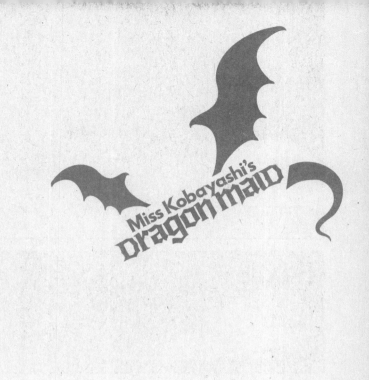

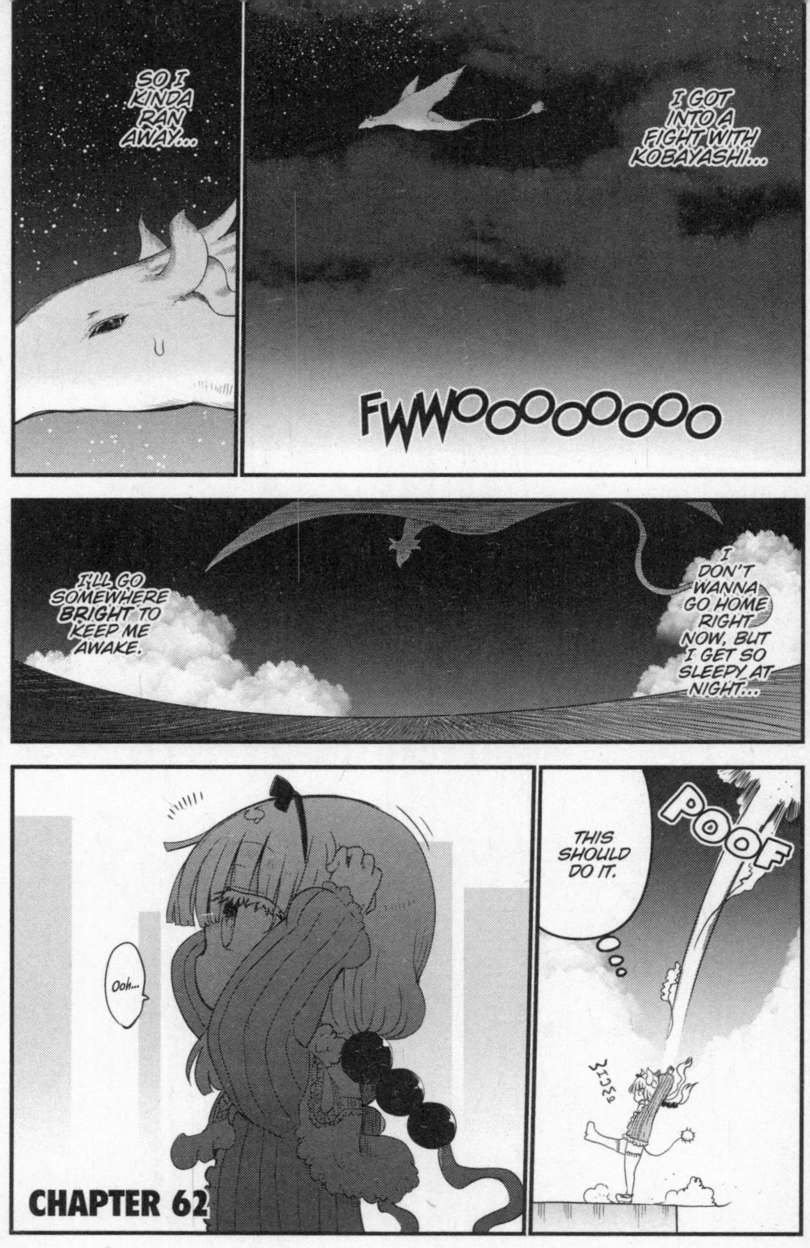
I GOT INTO A FIGHT WITH KOBAYASHI...
FWWOOOOOOOOOO
SO I KINDA RAN AWAY...
I DON'T WANNA GO HOME RIGHT NOW, BUT I GET SO SLEEPY AT NIGHT...
I'LL GO SOMEWHERE BRIGHT TO KEEP ME AWAKE.
POOF
THIS SHOULD DO IT.
Ooh...
CHAPTER 62

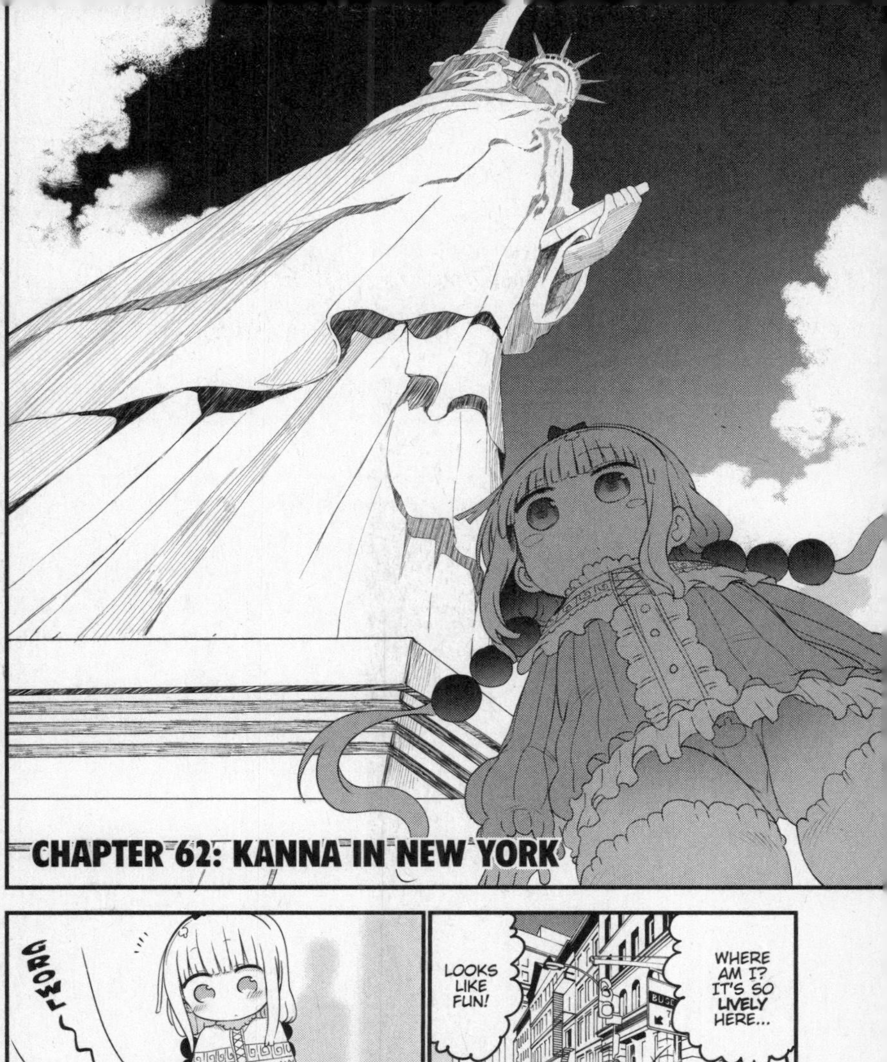
CHAPTER 62: KANNA IN NEW YORK
WHERE AM I? IT'S SO LIVELY HERE...
LOOKS LIKE FUN!
GROWL

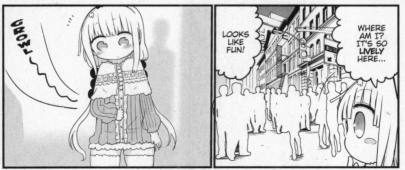

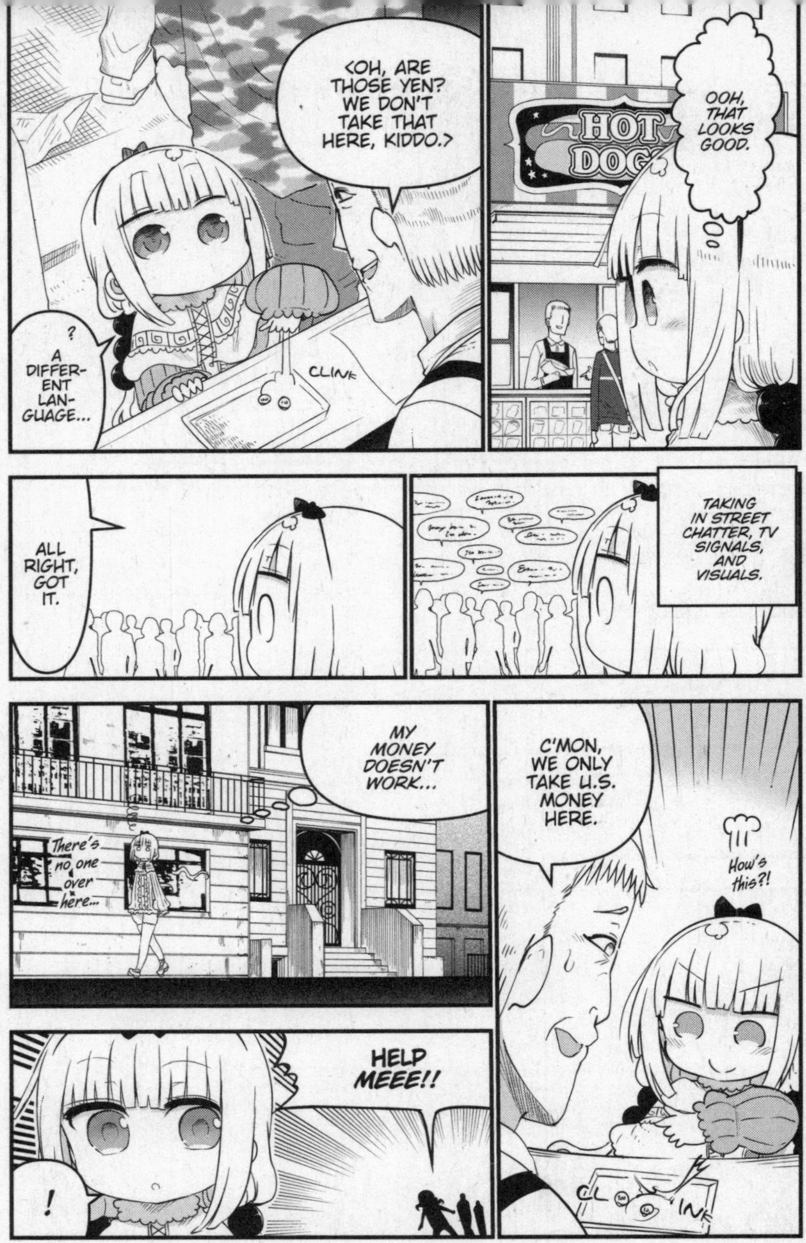
OOH, THAT LOOKS GOOD.
HOT DOG
<OH, ARE THOSE YEN? WE DON'T TAKE THAT HERE, KIDDO.>
CLINK
? A DIFFERENT LANGUAGE...
TAKING IN STREET CHATTER, TV SIGNALS, AND VISUALS.
ALL RIGHT, GOT IT.
C'MON, WE ONLY TAKE U.S. MONEY HERE.
How's this?!
CLINK
MY MONEY DOESN'T WORK...
There's no one over here...
HELP MEEE!!
!

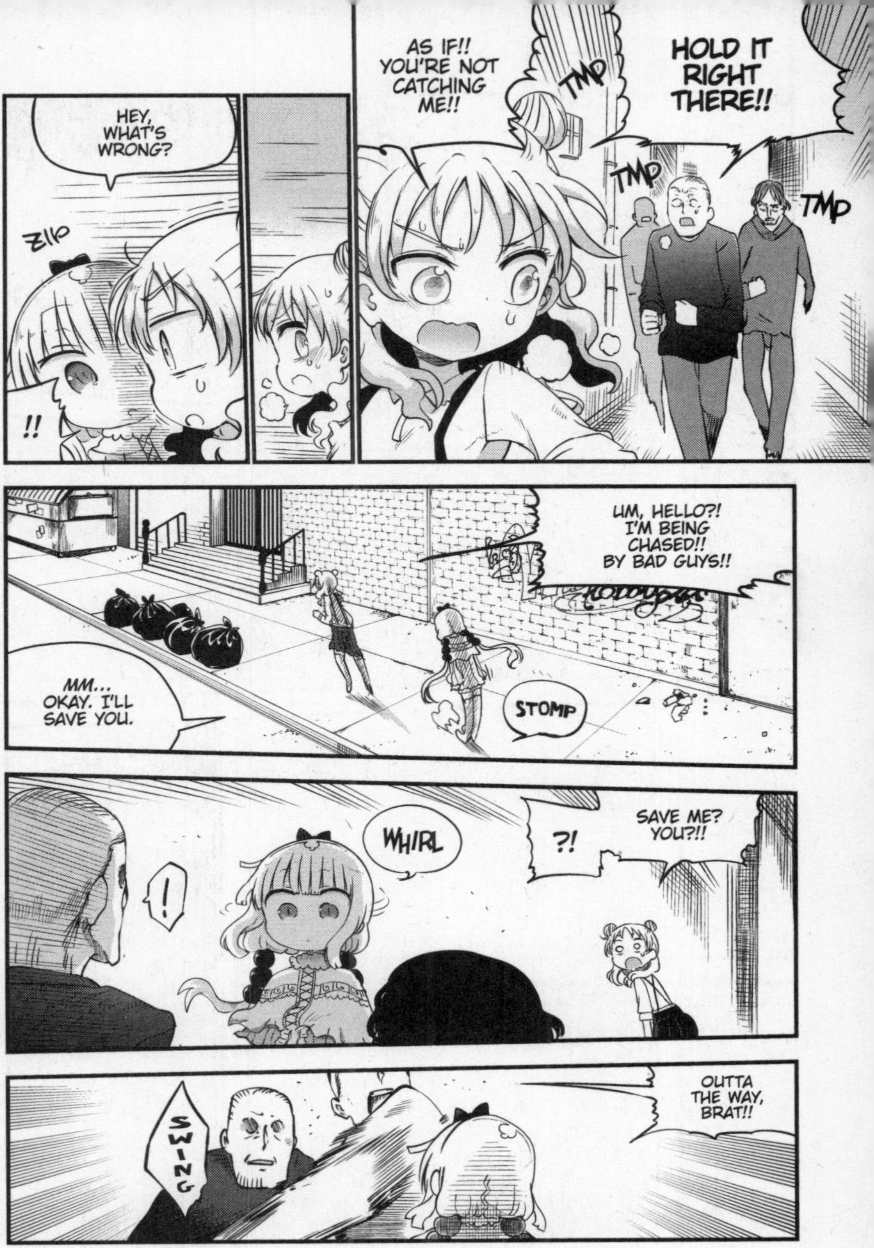
HOLD IT RIGHT THERE!!
TMP
TMP
TMP
AS IF!! YOU'RE NOT CATCHING ME!!
HEY, WHAT'S WRONG?
ZIP
!!
UM, HELLO?! I'M BEING CHASED!! BY BAD GUYS!!
STOMP
MM... OKAY. I'LL SAVE YOU.
SAVE ME? YOU?!!
?!
WHIRL
!
OUTTA THE WAY, BRAT!!
SWING

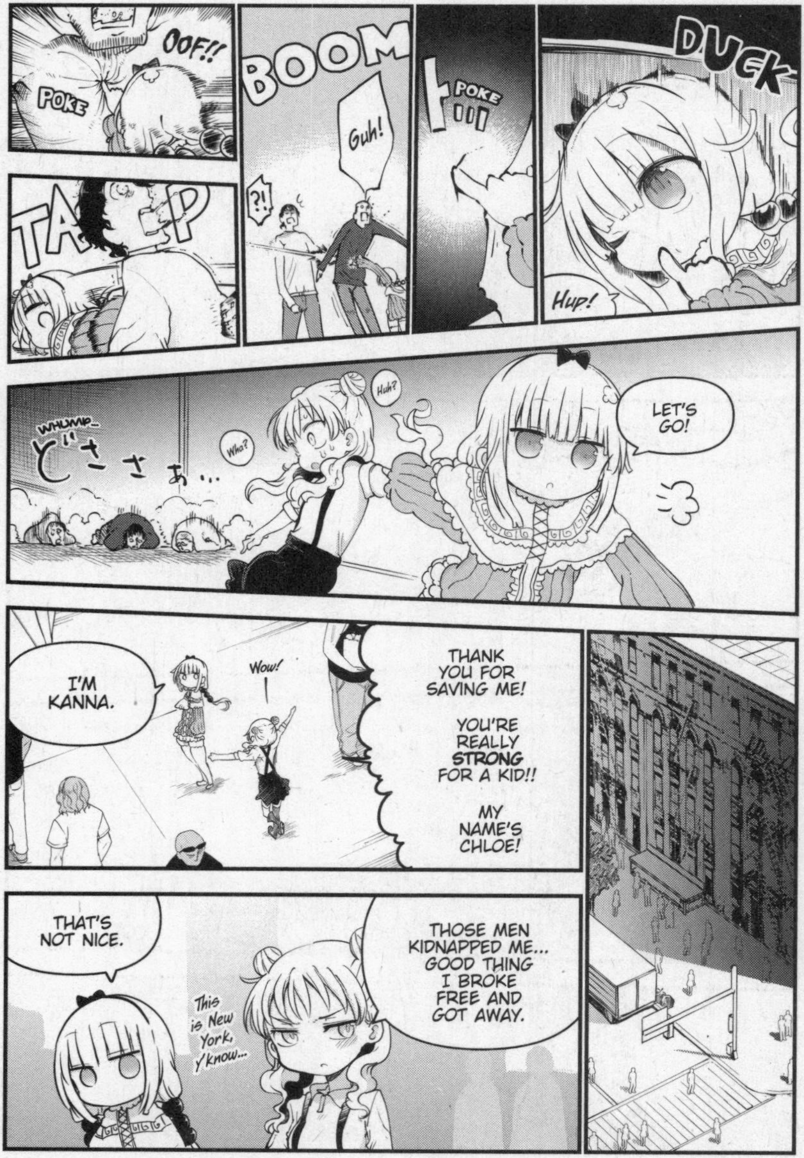
DUCK
Hup!
POKE
BOOM
Guh!
?!
OOF!!
POKE
TAP
LET'S GO!
Huh?
Wha?
WHUMP...
どささぁ…
THANK YOU FOR SAVING ME!
YOU'RE REALLY STRONG FOR A KID!!
MY NAME'S CHLOE!
Wow!
I'M KANNA.
THOSE MEN KIDNAPPED ME... GOOD THING I BROKE FREE AND GOT AWAY.
This is New York, y'know...
THAT'S NOT NICE.

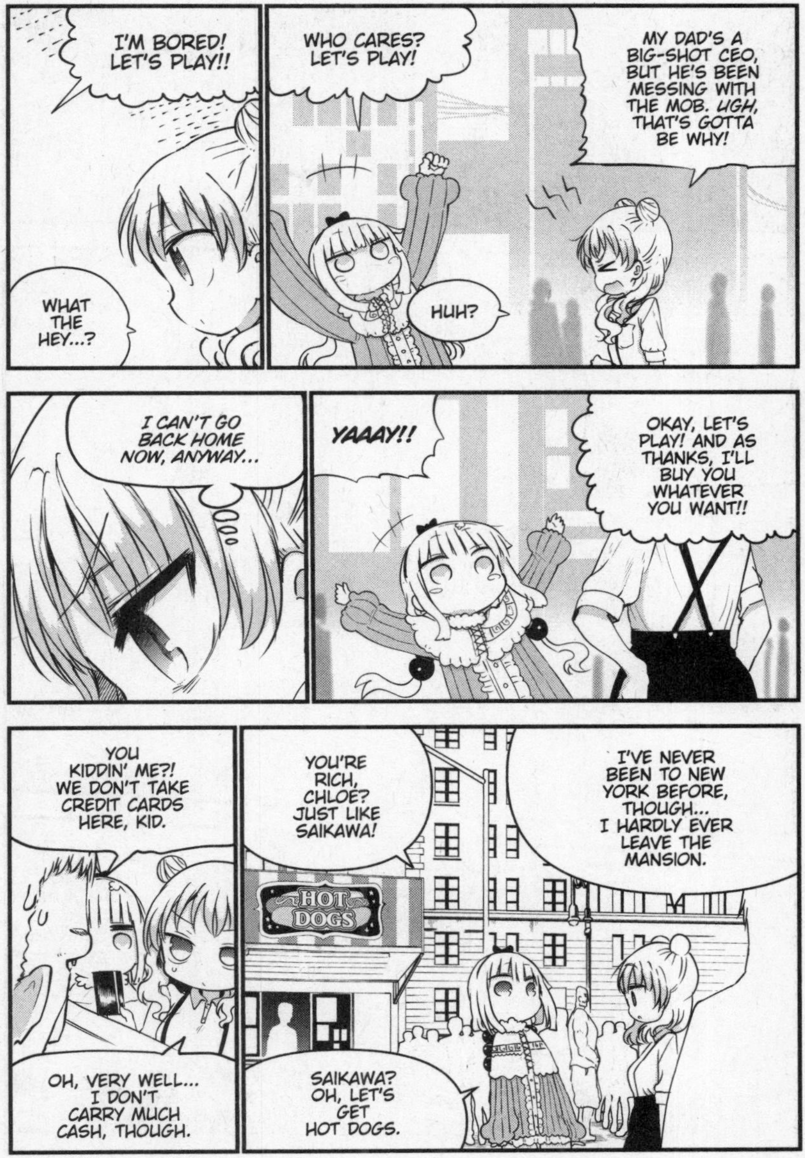
MY DAD'S A BIG-SHOT CEO, BUT HE'S BEEN MESSING WITH THE MOB. UGH, THAT'S GOTTA BE WHY!
WHO CARES? LET'S PLAY!
HUH?
I'M BORED! LET'S PLAY!!
WHAT THE HEY...?
OKAY, LET'S PLAY! AND AS THANKS, I'LL BUY YOU WHATEVER YOU WANT!!
YAAAY!!
I CAN'T GO BACK HOME NOW, ANYWAY...
I'VE NEVER BEEN TO NEW YORK BEFORE, THOUGH... I HARDLY EVER LEAVE THE MANSION.
YOU'RE RICH, CHLOE? JUST LIKE SAIKAWA!
HOT DOGS
SAIKAWA? OH, LET'S GET HOT DOGS.
YOU KIDDIN' ME?! WE DON'T TAKE CREDIT CARDS HERE, KID.
OH, VERY WELL... I DON'T CARRY MUCH CASH, THOUGH.

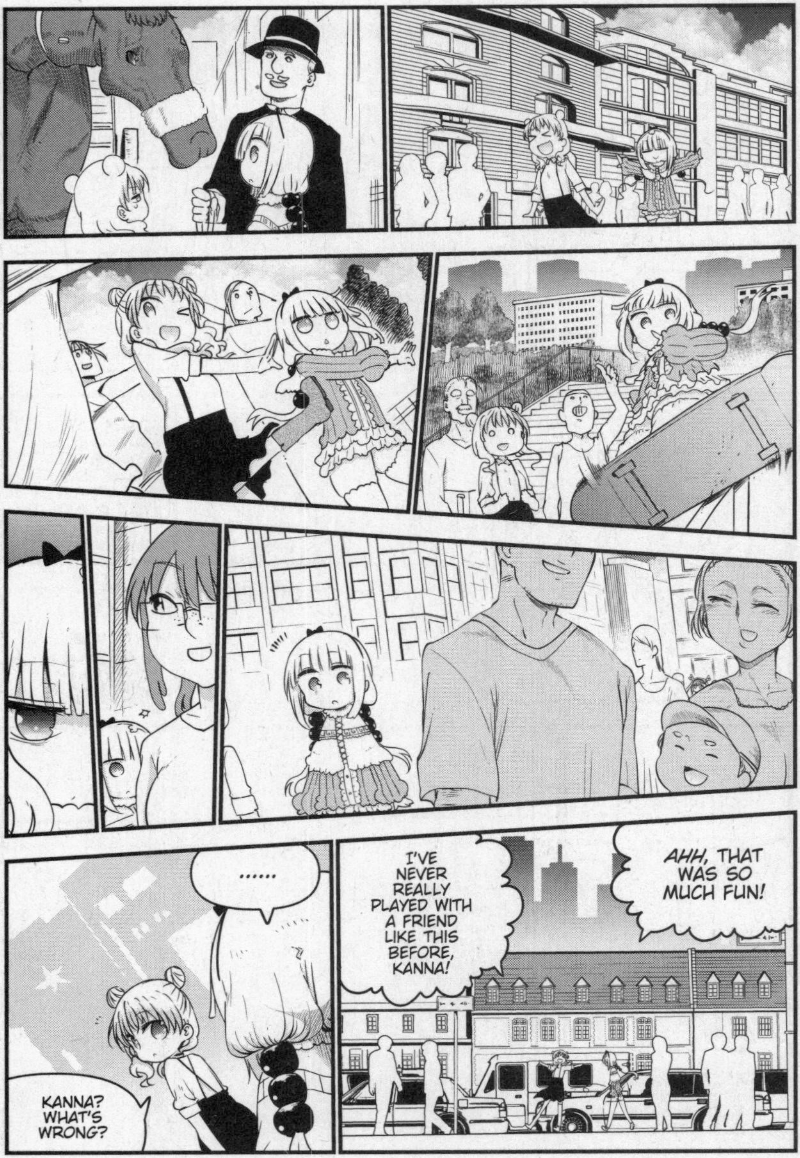
AHH, THAT WAS SO MUCH FUN!
I'VE NEVER REALLY PLAYED WITH A FRIEND LIKE THIS BEFORE, KANNA!
......
KANNA? WHAT'S WRONG?

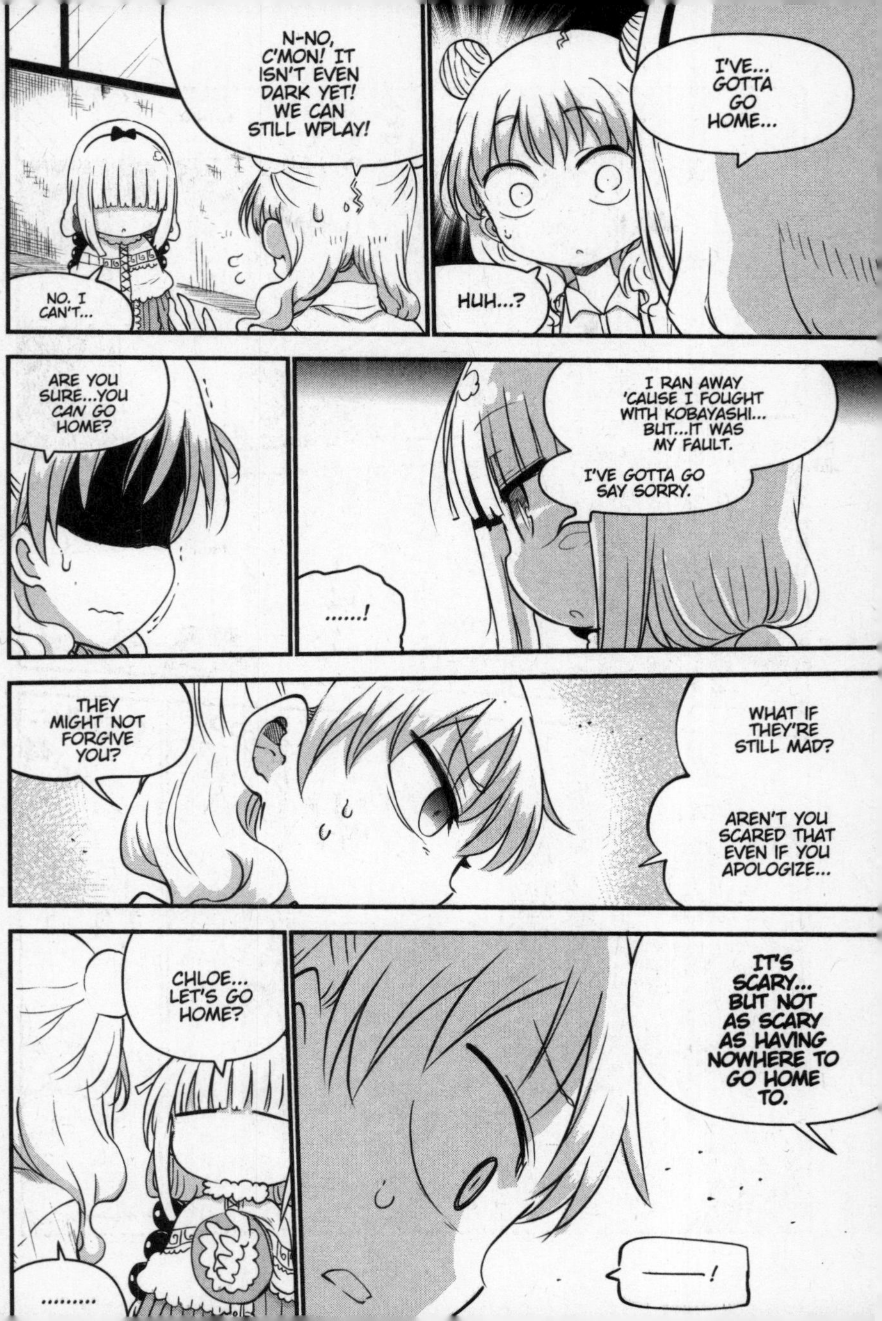
I'VE... GOTTA GO HOME...
HUH...?
N-NO, C'MON! IT ISN'T EVEN DARK YET! WE CAN STILL WPLAY!
NO. I CAN'T...
I RAN AWAY 'CAUSE I FOUGHT WITH KOBAYASHI... BUT...IT WAS MY FAULT.
I'VE GOTTA GO SAY SORRY.
......!
ARE YOU SURE...YOU CAN GO HOME?
WHAT IF THEY'RE STILL MAD?
AREN'T YOU SCARED THAT EVEN IF YOU APOLOGIZE...
THEY MIGHT NOT FORGIVE YOU?
IT'S SCARY... BUT NOT AS SCARY AS HAVING NOWHERE TO GO HOME TO.
——!
CHLOE... LET'S GO HOME?
....

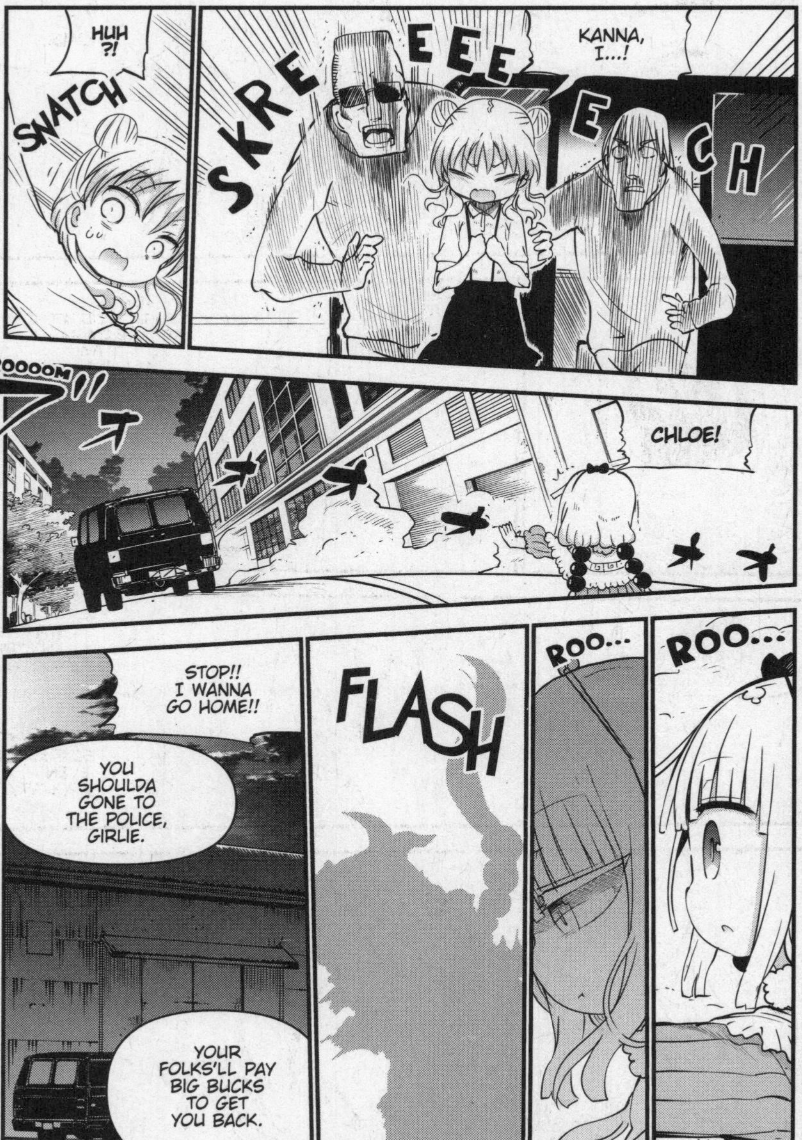
KANNA, I...!
SKREEEEECH
HUH ?!
SNATCH
VROOOOM
CHLOE!
ROO...
ROO...
FLASH
STOP!! I WANNA GO HOME!!
YOU SHOULDA GONE TO THE POLICE, GIRLIE.
YOUR FOLKS'LL PAY BIG BUCKS TO GET YOU BACK.

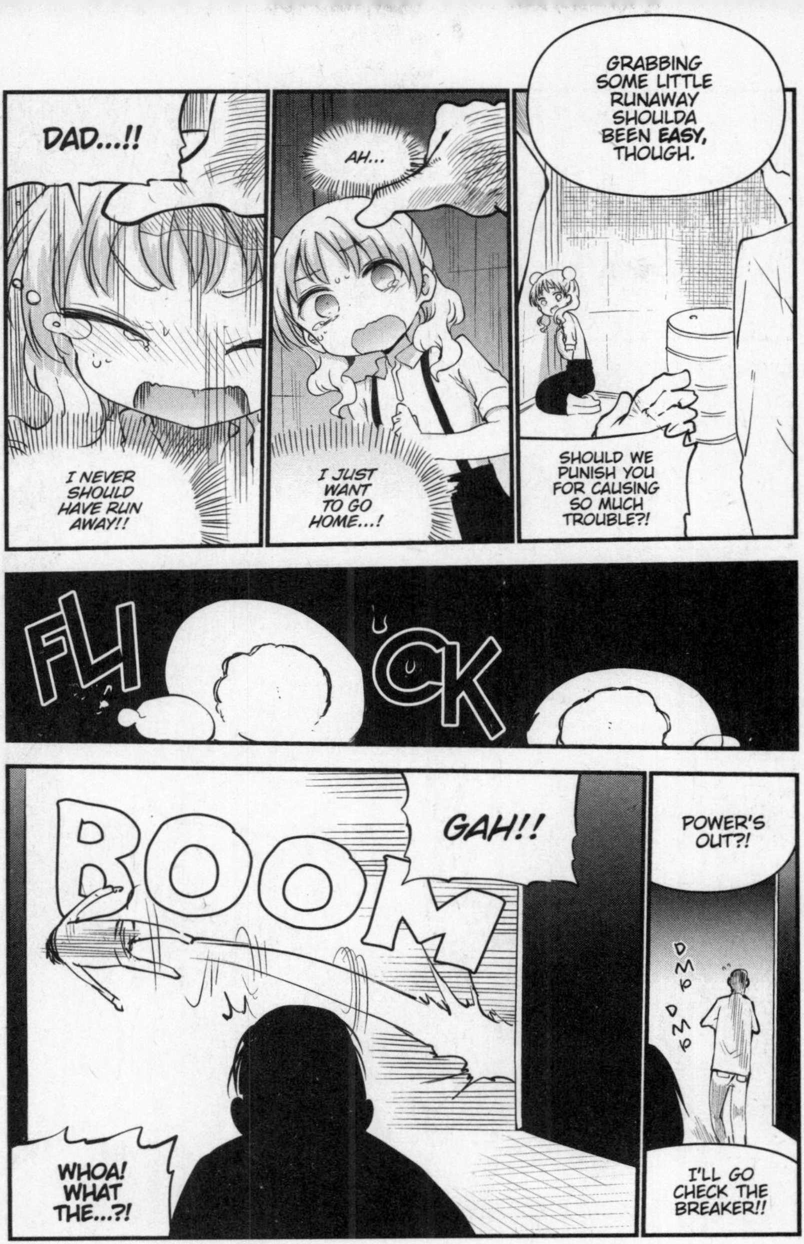
GRABBING SOME LITTLE RUNAWAY SHOULDA BEEN EASY, THOUGH.
SHOULD WE PUNISH YOU FOR CAUSING SO MUCH TROUBLE?!
AH...
I JUST WANT TO GO HOME...!
DAD...!!
I NEVER SHOULD HAVE RUN AWAY!!
FLICK
POWER'S OUT?!
DMP
DMP
I'LL GO CHECK THE BREAKER!!
GAH!!
BOOM
WHOA! WHAT THE...?!

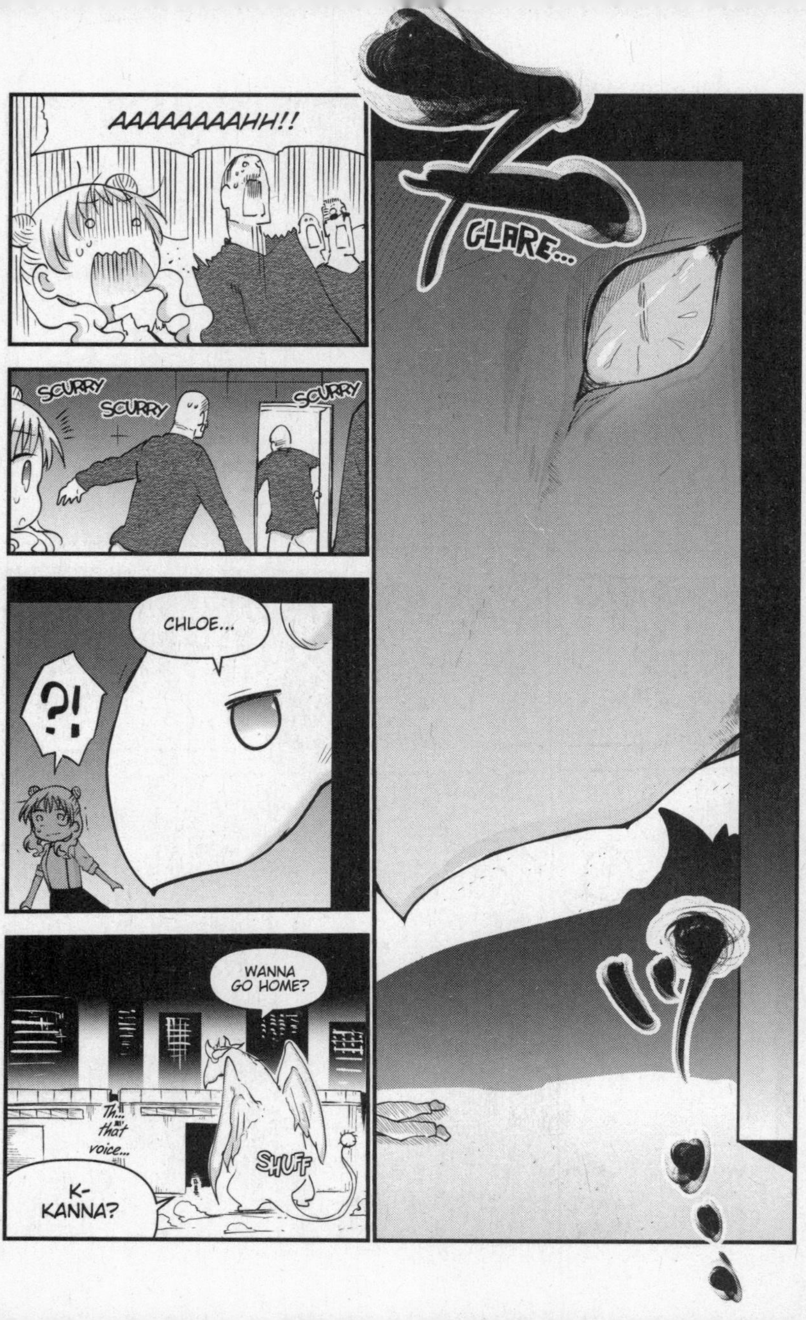
GLARE...
AAAAAAAAHH!!
SCURRY
SCURRY
SCURRY
CHLOE...
?!
WANNA GO HOME?
Th... that voice...
SHUFF
K-KANNA?

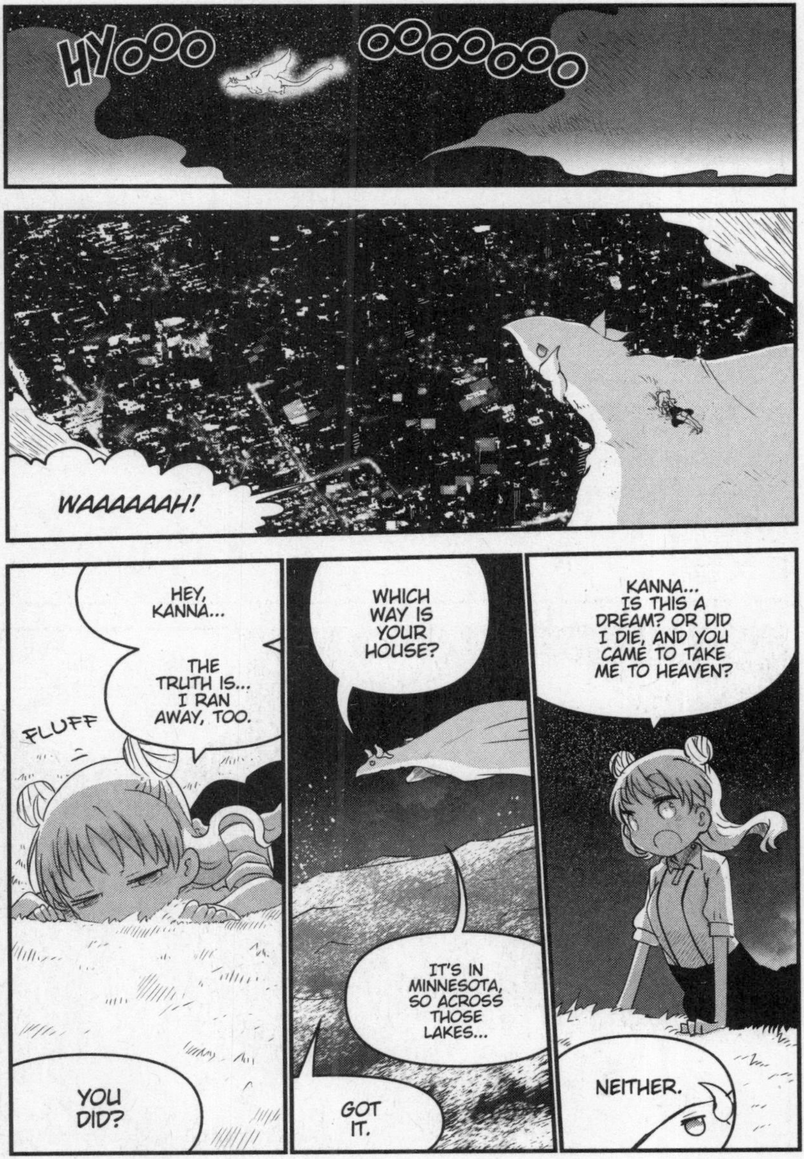
HYOOO
OOOOOOOO
WAAAAAAH!
KANNA... IS THIS A DREAM? OR DID I DIE, AND YOU CAME TO TAKE ME TO HEAVEN?
NEITHER.
WHICH WAY IS YOUR HOUSE?
IT'S IN MINNESOTA, SO ACROSS THOSE LAKES...
GOT IT.
HEY, KANNA...
THE TRUTH IS... I RAN AWAY, TOO.
FLUFF
YOU DID?

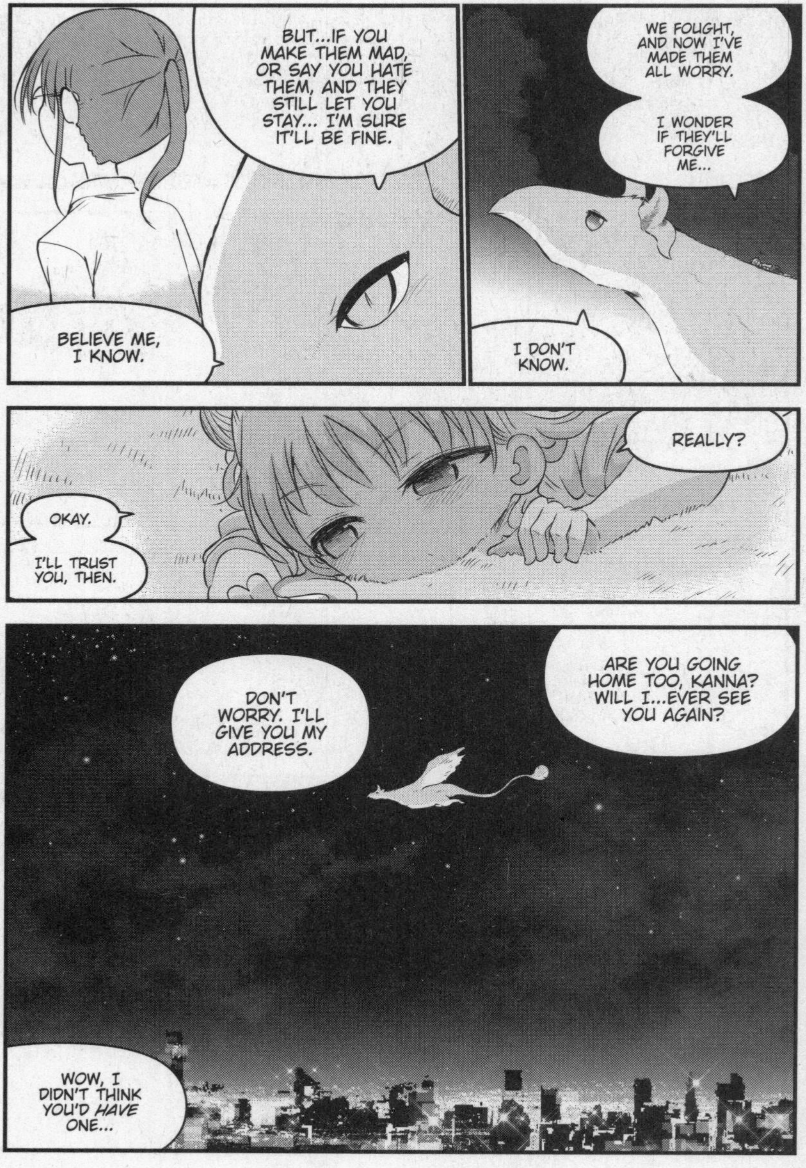
WE FOUGHT, AND NOW I'VE MADE THEM ALL WORRY.
I WONDER IF THEY'LL FORGIVE ME...
I DON'T KNOW.
BUT...IF YOU MAKE THEM MAD, OR SAY YOU HATE THEM, AND THEY STILL LET YOU STAY... I'M SURE IT'LL BE FINE.
BELIEVE ME, I KNOW.
REALLY?
OKAY.
I'LL TRUST YOU, THEN.
ARE YOU GOING HOME TOO, KANNA? WILL I...EVER SEE YOU AGAIN?
DON'T WORRY. I'LL GIVE YOU MY ADDRESS.
WOW, I DIDN'T THINK YOU'D *HAVE* ONE...

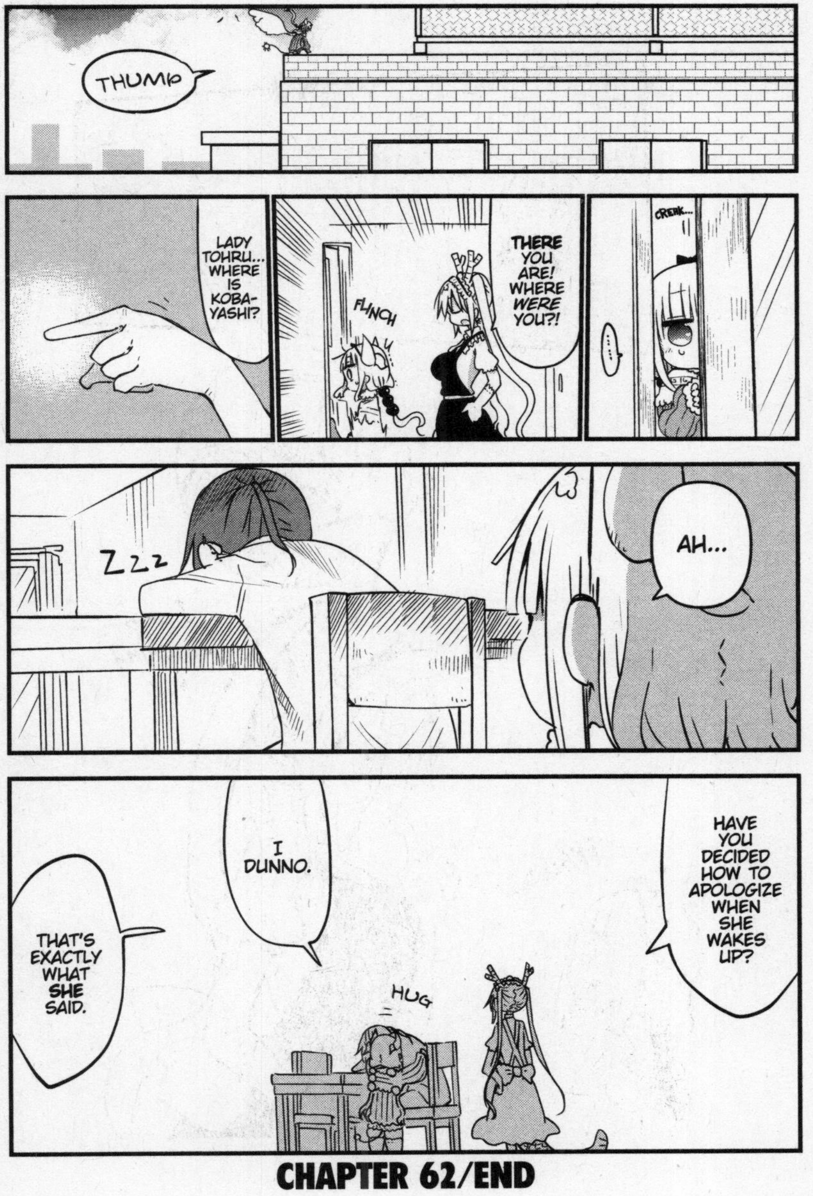
THUMP
CREAK...
...
THERE YOU ARE! WHERE WERE YOU?!
FLINCH
LADY TOHRU... WHERE IS KOBAYASHI?
AH...
Zzz
HAVE YOU DECIDED HOW TO APOLOGIZE WHEN SHE WAKES UP?
I DUNNO.
HUG
THAT'S EXACTLY WHAT SHE SAID.

CHAPTER 62/END

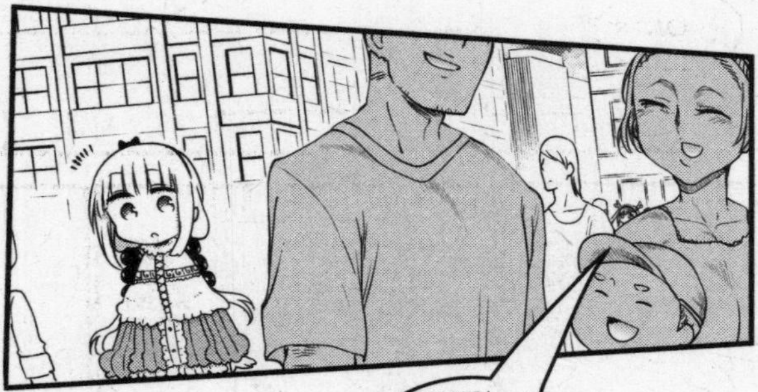

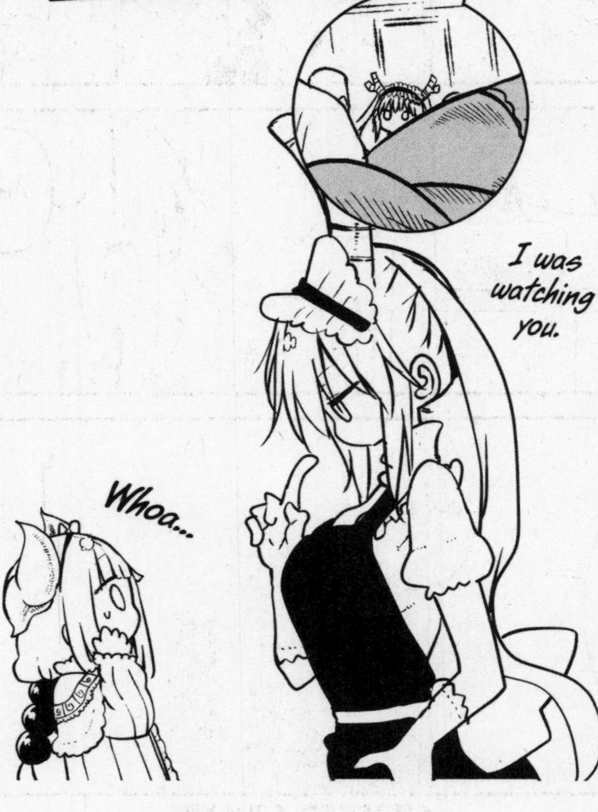
I was watching you.
Whoa...

Miss Kobayashi's
DRAGON MAID

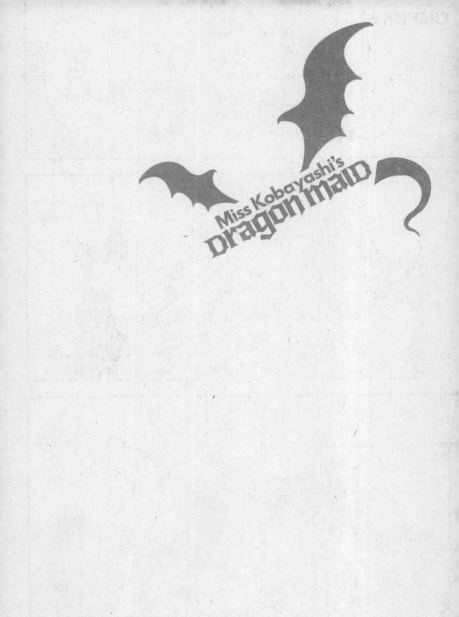

CHAPTER 63

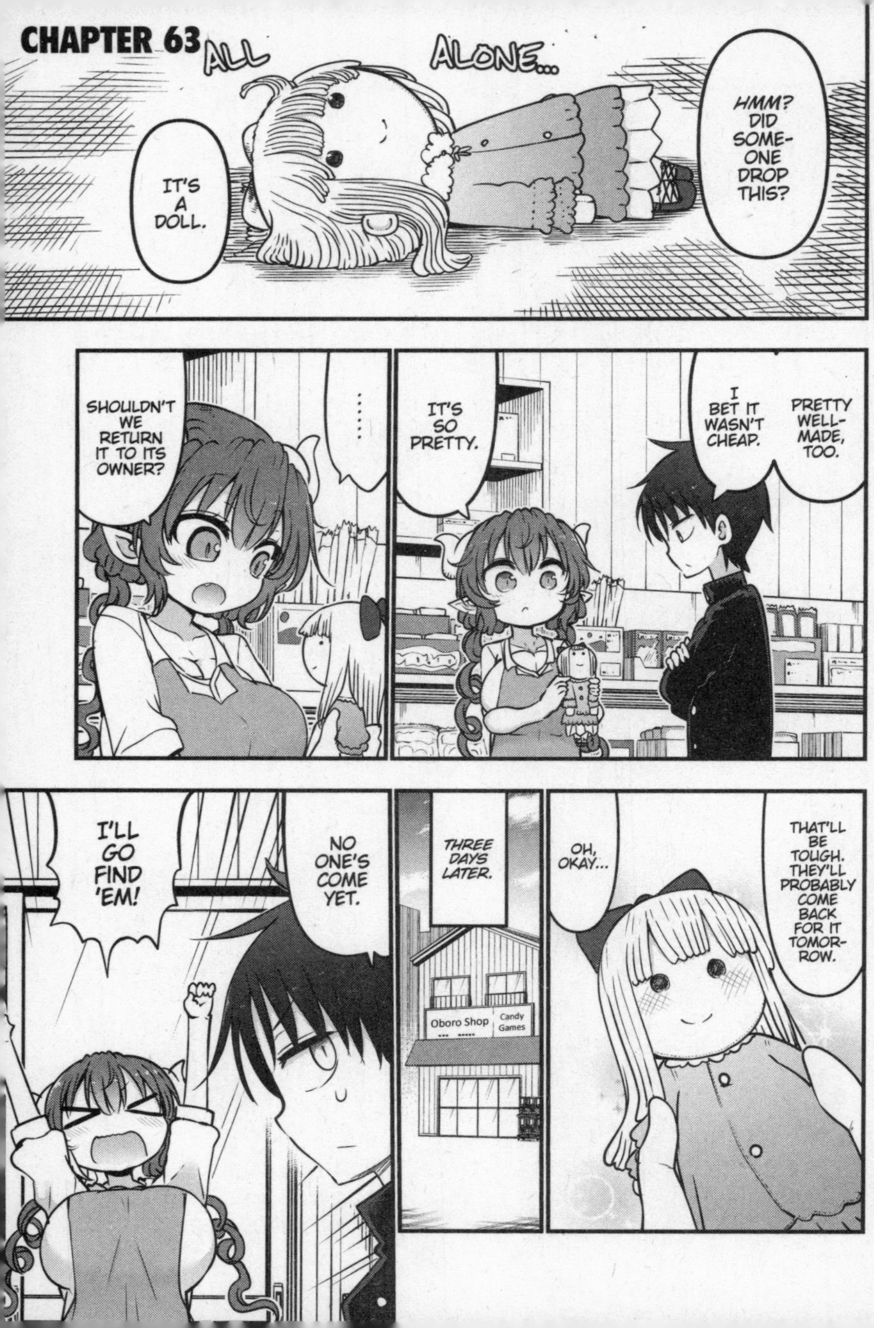
ALL ALONE...
HMM? DID SOME-ONE DROP THIS?
IT'S A DOLL.
PRETTY WELL-MADE, TOO.
I BET IT WASN'T CHEAP.
IT'S SO PRETTY.
......
SHOULDN'T WE RETURN IT TO ITS OWNER?
THAT'LL BE TOUGH. THEY'LL PROBABLY COME BACK FOR IT TOMOR-ROW.
OH, OKAY...
THREE DAYS LATER.
Oboro Shop
Candy Games
NO ONE'S COME YET.
I'LL GO FIND 'EM!

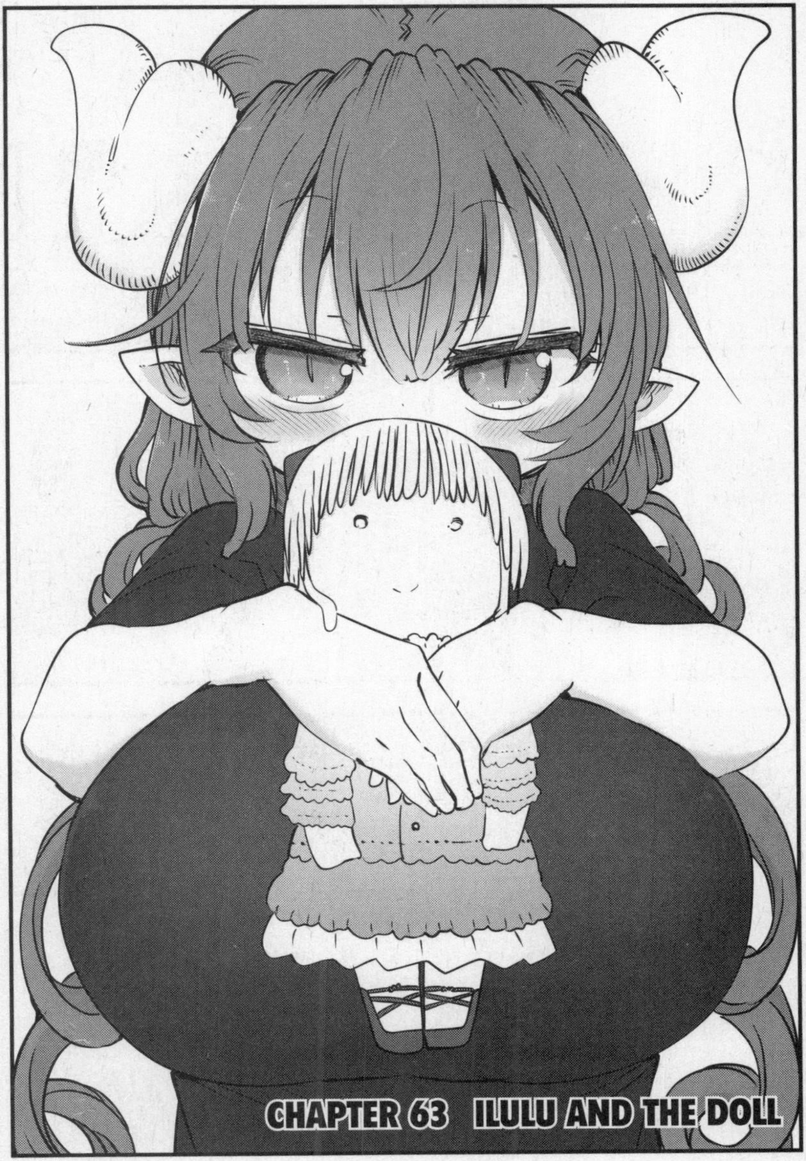

CHAPTER 63 ILULU AND THE DOLL

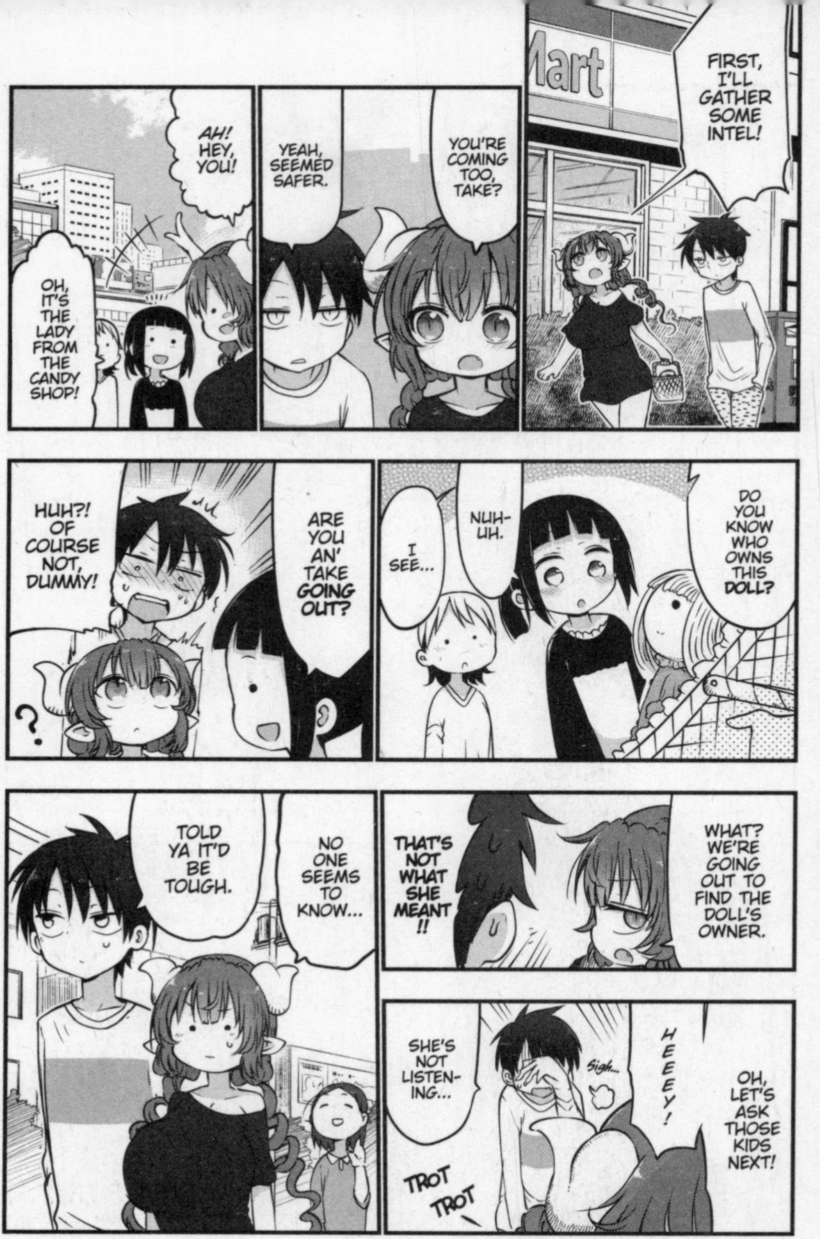
Mart
FIRST, I'LL GATHER SOME INTEL!
YOU'RE COMING TOO, TAKE?
YEAH, SEEMED SAFER.
AH! HEY, YOU!
OH, IT'S THE LADY FROM THE CANDY SHOP!
DO YOU KNOW WHO OWNS THIS DOLL?
NUH-UH.
I SEE...
ARE YOU AN' TAKE GOING OUT?
HUH?! OF COURSE NOT, DUMMY!
WHAT? WE'RE GOING OUT TO FIND THE DOLL'S OWNER.
THAT'S NOT WHAT SHE MEANT!!
OH, LET'S ASK THOSE KIDS NEXT!
HEEEY!
Sigh...
SHE'S NOT LISTENING...
TROT TROT
NO ONE SEEMS TO KNOW...
TOLD YA IT'D BE TOUGH.

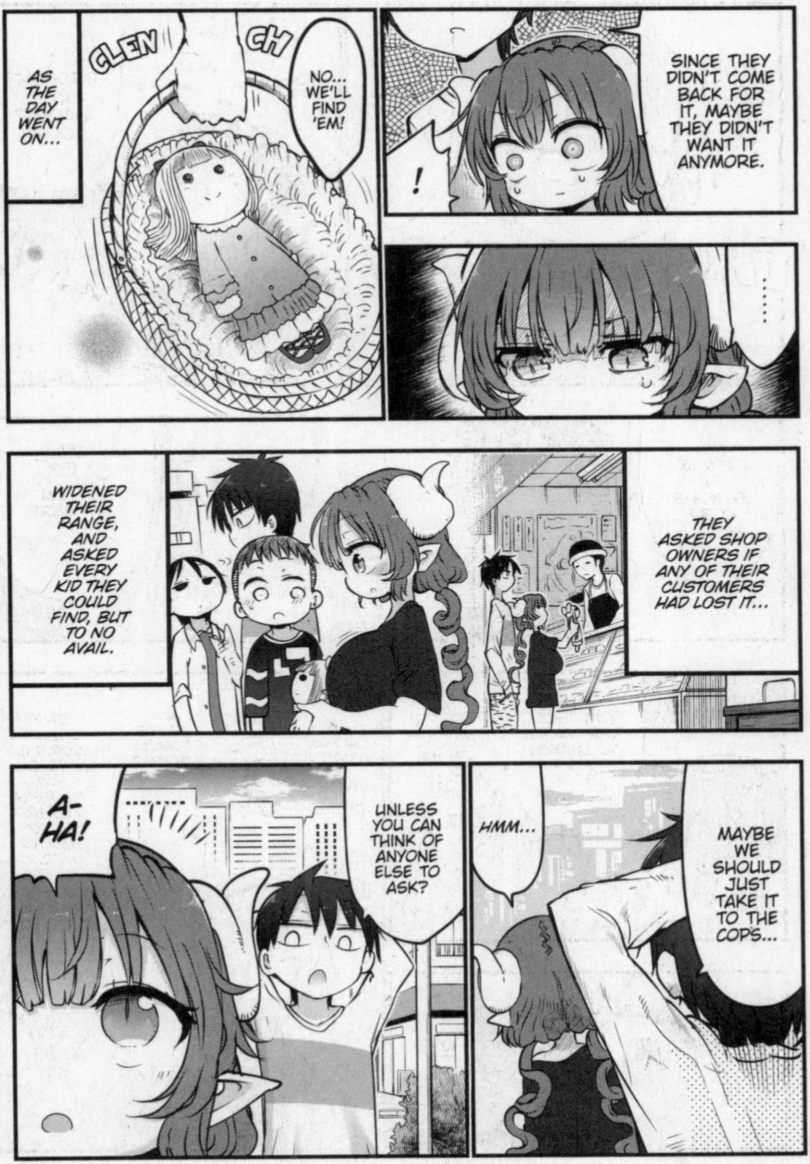
SINCE THEY DIDN'T COME BACK FOR IT, MAYBE THEY DIDN'T WANT IT ANYMORE.
!
......
NO... WE'LL FIND 'EM!
CLENCH
AS THE DAY WENT ON...
THEY ASKED SHOP OWNERS IF ANY OF THEIR CUSTOMERS HAD LOST IT...
WIDENED THEIR RANGE, AND ASKED EVERY KID THEY COULD FIND, BUT TO NO AVAIL.
MAYBE WE SHOULD JUST TAKE IT TO THE COPS...
HMM...
UNLESS YOU CAN THINK OF ANYONE ELSE TO ASK?
A-HA!

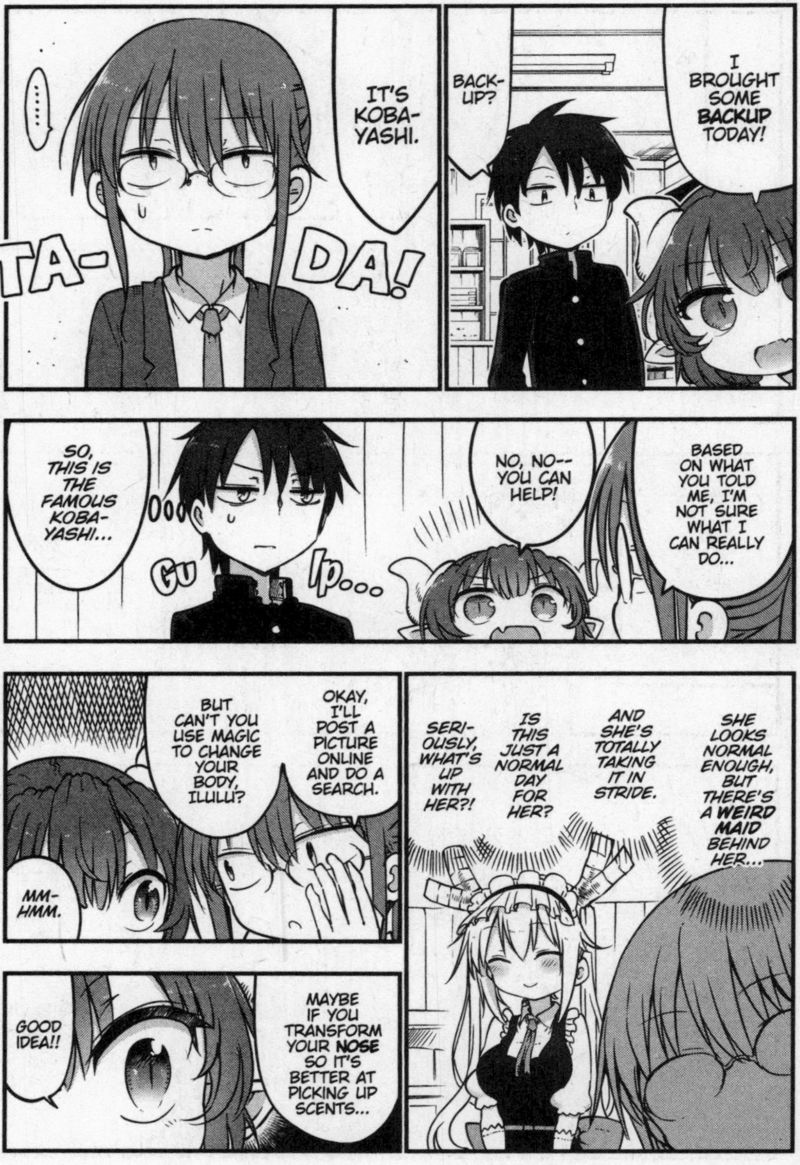
I BROUGHT SOME BACKUP TODAY!
BACK-UP?
IT'S KOBA-YASHI.
TA-DA!
......
BASED ON WHAT YOU TOLD ME, I'M NOT SURE WHAT I CAN REALLY DO...
NO, NO-- YOU CAN HELP!
GULP...
SO, THIS IS THE FAMOUS KOBA-YASHI...
SHE LOOKS NORMAL ENOUGH, BUT THERE'S A WEIRD MAID BEHIND HER...
AND SHE'S TOTALLY TAKING IT IN STRIDE.
IS THIS JUST A NORMAL DAY FOR HER?
SERI-OUSLY, WHAT'S UP WITH HER?!
OKAY, I'LL POST A PICTURE ONLINE AND DO A SEARCH.
BUT CAN'T YOU USE MAGIC TO CHANGE YOUR BODY, ILULU?
MM-HMM.
MAYBE IF YOU TRANSFORM YOUR NOSE SO IT'S BETTER AT PICKING UP SCENTS...
GOOD IDEA!!

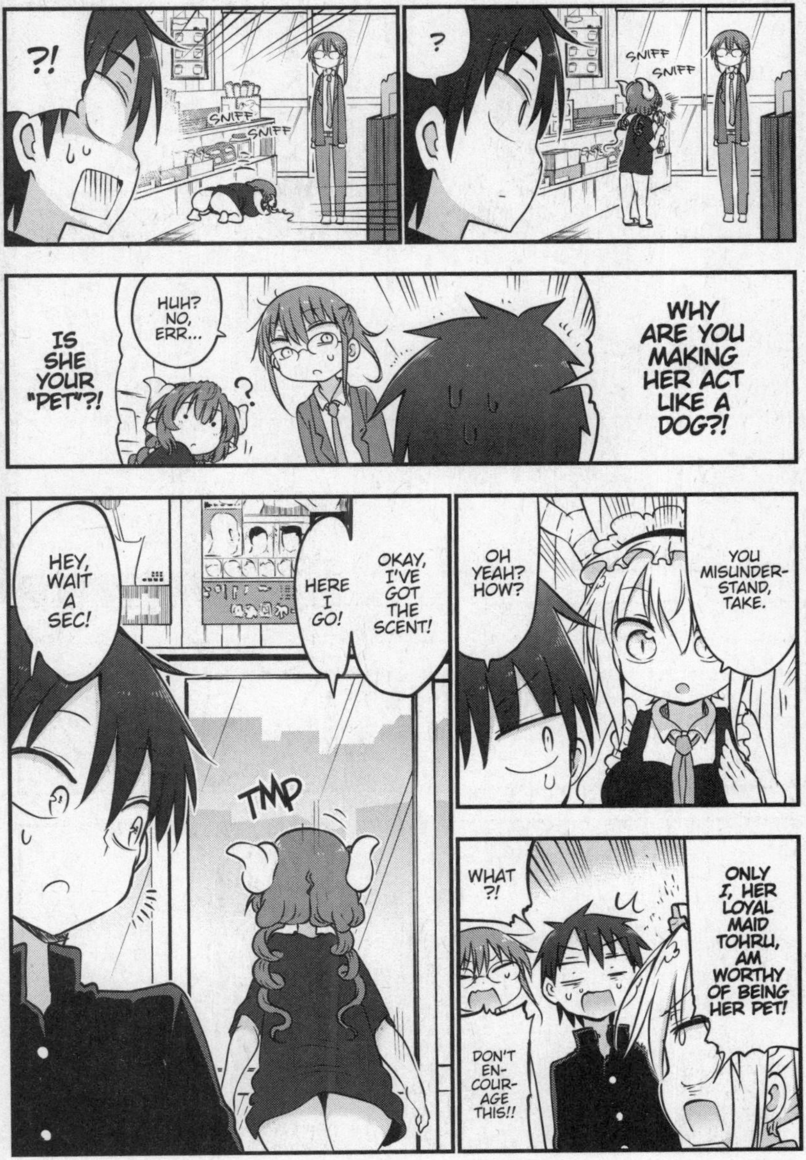
?
SNIFF SNIFF
?!
SNIFF SNIFF
WHY ARE YOU MAKING HER ACT LIKE A DOG?!
HUH? NO, ERR...
?
IS SHE YOUR "PET"?!
YOU MISUNDERSTAND, TAKE.
OH YEAH? HOW?
ONLY I, HER LOYAL MAID TOHRU, AM WORTHY OF BEING HER PET!
WHAT?!
DON'T ENCOURAGE THIS!!
OKAY, I'VE GOT THE SCENT!
HERE I GO!
HEY, WAIT A SEC!
TMP

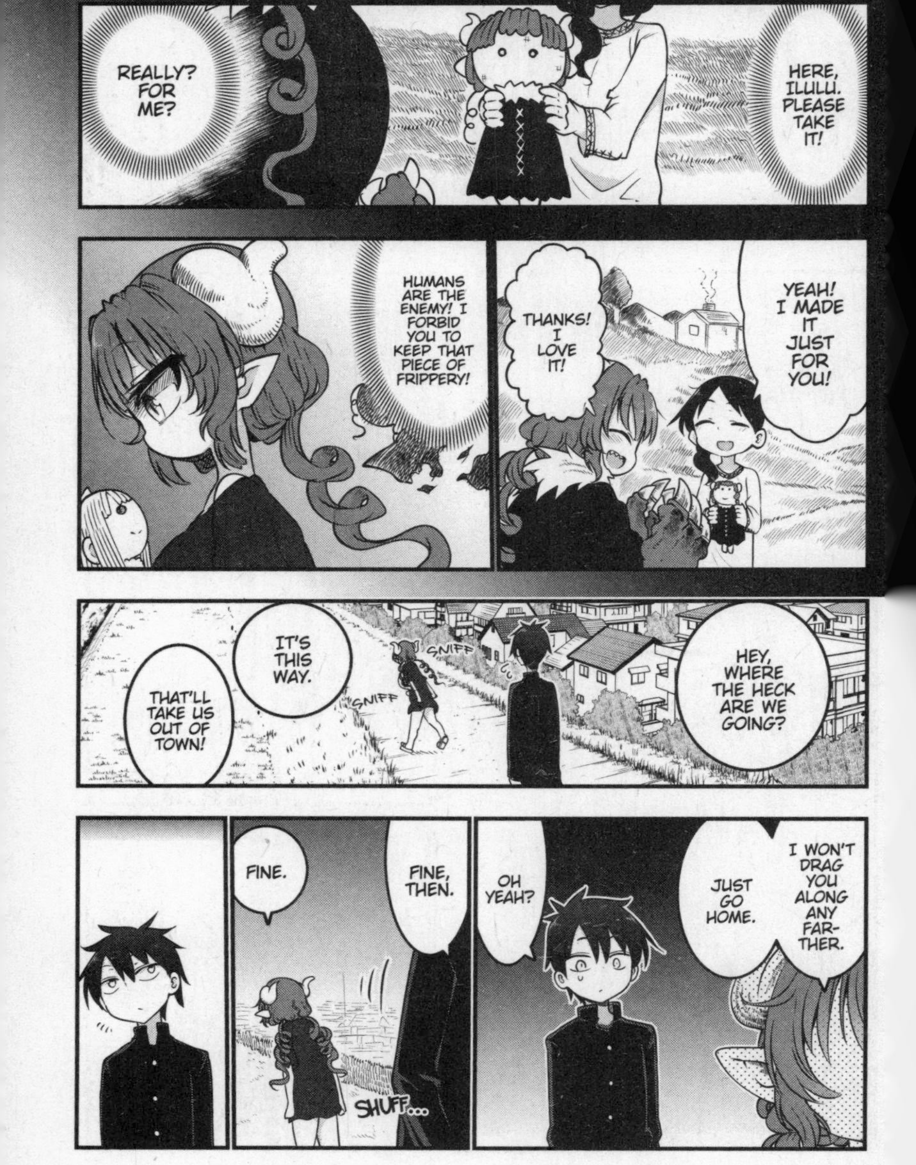
HERE, ILULU. PLEASE TAKE IT!
REALLY? FOR ME?
YEAH! I MADE IT JUST FOR YOU!
THANKS! I LOVE IT!
HUMANS ARE THE ENEMY! I FORBID YOU TO KEEP THAT PIECE OF FRIPPERY!
HEY, WHERE THE HECK ARE WE GOING?
SNIFF
IT'S THIS WAY.
SNIFF
THAT'LL TAKE US OUT OF TOWN!
I WON'T DRAG YOU ALONG ANY FAR-THER.
JUST GO HOME.
OH YEAH?
FINE, THEN.
FINE.
SHUFF...

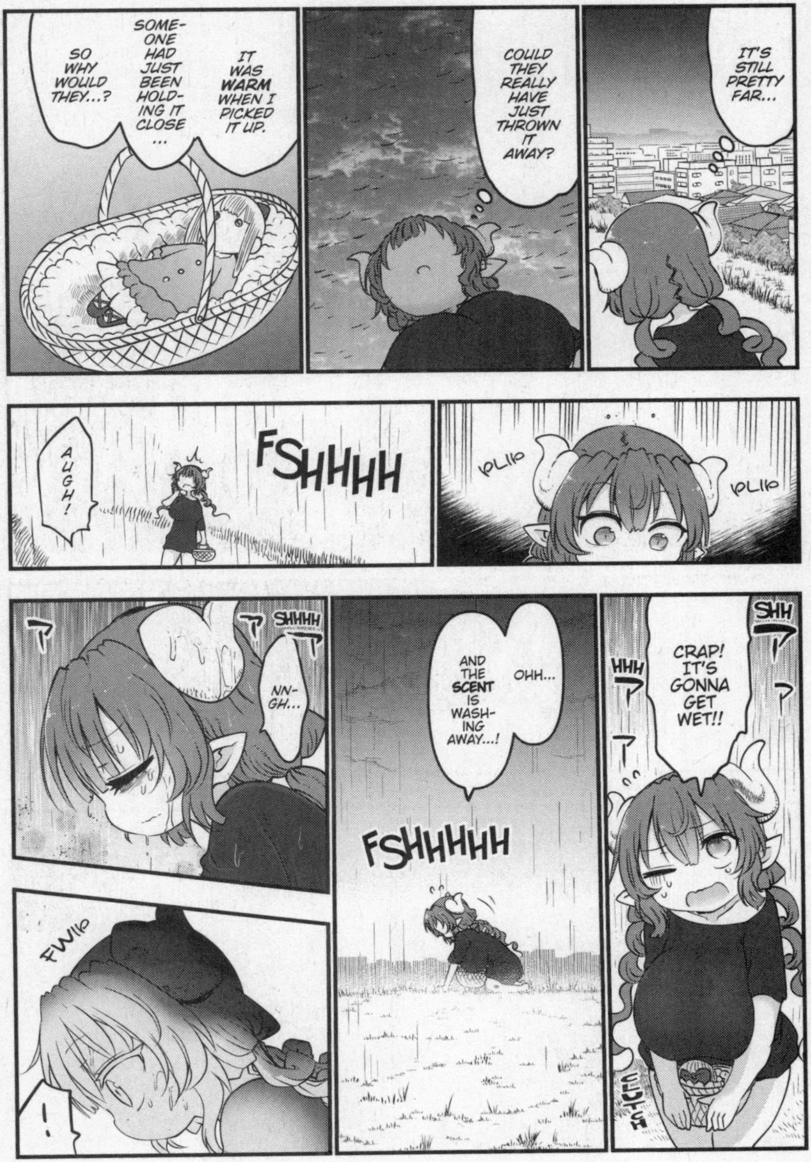
IT'S STILL PRETTY FAR...
COULD THEY REALLY HAVE JUST THROWN IT AWAY?
IT WAS WARM WHEN I PICKED IT UP.
SOME-ONE HAD JUST BEEN HOLD-ING IT CLOSE...
SO WHY WOULD THEY...?
PLIP
PLIP
FSHHHH
AUGH!
SHHHHH
CRAP! IT'S GONNA GET WET!!
CLUTCH
OHH...
AND THE SCENT IS WASH-ING AWAY...!
FSHHHHH
SHHHH
NN-GH...
FWIP
!

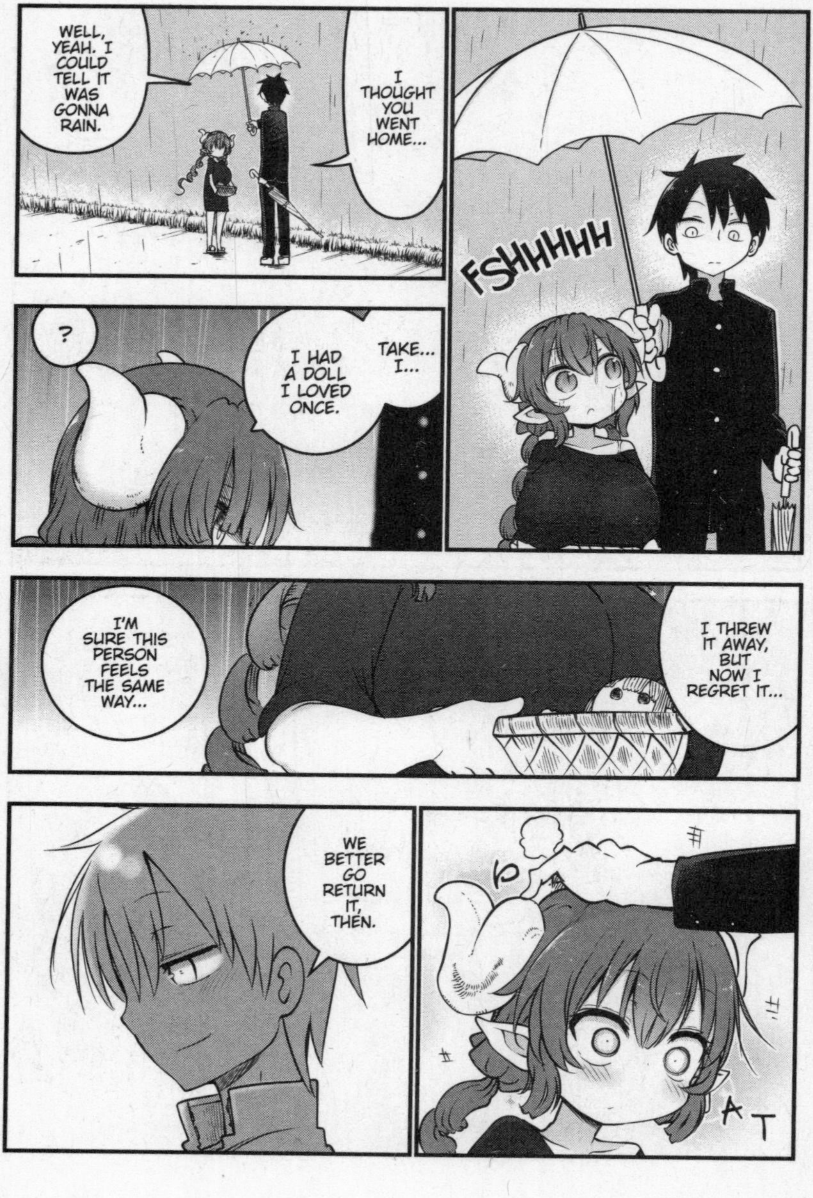
FSHHHHH
I THOUGHT YOU WENT HOME...
WELL, YEAH. I COULD TELL IT WAS GONNA RAIN.
TAKE... I...
I HAD A DOLL I LOVED ONCE.
?
I THREW IT AWAY, BUT NOW I REGRET IT...
I'M SURE THIS PERSON FEELS THE SAME WAY...
AT
WE BETTER GO RETURN IT, THEN.

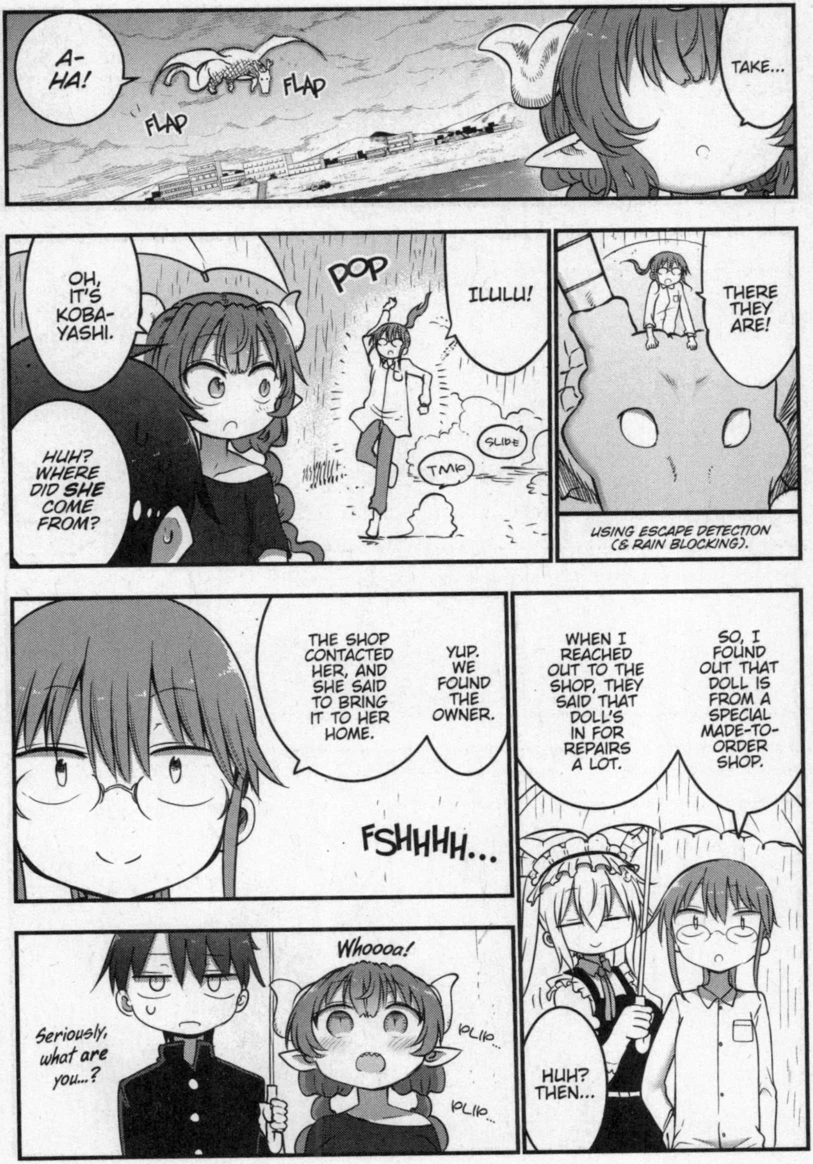
TAKE...
FLAP
FLAP
A-HA!
THERE THEY ARE!
USING ESCAPE DETECTION (& RAIN BLOCKING).
ILULU!
POP
SLIDE
TMP
OH, IT'S KOBA-YASHI.
HUH? WHERE DID SHE COME FROM?
SO, I FOUND OUT THAT DOLL IS FROM A SPECIAL MADE-TO-ORDER SHOP.
WHEN I REACHED OUT TO THE SHOP, THEY SAID THAT DOLL'S IN FOR REPAIRS A LOT.
HUH? THEN...
YUP. WE FOUND THE OWNER.
THE SHOP CONTACTED HER, AND SHE SAID TO BRING IT TO HER HOME.
FSHHHH...
Whoooa!
PLIP...
PLIP...
Seriously, what are you...?

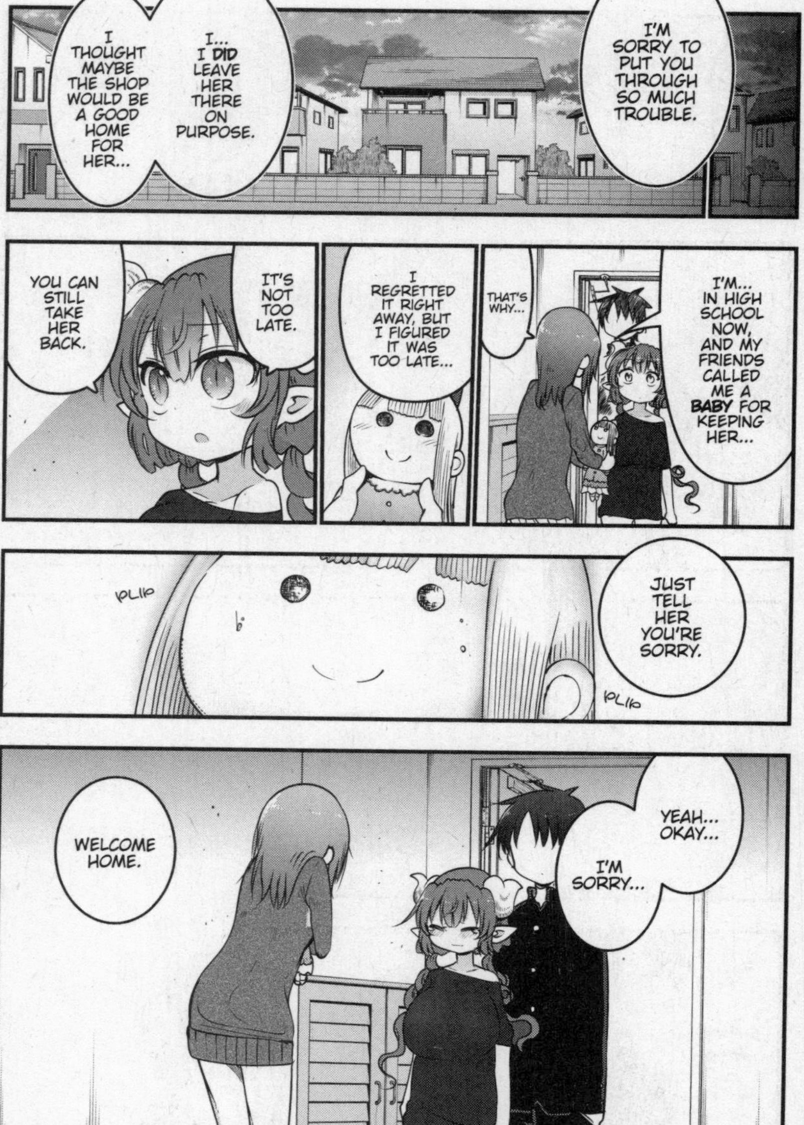
I'M SORRY TO PUT YOU THROUGH SO MUCH TROUBLE.
I... I **DID** LEAVE HER THERE ON PURPOSE.
I THOUGHT MAYBE THE SHOP WOULD BE A GOOD HOME FOR HER...
I'M... IN HIGH SCHOOL NOW, AND MY FRIENDS CALLED ME A **BABY** FOR KEEPING HER...
THAT'S WHY...
I REGRETTED IT RIGHT AWAY, BUT I FIGURED IT WAS TOO LATE...
IT'S NOT TOO LATE.
YOU CAN STILL TAKE HER BACK.
JUST TELL HER YOU'RE SORRY.
PLIP
PLIP
YEAH... OKAY...
I'M SORRY...
WELCOME HOME.

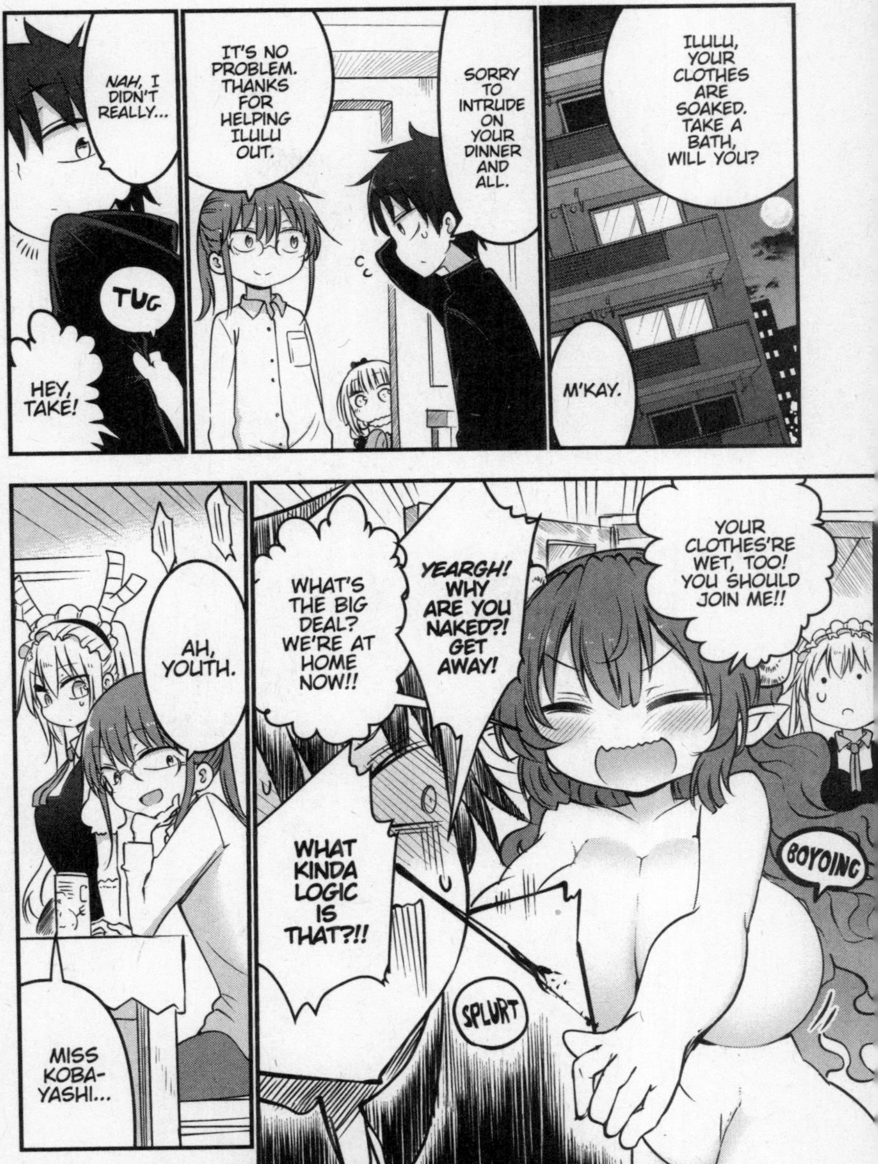
ILULU, YOUR CLOTHES ARE SOAKED. TAKE A BATH, WILL YOU?
M'KAY.
SORRY TO INTRUDE ON YOUR DINNER AND ALL.
IT'S NO PROBLEM. THANKS FOR HELPING ILULU OUT.
NAH, I DIDN'T REALLY...
TUG
HEY, TAKE!
YOUR CLOTHES'RE WET, TOO! YOU SHOULD JOIN ME!!
YEARGH! WHY ARE YOU NAKED?! GET AWAY!
WHAT'S THE BIG DEAL? WE'RE AT HOME NOW!!
BOYOING
WHAT KINDA LOGIC IS THAT?!!
SPLURT
AH, YOUTH.
MISS KOBAYASHI...

CHAPTER 63/END

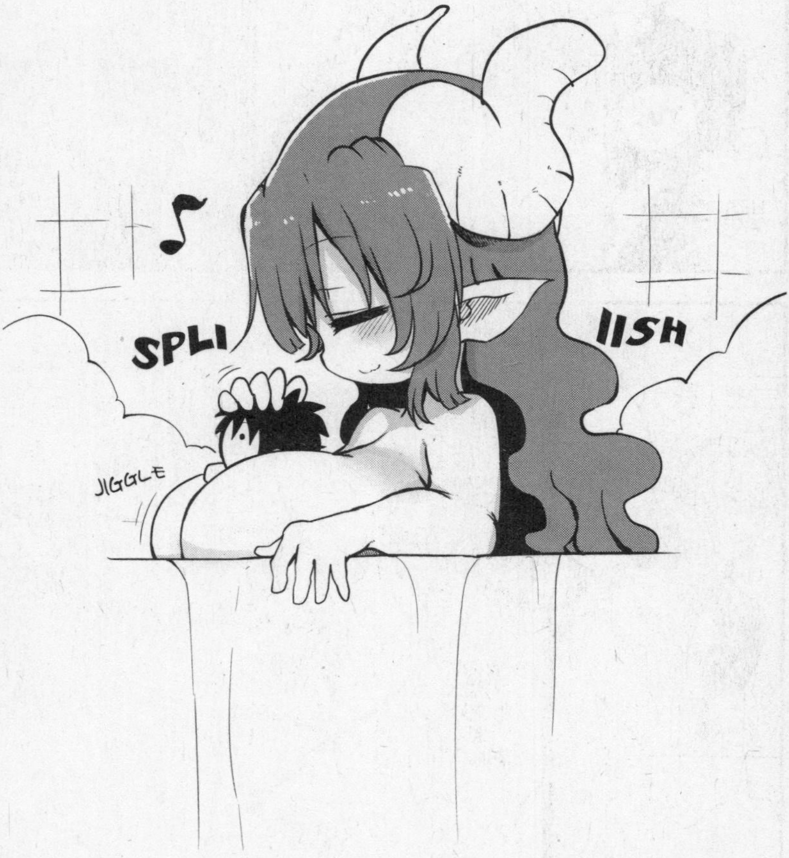
SPLI
IISH
JIGGLE

Miss Kobayashi's
DRAGON MAID

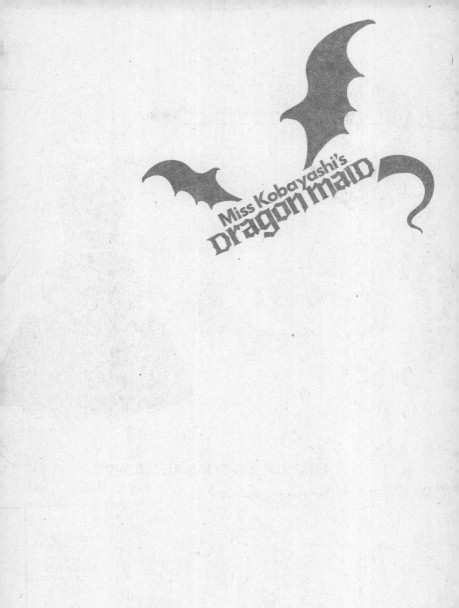

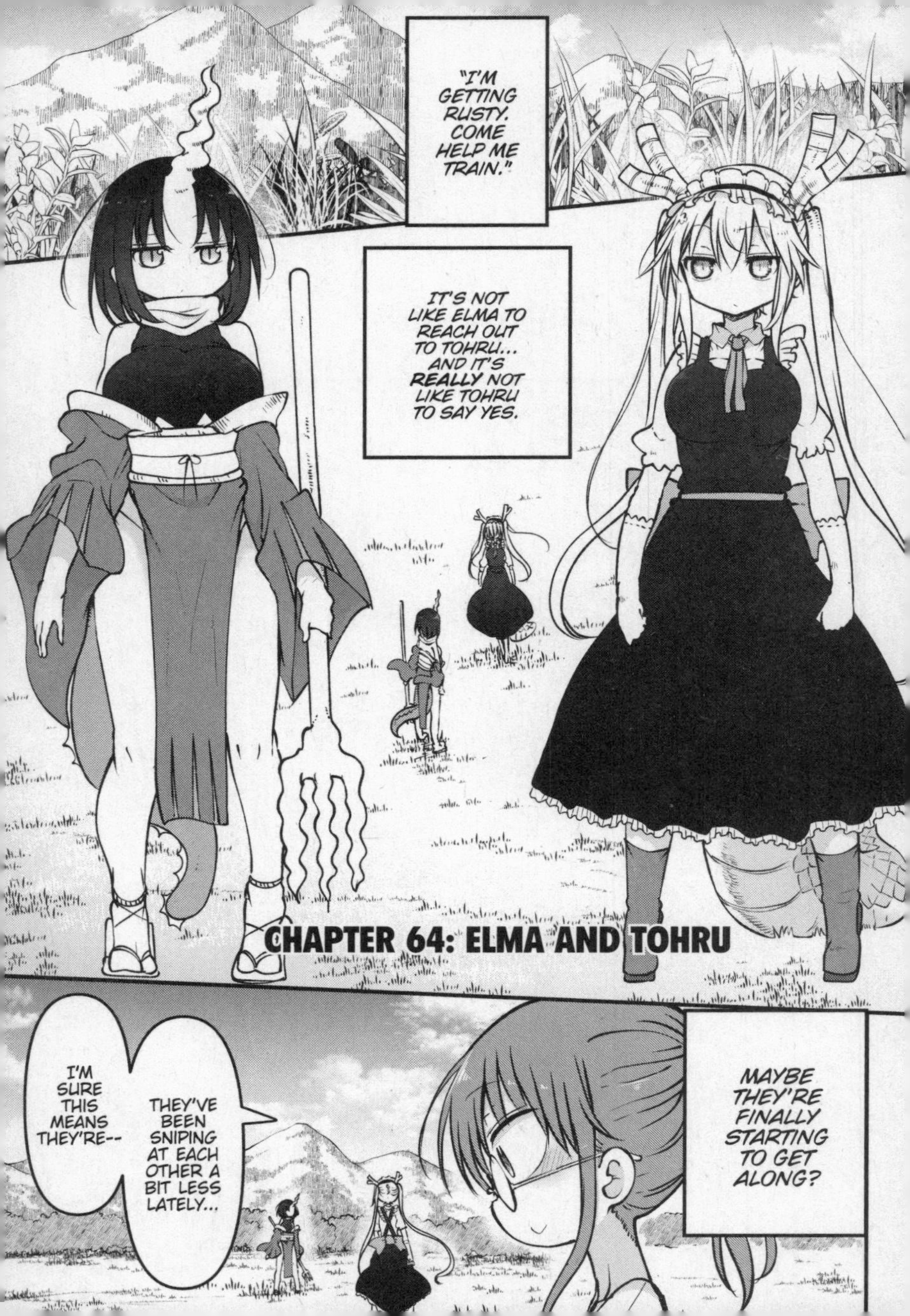
"I'M GETTING RUSTY. COME HELP ME TRAIN."
IT'S NOT LIKE ELMA TO REACH OUT TO TOHRU... AND IT'S REALLY NOT LIKE TOHRU TO SAY YES.
CHAPTER 64: ELMA AND TOHRU
MAYBE THEY'RE FINALLY STARTING TO GET ALONG?
THEY'VE BEEN SNIPING AT EACH OTHER A BIT LESS LATELY...
I'M SURE THIS MEANS THEY'RE--

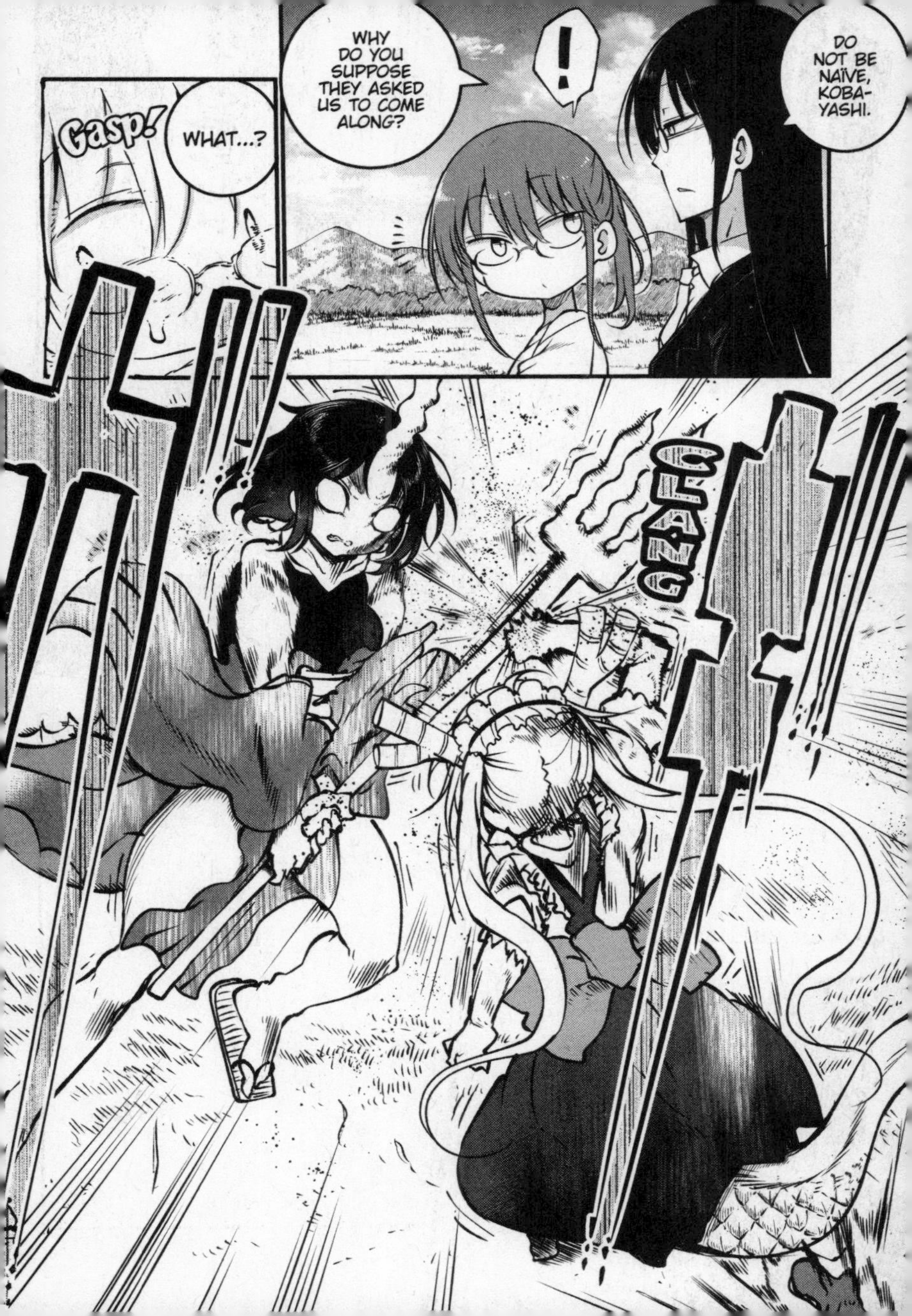
DO NOT BE NAÏVE, KOBAYASHI.
!
WHY DO YOU SUPPOSE THEY ASKED US TO COME ALONG?
WHAT...?
Gasp!
CLANG

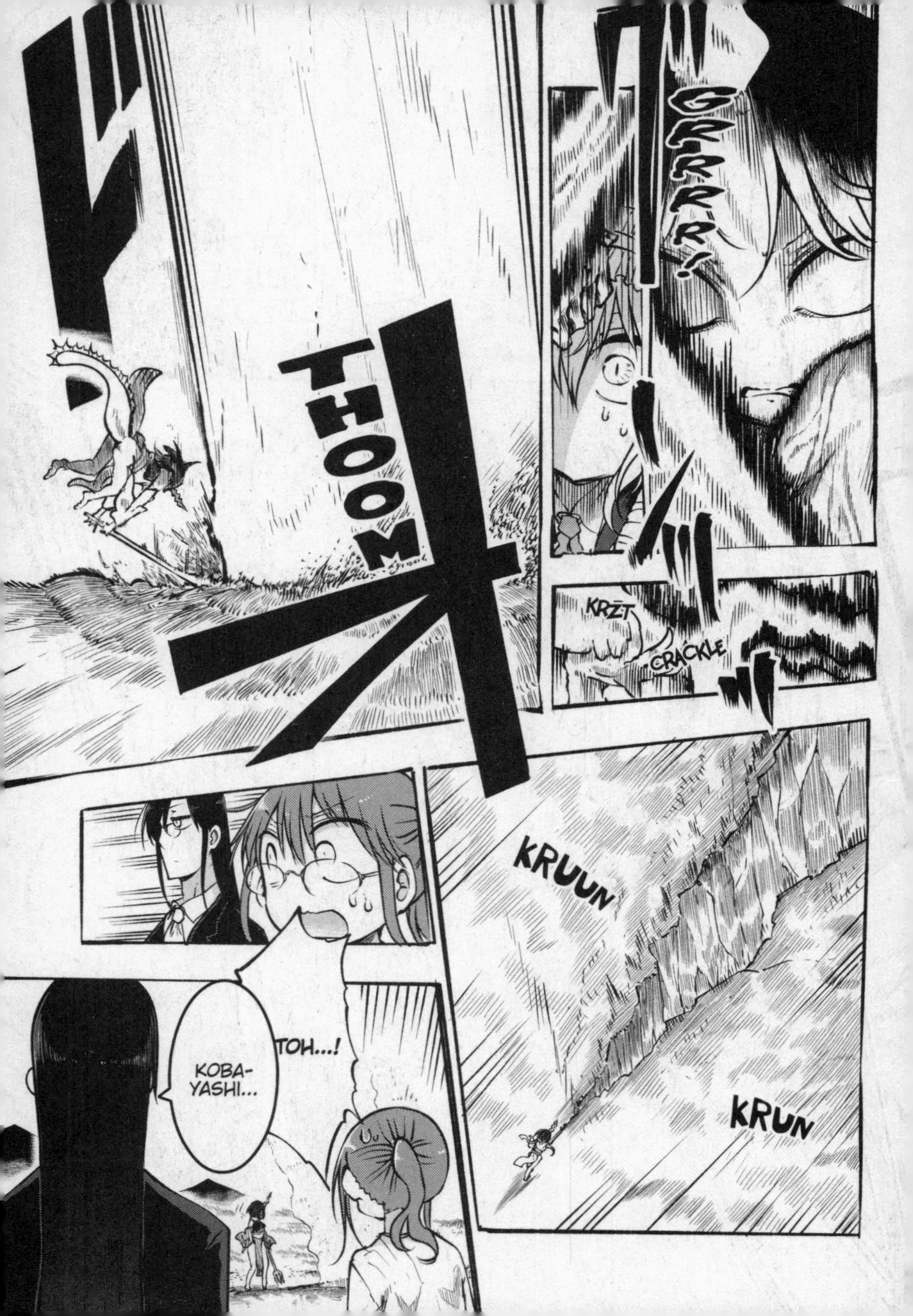
GRRRR!
KRZT
CRACKLE
THOOM
KRUUN
KRUN
KOBA-YASHI...
TOH...!

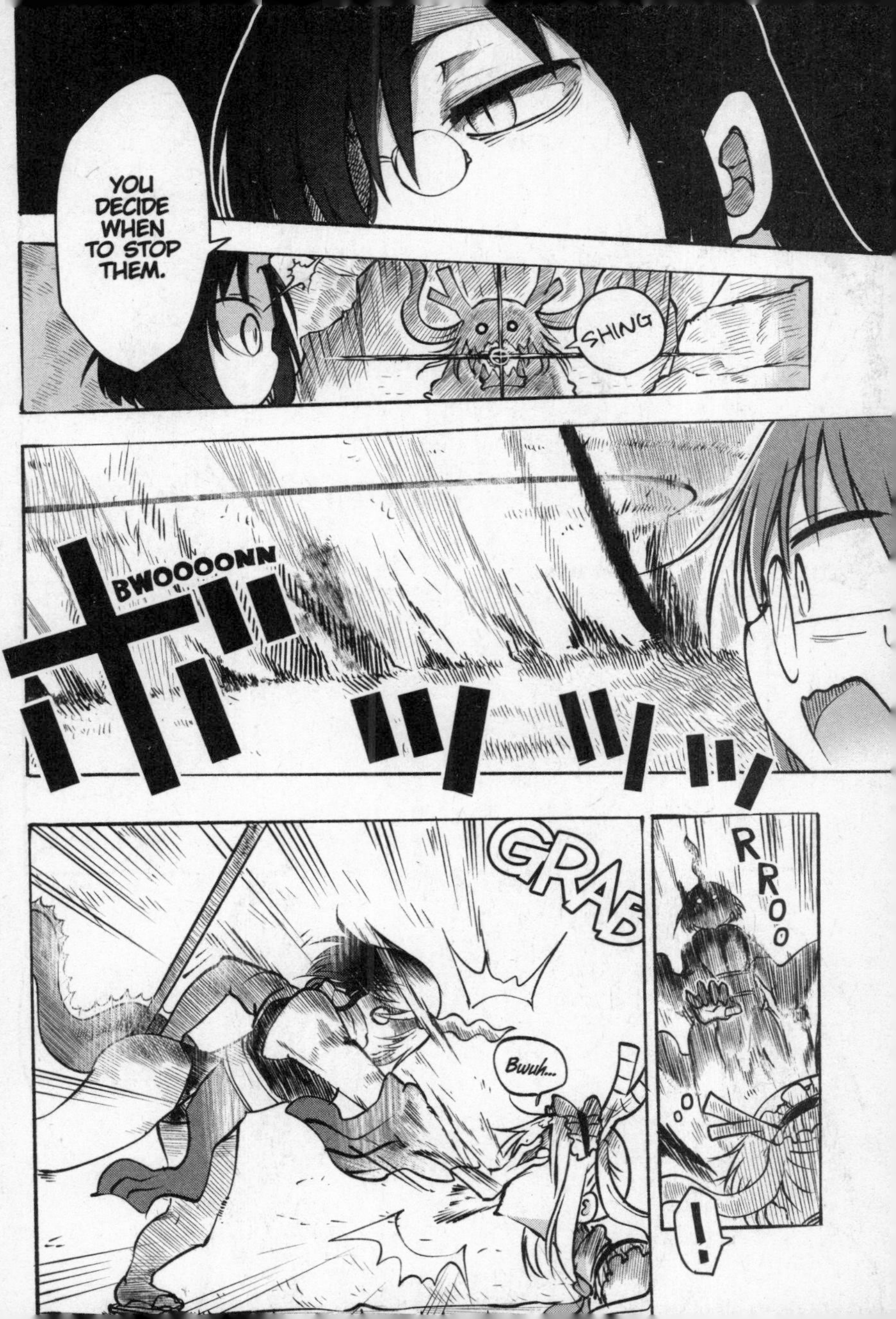
YOU DECIDE WHEN TO STOP THEM.
SHING
BWOOOONN
RROO
!
GRAB
Bwuh...

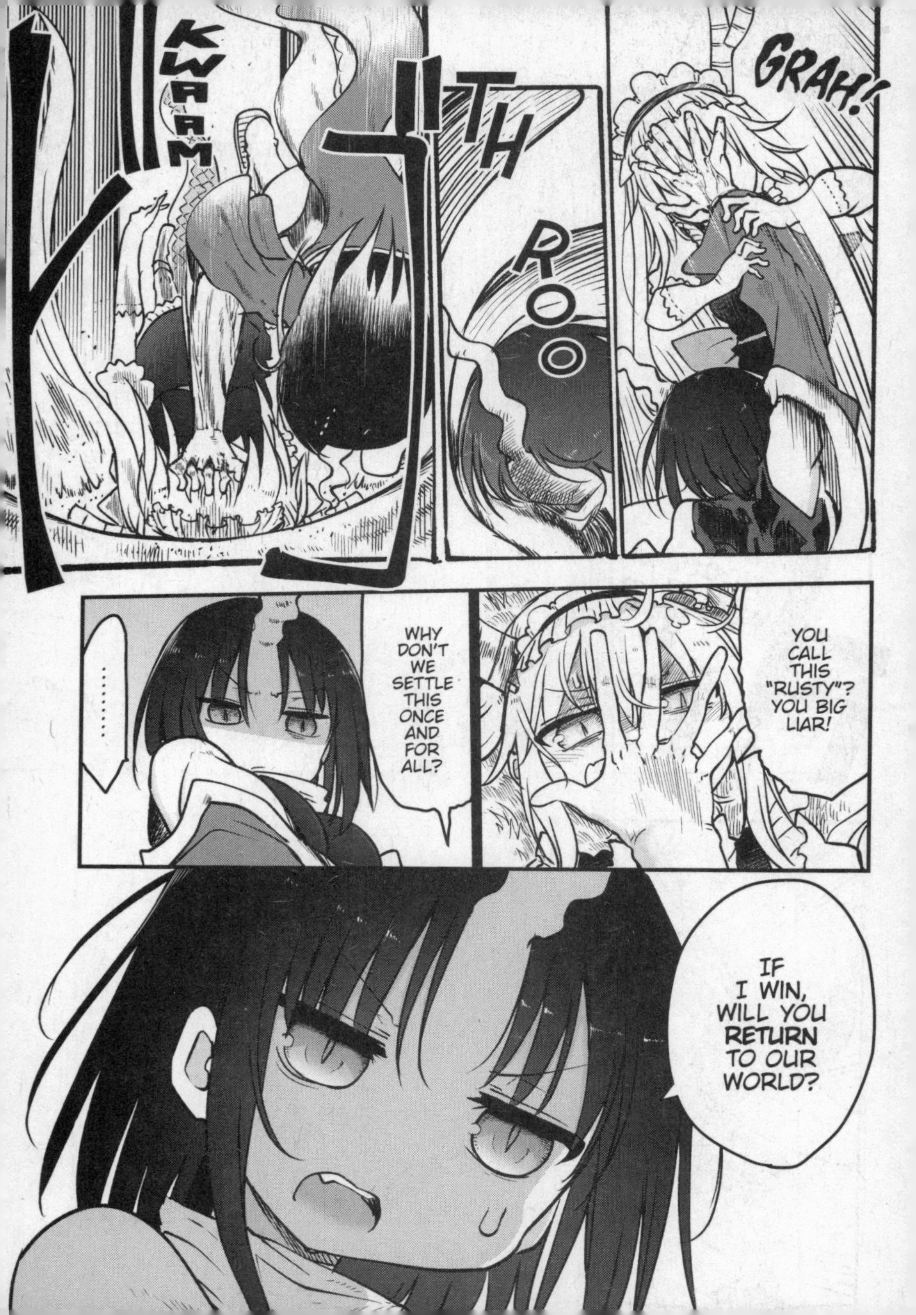
GRAH!!
TH
ROOO
KWRAM
YOU CALL THIS "RUSTY"? YOU BIG LIAR!
WHY DON'T WE SETTLE THIS ONCE AND FOR ALL?
......
IF I WIN, WILL YOU RETURN TO OUR WORLD?

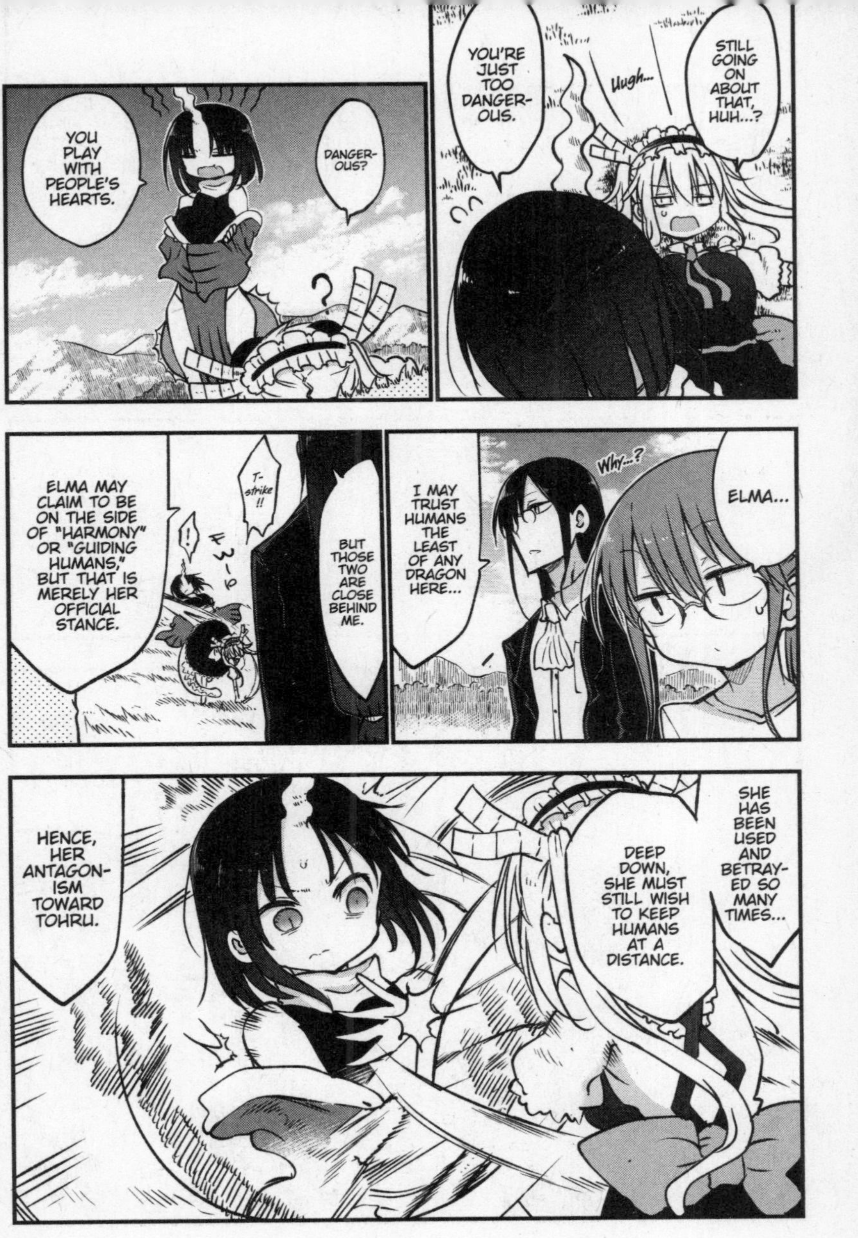
STILL GOING ON ABOUT THAT, HUH...?
Uugh...
YOU'RE JUST TOO DANGER-OUS.
DANGER-OUS?
YOU PLAY WITH PEOPLE'S HEARTS.
ELMA...
Why...?
I MAY TRUST HUMANS THE LEAST OF ANY DRAGON HERE...
BUT THOSE TWO ARE CLOSE BEHIND ME.
T-strike!!
!
ELMA MAY CLAIM TO BE ON THE SIDE OF "HARMONY" OR "GUIDING HUMANS," BUT THAT IS MERELY HER OFFICIAL STANCE.
SHE HAS BEEN USED AND BETRAYED SO MANY TIMES...
DEEP DOWN, SHE MUST STILL WISH TO KEEP HUMANS AT A DISTANCE.
HENCE, HER ANTAGONISM TOWARD TOHRU.

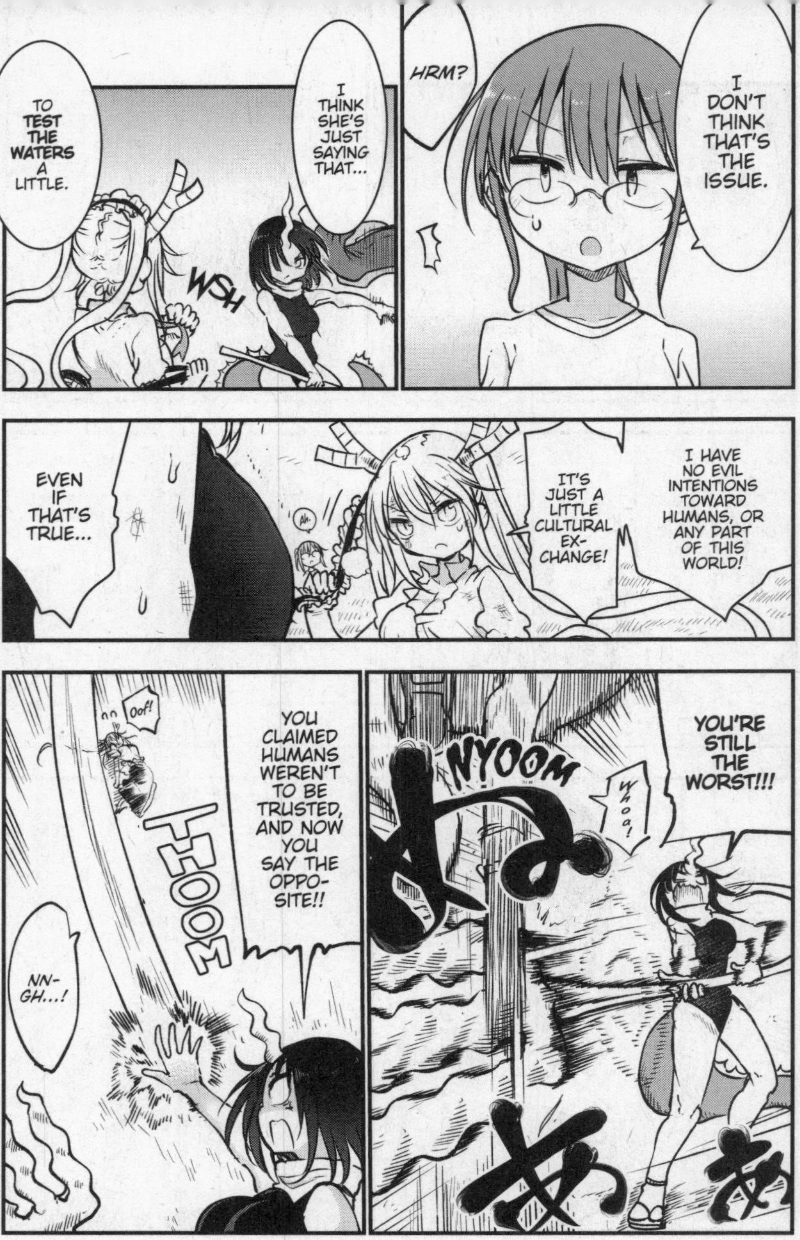
I DON'T THINK THAT'S THE ISSUE.
HRM?
I THINK SHE'S JUST SAYING THAT...
TO TEST THE WATERS A LITTLE.
WSH
I HAVE NO EVIL INTENTIONS TOWARD HUMANS, OR ANY PART OF THIS WORLD!
IT'S JUST A LITTLE CULTURAL EX-CHANGE!
Ah.
EVEN IF THAT'S TRUE...
YOU'RE STILL THE WORST!!!
Whoa!
NYOOM
YOU CLAIMED HUMANS WEREN'T TO BE TRUSTED, AND NOW YOU SAY THE OPPO-SITE!!
Oof!
THOOM
NN-GH...!

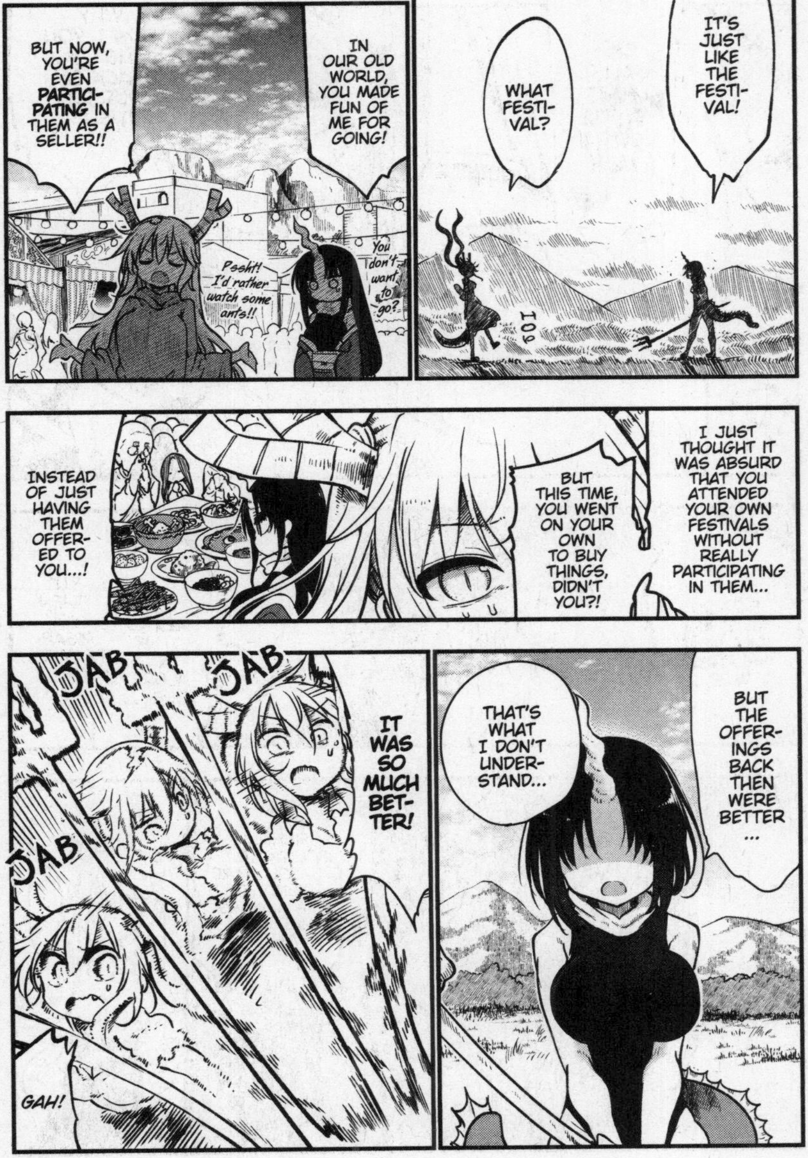
IT'S JUST LIKE THE FESTIVAL!
WHAT FESTIVAL?
IN OUR OLD WORLD, YOU MADE FUN OF ME FOR GOING!
BUT NOW, YOU'RE EVEN **PARTICIPATING** IN THEM AS A SELLER!!
You don't want to go?
Pssht! I'd rather watch some ants!!
I JUST THOUGHT IT WAS ABSURD THAT YOU ATTENDED YOUR OWN FESTIVALS WITHOUT REALLY PARTICIPATING IN THEM...
BUT THIS TIME, YOU WENT ON YOUR OWN TO BUY THINGS, DIDN'T YOU?!
INSTEAD OF JUST HAVING THEM OFFERED TO YOU...!
BUT THE OFFERINGS BACK THEN WERE BETTER...
THAT'S WHAT I DON'T UNDERSTAND...
IT WAS SO MUCH BETTER!
JAB
JAB
JAB
GAH!

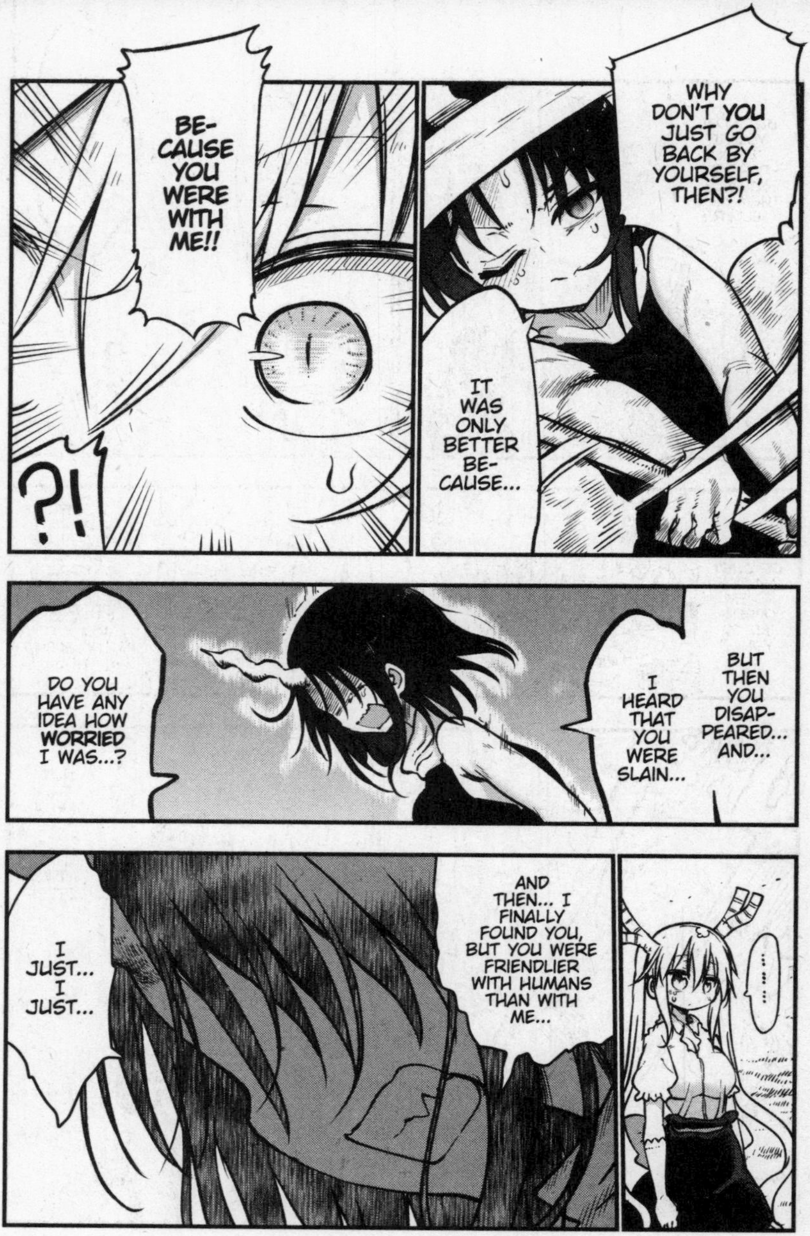
WHY DON'T YOU JUST GO BACK BY YOURSELF, THEN?!
IT WAS ONLY BETTER BE-CAUSE...
BE-CAUSE YOU WERE WITH ME!!
?!
BUT THEN YOU DISAP-PEARED... AND...
I HEARD THAT YOU WERE SLAIN...
DO YOU HAVE ANY IDEA HOW WORRIED I WAS...?
......
AND THEN... I FINALLY FOUND YOU, BUT YOU WERE FRIENDLIER WITH HUMANS THAN WITH ME...
I JUST... I JUST...

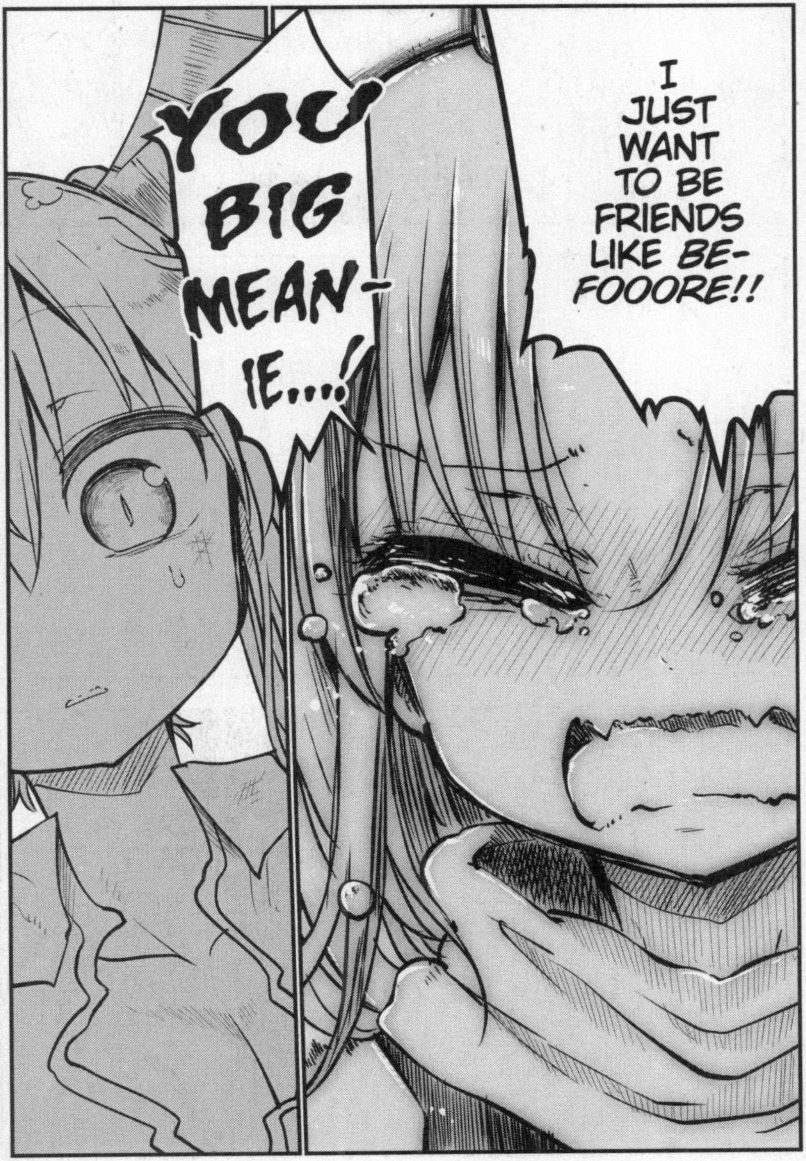
I JUST WANT TO BE FRIENDS LIKE *BE-FOOORE!!*
YOU BIG MEAN-IE....!

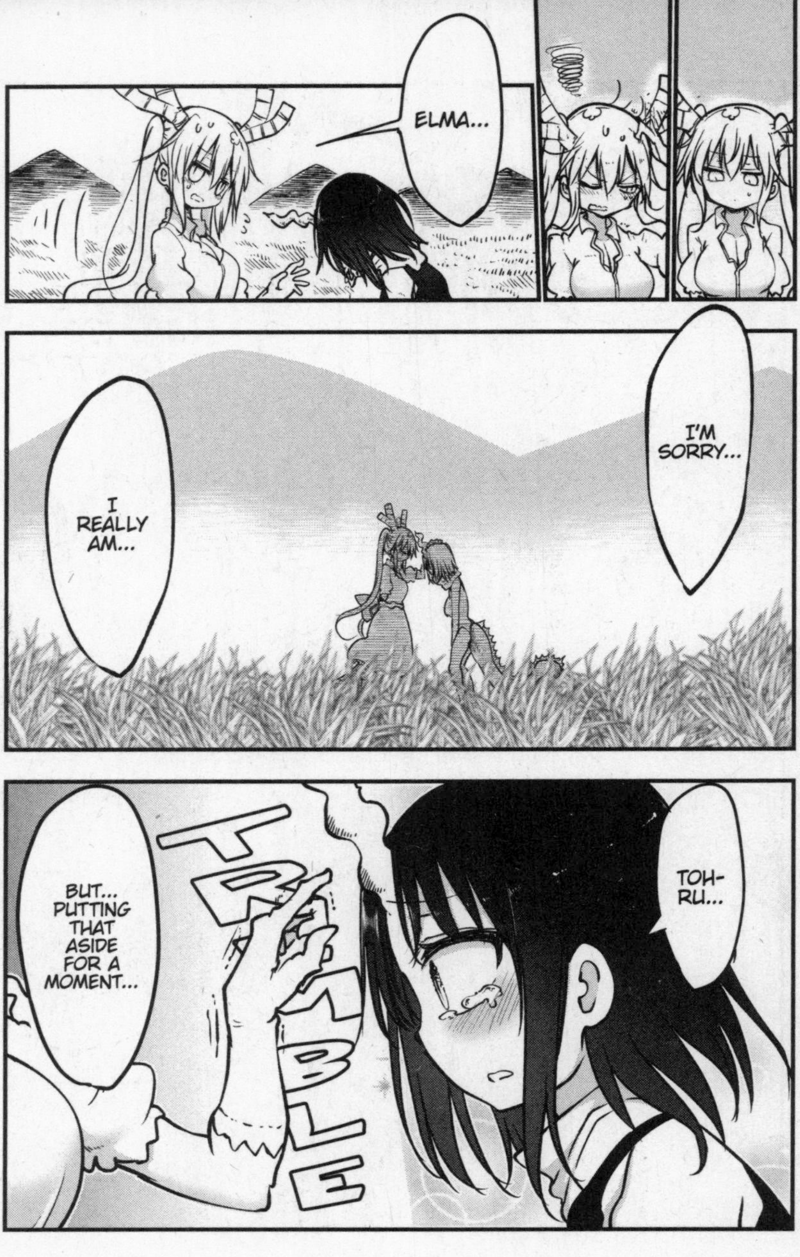
ELMA...
I'M SORRY...
I REALLY AM...
TOH-RU...
BUT... PUTTING THAT ASIDE FOR A MOMENT...
TREMBLE

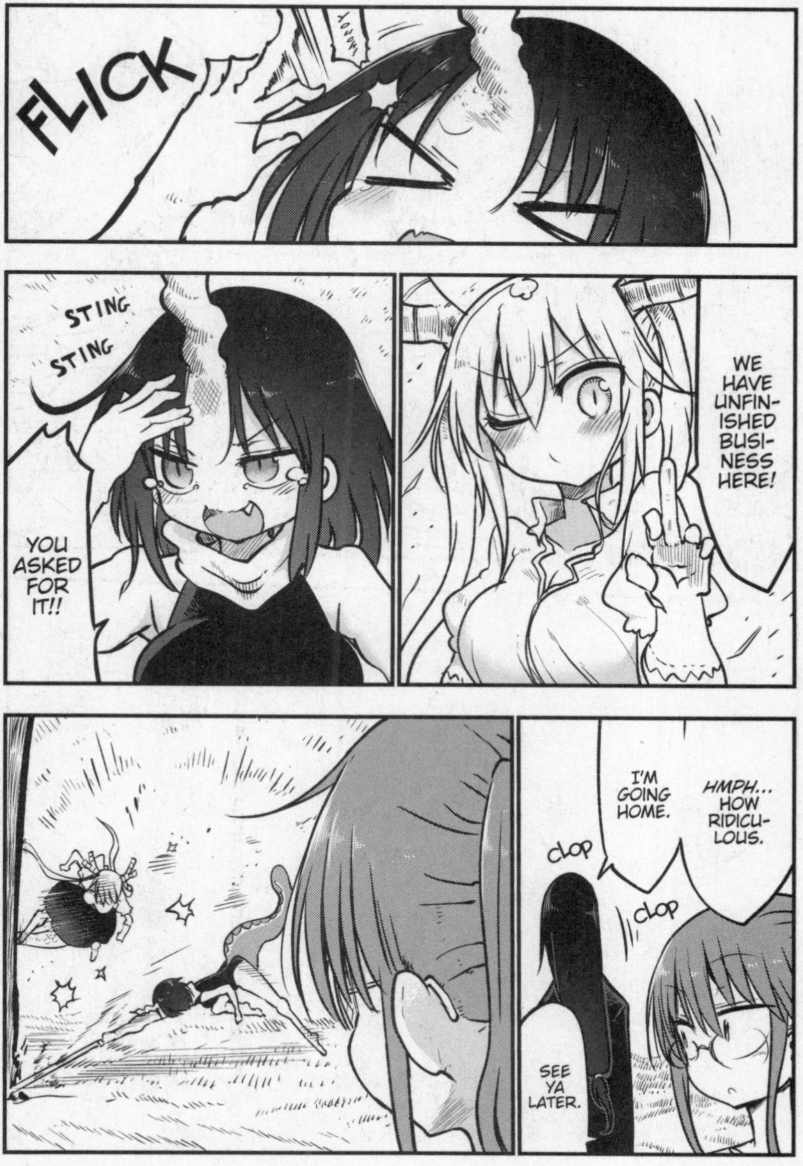
YOOOW!
FLICK
WE HAVE UNFINISHED BUSINESS HERE!
STING
STING
YOU ASKED FOR IT!!
HMPH... HOW RIDICULOUS.
I'M GOING HOME.
CLOP
CLOP
SEE YA LATER.

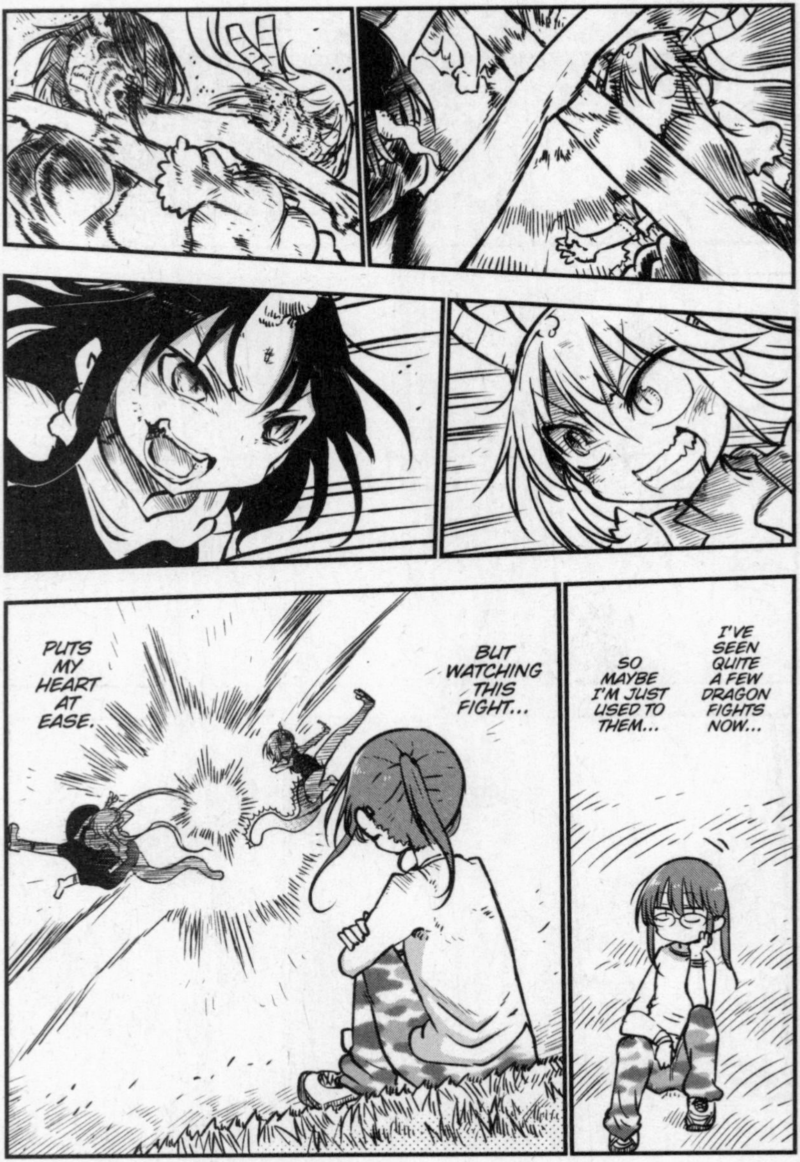
I'VE SEEN QUITE A FEW DRAGON FIGHTS NOW...
SO MAYBE I'M JUST USED TO THEM...
BUT WATCHING THIS FIGHT...
PUTS MY HEART AT EASE.

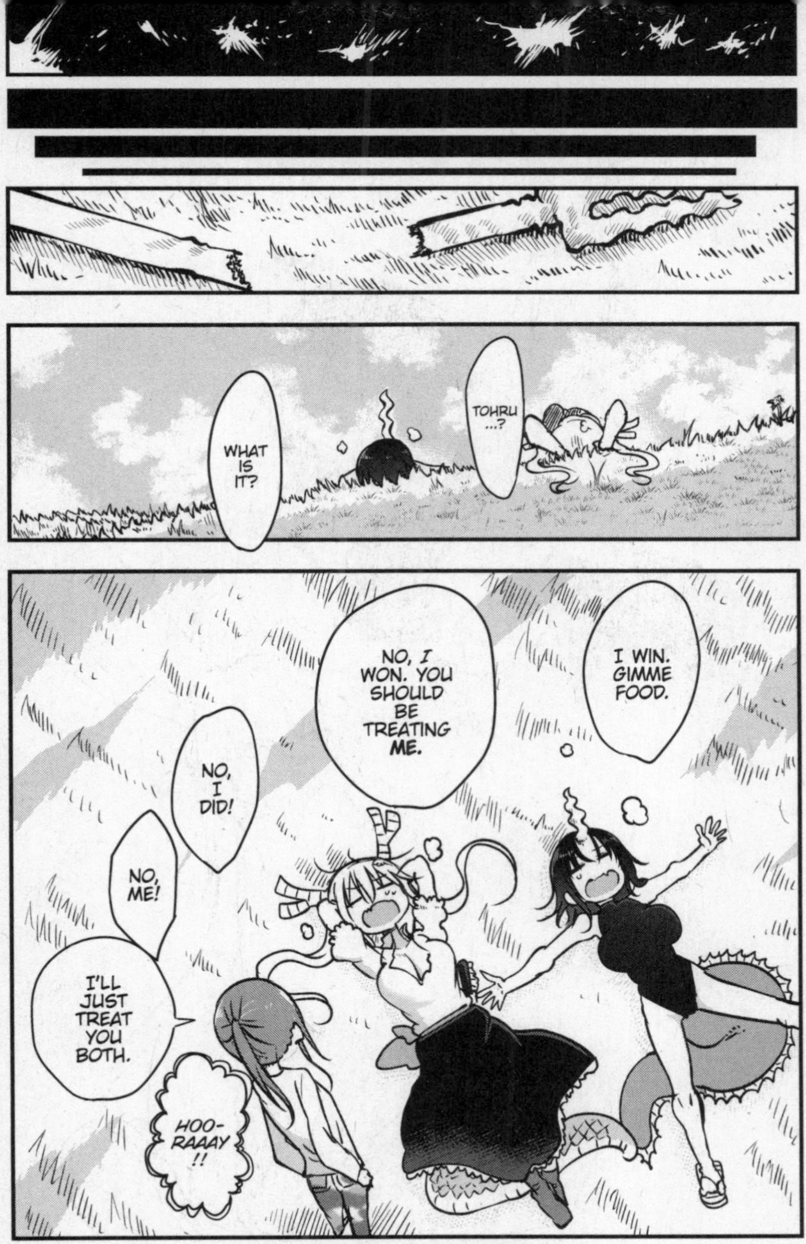
TOHRU ...?
WHAT IS IT?
I WIN. GIMME FOOD.
NO, I WON. YOU SHOULD BE TREATING ME.
NO, I DID!
NO, ME!
I'LL JUST TREAT YOU BOTH.
HOO-RAAAY!!

CHAPTER 64/END

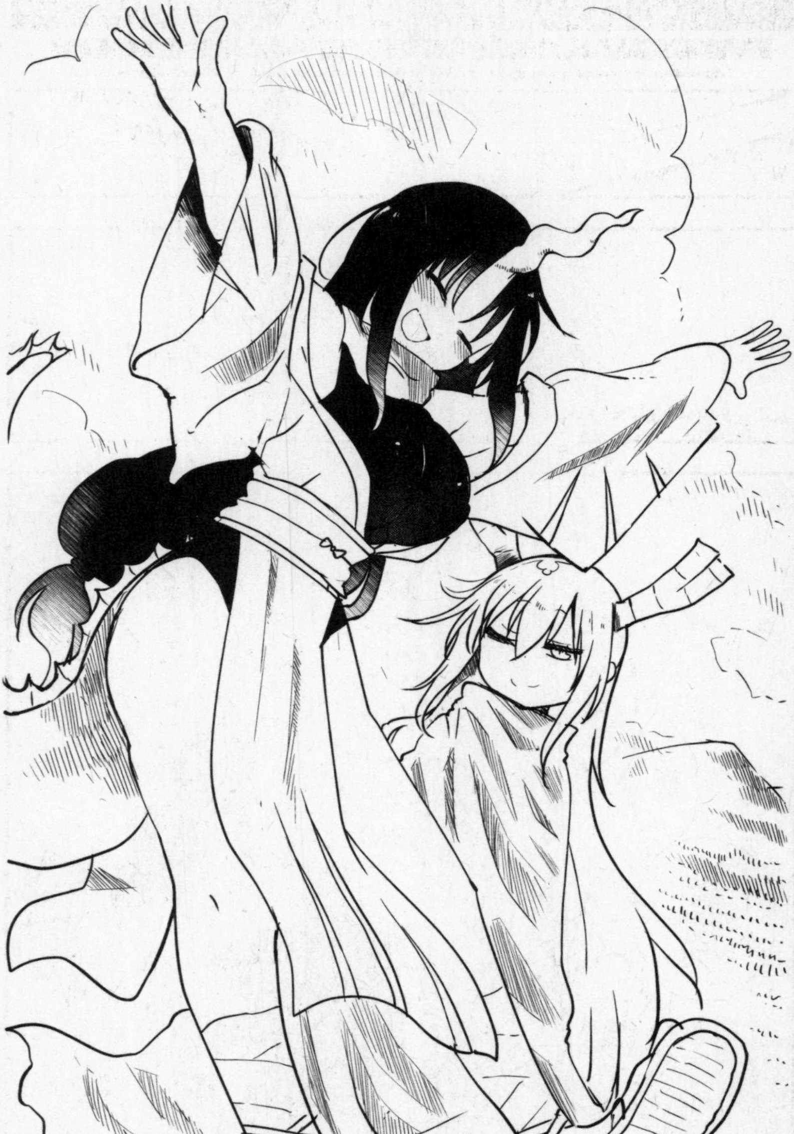

Miss Kobayashi's Dragon Maid

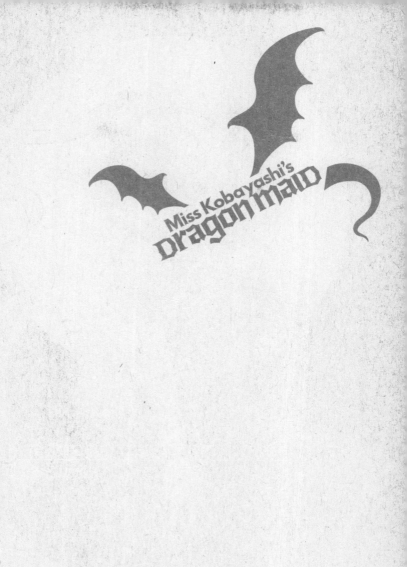

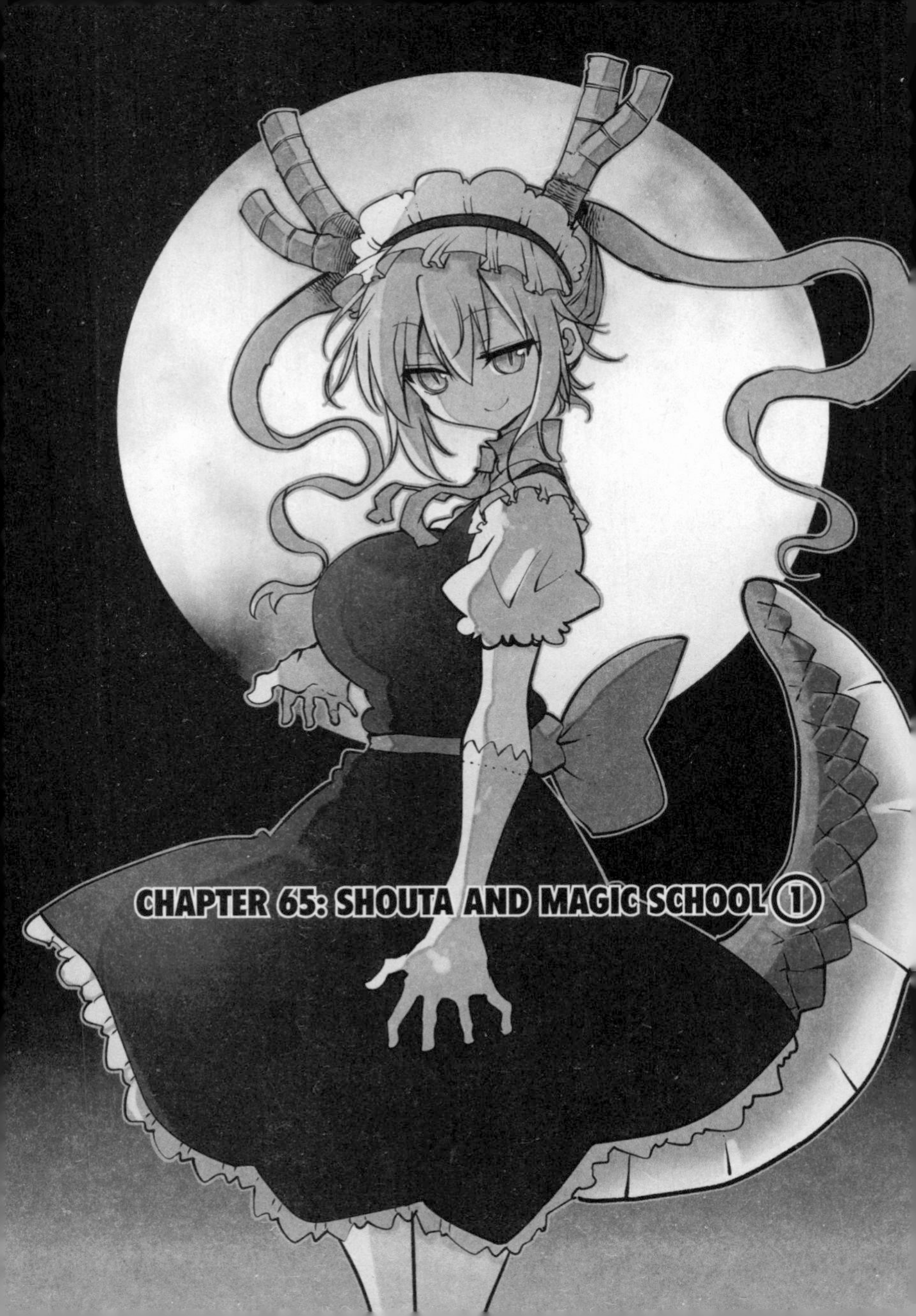
CHAPTER 65: SHOUTA AND MAGIC SCHOOL ①

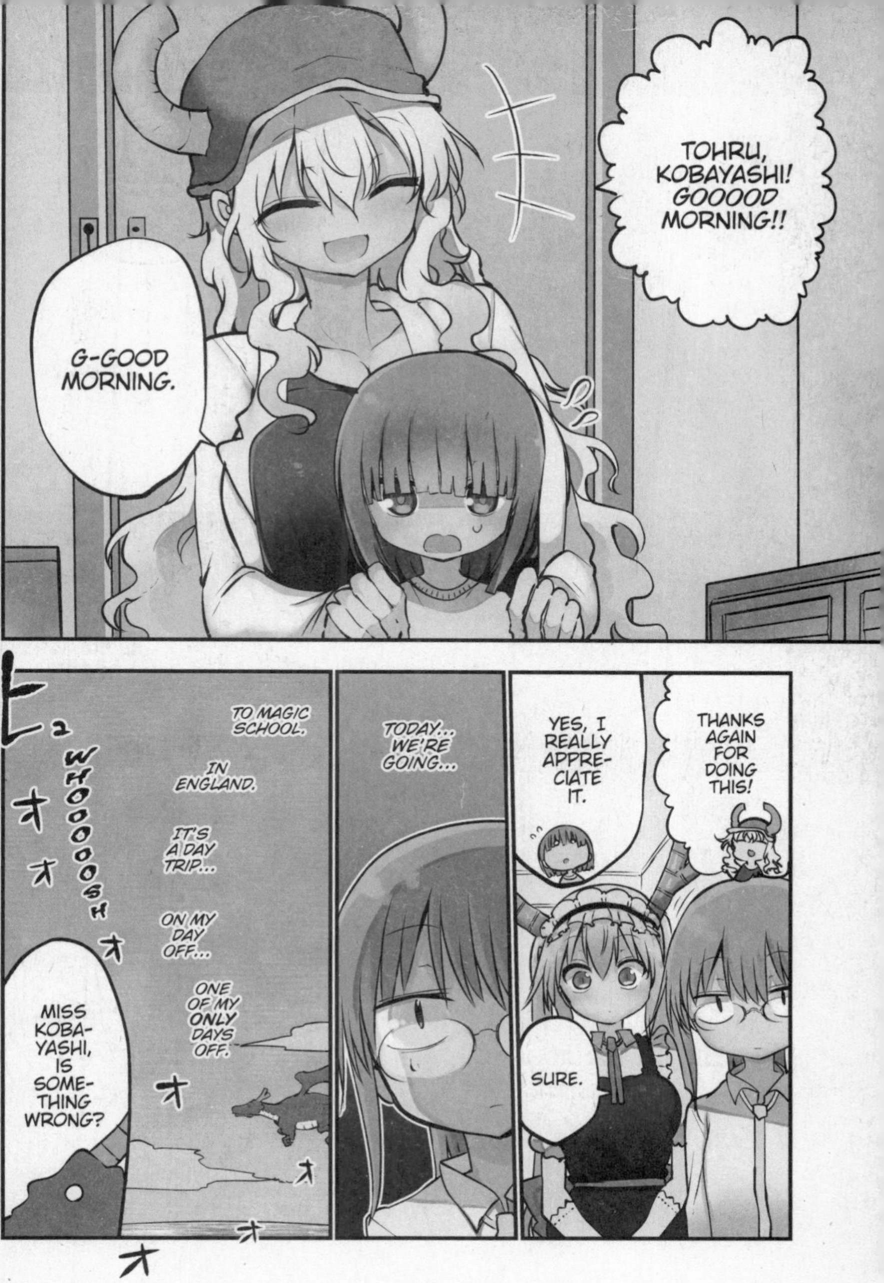
TOHRU, KOBAYASHI! GOOOOD MORNING!!
G-GOOD MORNING.
THANKS AGAIN FOR DOING THIS!
YES, I REALLY APPRE-CIATE IT.
SURE.
TODAY... WE'RE GOING...
TO MAGIC SCHOOL.
IN ENGLAND.
IT'S A DAY TRIP...
ON MY DAY OFF...
ONE OF MY ONLY DAYS OFF.
WHOOOOOOSH
MISS KOBA-YASHI, IS SOME-THING WRONG?

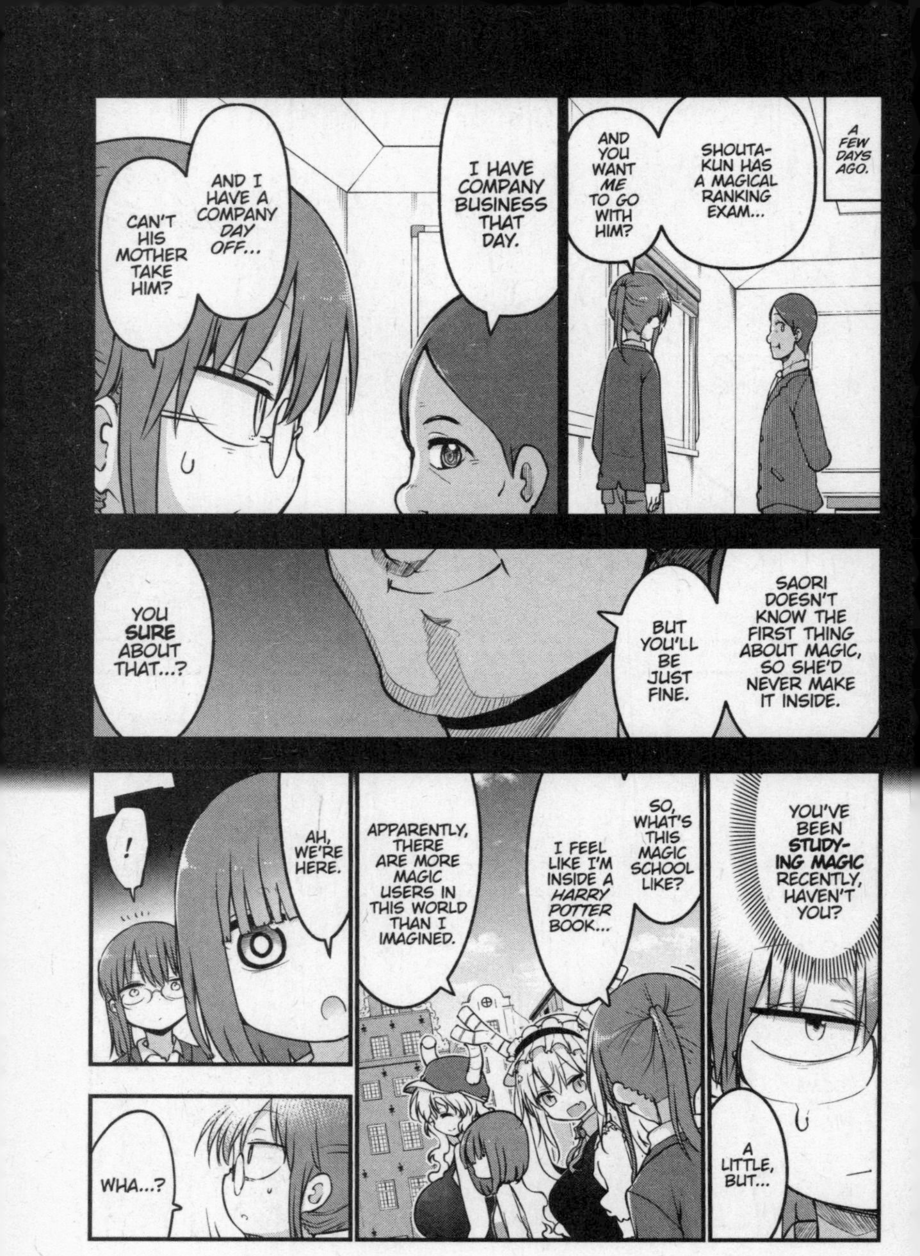
A FEW DAYS AGO.
SHOUTA-KUN HAS A MAGICAL RANKING EXAM...
AND YOU WANT ME TO GO WITH HIM?
I HAVE COMPANY BUSINESS THAT DAY.
AND I HAVE A COMPANY DAY OFF...
CAN'T HIS MOTHER TAKE HIM?
SAORI DOESN'T KNOW THE FIRST THING ABOUT MAGIC, SO SHE'D NEVER MAKE IT INSIDE.
BUT YOU'LL BE JUST FINE.
YOU SURE ABOUT THAT...?
YOU'VE BEEN STUDYING MAGIC RECENTLY, HAVEN'T YOU?
A LITTLE, BUT...
SO, WHAT'S THIS MAGIC SCHOOL LIKE?
I FEEL LIKE I'M INSIDE A HARRY POTTER BOOK...
APPARENTLY, THERE ARE MORE MAGIC USERS IN THIS WORLD THAN I IMAGINED.
AH, WE'RE HERE.
!
WHA...?

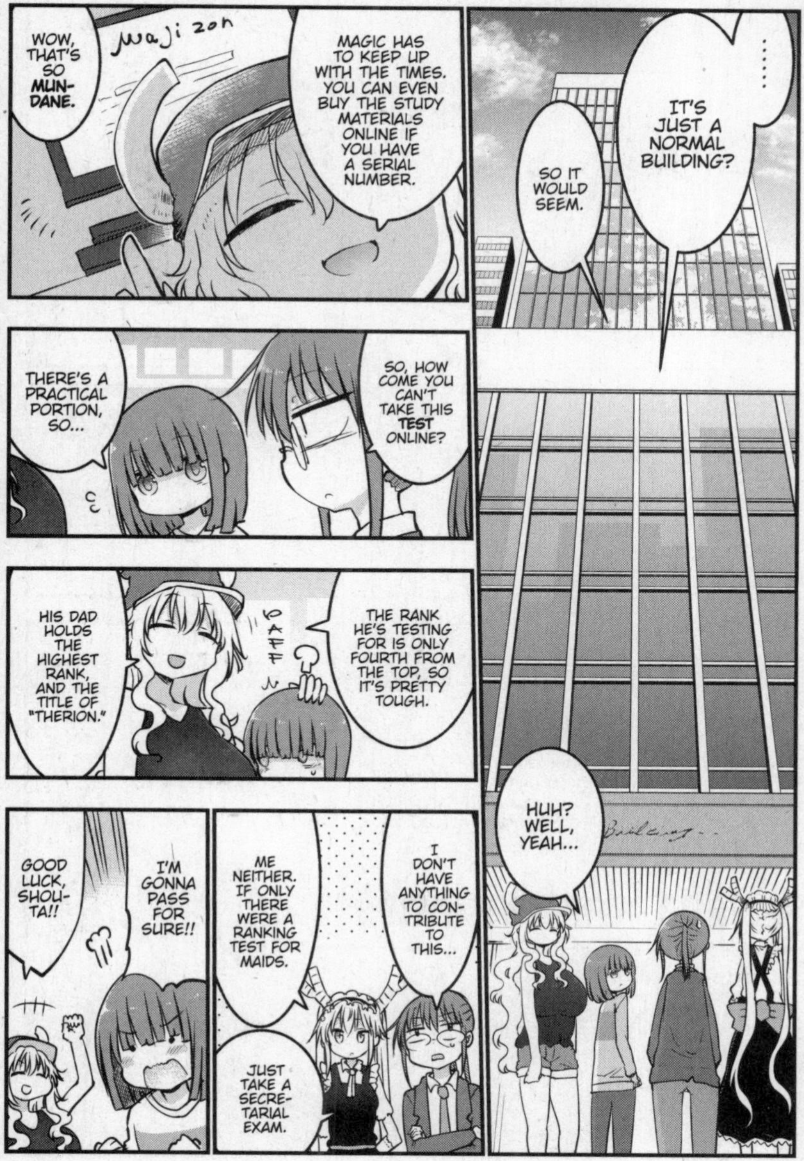
......
IT'S JUST A NORMAL BUILDING?
SO IT WOULD SEEM.
HUH? WELL, YEAH...
MAGIC HAS TO KEEP UP WITH THE TIMES. YOU CAN EVEN BUY THE STUDY MATERIALS ONLINE IF YOU HAVE A SERIAL NUMBER.
majizon
WOW, THAT'S SO **MUNDANE.**
SO, HOW COME YOU CAN'T TAKE THIS **TEST** ONLINE?
THERE'S A PRACTICAL PORTION, SO...
THE RANK HE'S TESTING FOR IS ONLY FOURTH FROM THE TOP, SO IT'S PRETTY TOUGH.
PAFF
HIS DAD HOLDS THE HIGHEST RANK, AND THE TITLE OF "THERION."
I DON'T HAVE ANYTHING TO CONTRIBUTE TO THIS...
ME NEITHER. IF ONLY THERE WERE A RANKING TEST FOR MAIDS.
JUST TAKE A SECRETARIAL EXAM.
I'M GONNA PASS FOR SURE!!
GOOD LUCK, SHOUTA!!

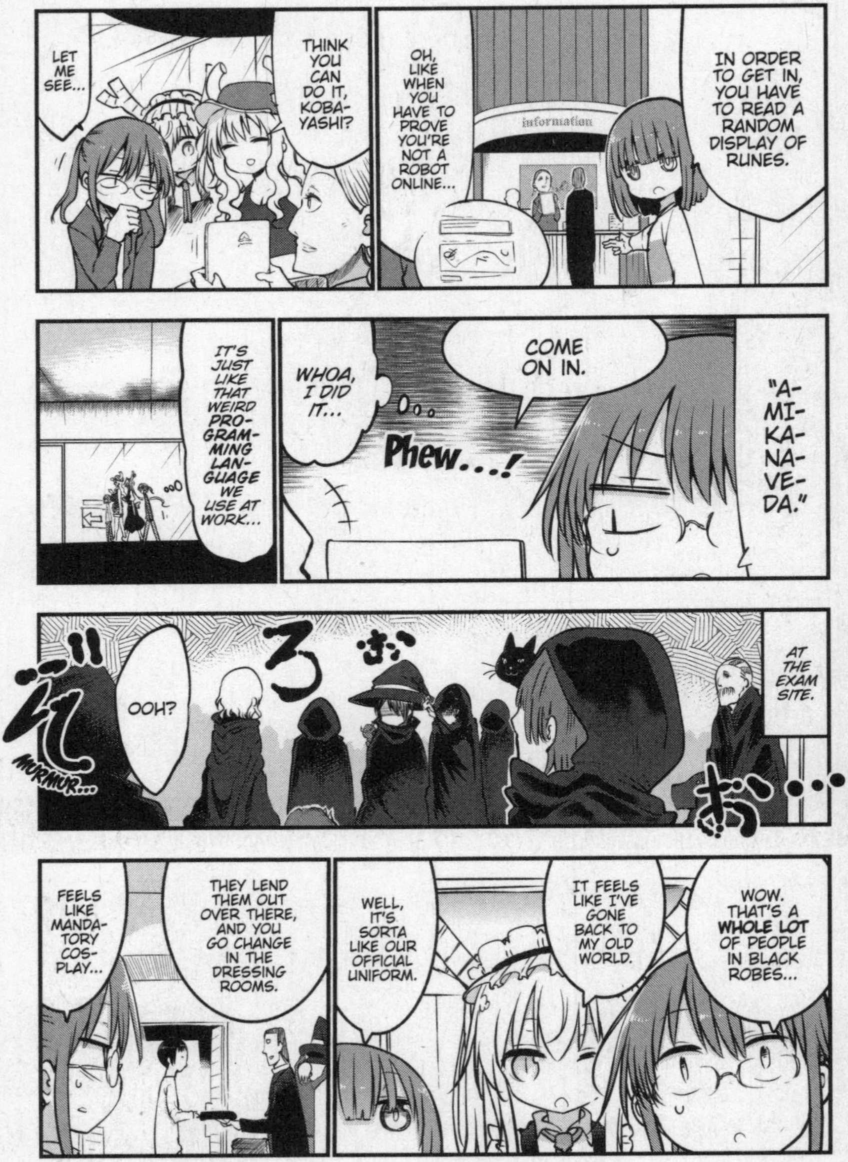
IN ORDER TO GET IN, YOU HAVE TO READ A RANDOM DISPLAY OF RUNES.
information
OH, LIKE WHEN YOU HAVE TO PROVE YOU'RE NOT A ROBOT ONLINE...
THINK YOU CAN DO IT, KOBAYASHI?
LET ME SEE...
"A-MI-KA-NA-VE-DA."
COME ON IN.
Phew...!
WHOA, I DID IT...
IT'S JUST LIKE THAT WEIRD PROGRAMMING LANGUAGE WE USE AT WORK...
AT THE EXAM SITE.
OOH?
MURMUR...
WOW. THAT'S A **WHOLE LOT** OF PEOPLE IN BLACK ROBES...
IT FEELS LIKE I'VE GONE BACK TO MY OLD WORLD.
WELL, IT'S SORTA LIKE OUR OFFICIAL UNIFORM.
THEY LEND THEM OUT OVER THERE, AND YOU GO CHANGE IN THE DRESSING ROOMS.
FEELS LIKE MANDATORY COSPLAY...

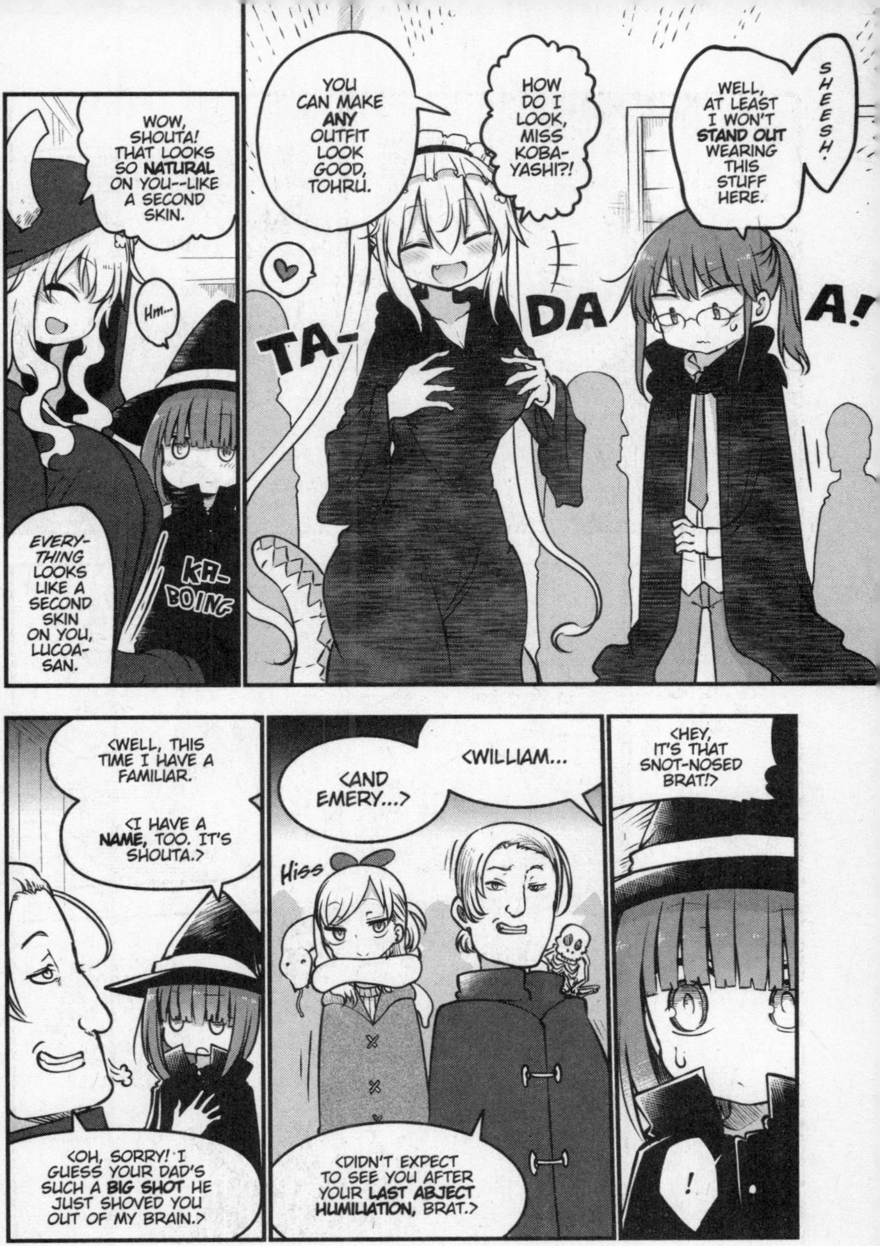
SHEESH!
WELL, AT LEAST I WON'T STAND OUT WEARING THIS STUFF HERE.
HOW DO I LOOK, MISS KOBA-YASHI?!
YOU CAN MAKE ANY OUTFIT LOOK GOOD, TOHRU.
TA- DA A!
WOW, SHOUTA! THAT LOOKS SO NATURAL ON YOU--LIKE A SECOND SKIN.
Hm...
KA-BOING
EVERY-THING LOOKS LIKE A SECOND SKIN ON YOU, LUCOA-SAN.
<HEY, IT'S THAT SNOT-NOSED BRAT!>
!
<WILLIAM...
<AND EMERY...>
Hiss
<DIDN'T EXPECT TO SEE YOU AFTER YOUR LAST ABJECT HUMILIATION, BRAT.>
<WELL, THIS TIME I HAVE A FAMILIAR.
<I HAVE A NAME, TOO. IT'S SHOUTA.>
<OH, SORRY! I GUESS YOUR DAD'S SUCH A BIG SHOT HE JUST SHOVED YOU OUT OF MY BRAIN.>

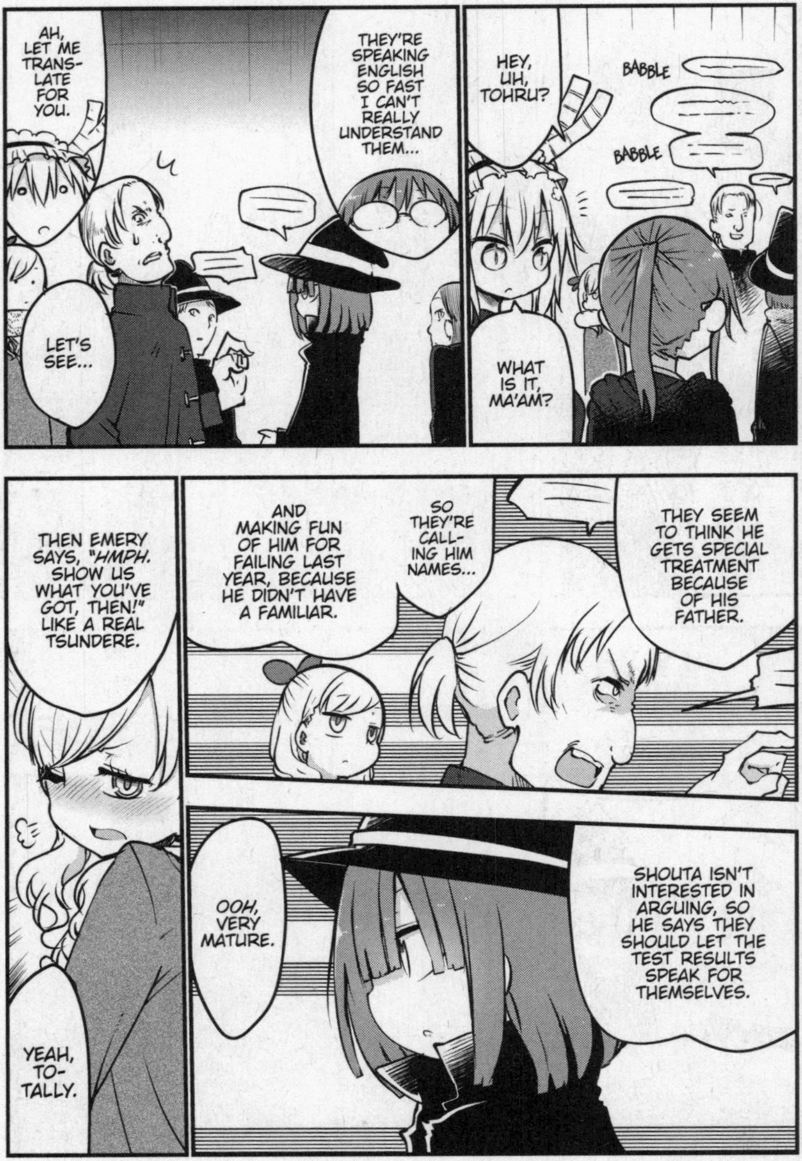
HEY, UH, TOHRU?
BABBLE
BABBLE
WHAT IS IT, MA'AM?
THEY'RE SPEAKING ENGLISH SO FAST I CAN'T REALLY UNDERSTAND THEM...
AH, LET ME TRANSLATE FOR YOU.
LET'S SEE...
THEY SEEM TO THINK HE GETS SPECIAL TREATMENT BECAUSE OF HIS FATHER.
SO THEY'RE CALLING HIM NAMES...
AND MAKING FUN OF HIM FOR FAILING LAST YEAR, BECAUSE HE DIDN'T HAVE A FAMILIAR.
SHOUTA ISN'T INTERESTED IN ARGUING, SO HE SAYS THEY SHOULD LET THE TEST RESULTS SPEAK FOR THEMSELVES.
OOH, VERY MATURE.
THEN EMERY SAYS, "*HMPH.* SHOW US WHAT YOU'VE GOT, THEN!" LIKE A REAL TSUNDERE.
YEAH, TOTALLY.

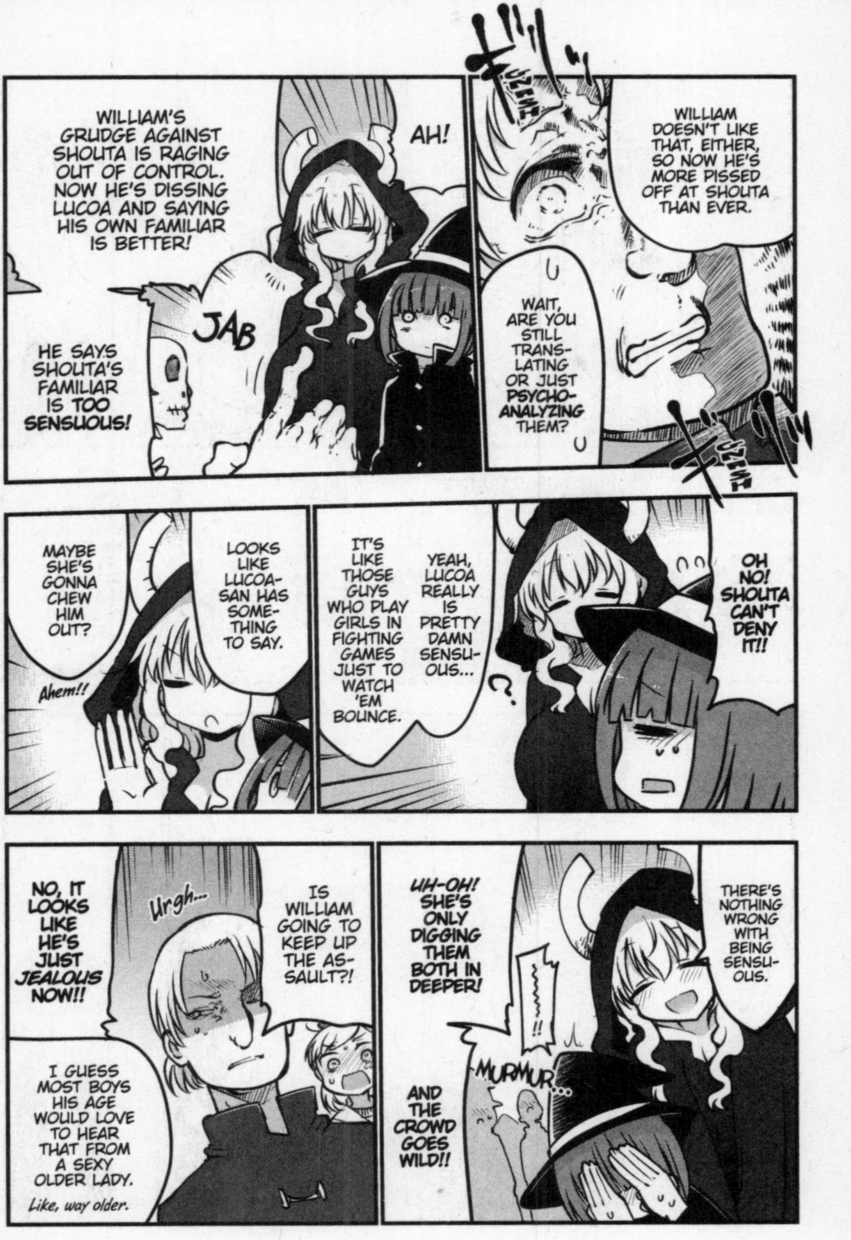
WILLIAM DOESN'T LIKE THAT, EITHER, SO NOW HE'S MORE PISSED OFF AT SHOUTA THAN EVER.
WAIT, ARE YOU STILL TRANS-LATING OR JUST PSYCHO-ANALYZING THEM?
AH!
WILLIAM'S GRUDGE AGAINST SHOUTA IS RAGING OUT OF CONTROL. NOW HE'S DISSING LUCOA AND SAYING HIS OWN FAMILIAR IS BETTER!
JAB
HE SAYS SHOUTA'S FAMILIAR IS TOO SENSUOUS!
OH NO! SHOUTA CAN'T DENY IT!!
YEAH, LUCOA REALLY IS PRETTY DAMN SENSU-OUS...
IT'S LIKE THOSE GUYS WHO PLAY GIRLS IN FIGHTING GAMES JUST TO WATCH 'EM BOUNCE.
LOOKS LIKE LUCOA-SAN HAS SOME-THING TO SAY.
MAYBE SHE'S GONNA CHEW HIM OUT?
Ahem!!
THERE'S NOTHING WRONG WITH BEING SENSU-OUS.
UH-OH! SHE'S ONLY DIGGING THEM BOTH IN DEEPER!
MURMUR...
AND THE CROWD GOES WILD!!
IS WILLIAM GOING TO KEEP UP THE AS-SAULT?!
Urgh...
NO, IT LOOKS LIKE HE'S JUST JEALOUS NOW!!
I GUESS MOST BOYS HIS AGE WOULD LOVE TO HEAR THAT FROM A SEXY OLDER LADY.
Like, way older.

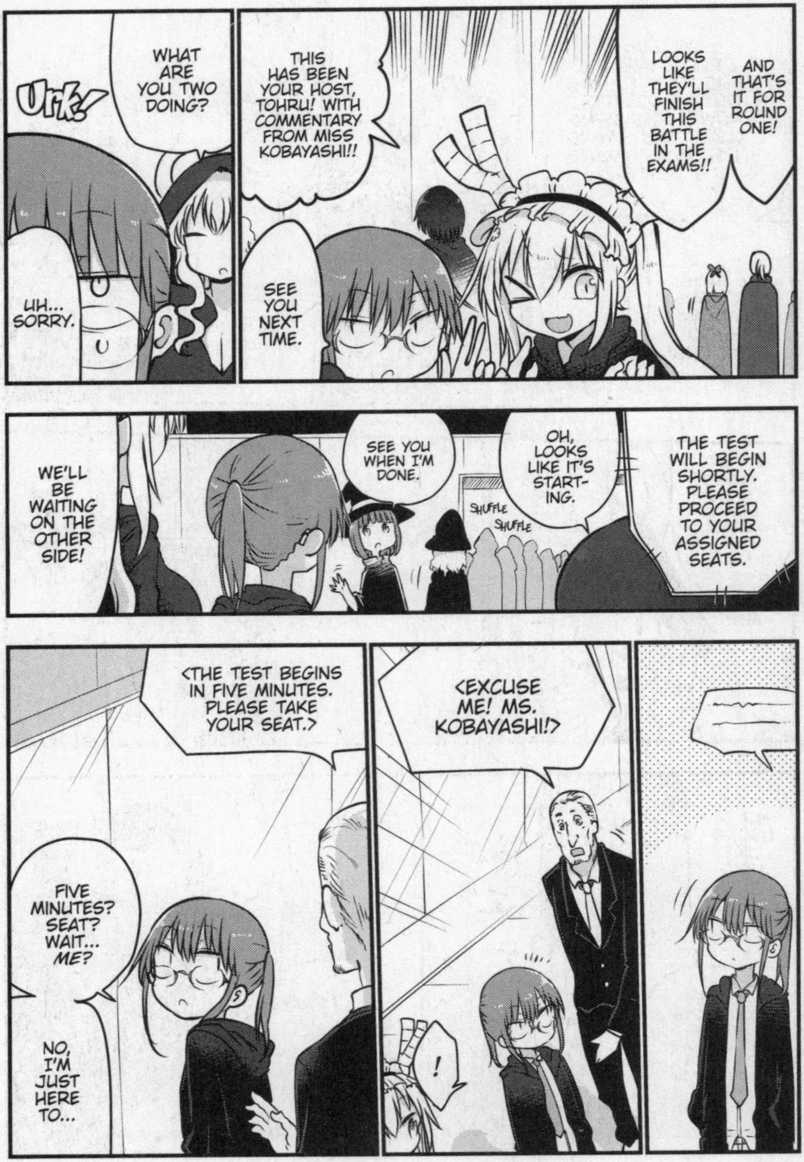
AND THAT'S IT FOR ROUND ONE!
LOOKS LIKE THEY'LL FINISH THIS BATTLE IN THE EXAMS!!
THIS HAS BEEN YOUR HOST, TOHRU! WITH COMMENTARY FROM MISS KOBAYASHI!!
SEE YOU NEXT TIME.
WHAT ARE YOU TWO DOING?
Urk!
UH... SORRY.
THE TEST WILL BEGIN SHORTLY. PLEASE PROCEED TO YOUR ASSIGNED SEATS.
OH, LOOKS LIKE IT'S STARTING.
SEE YOU WHEN I'M DONE.
SHUFFLE SHUFFLE
WE'LL BE WAITING ON THE OTHER SIDE!
<EXCUSE ME! MS. KOBAYASHI!>
!
<THE TEST BEGINS IN FIVE MINUTES. PLEASE TAKE YOUR SEAT.>
FIVE MINUTES? SEAT? WAIT... ME?
NO, I'M JUST HERE TO...

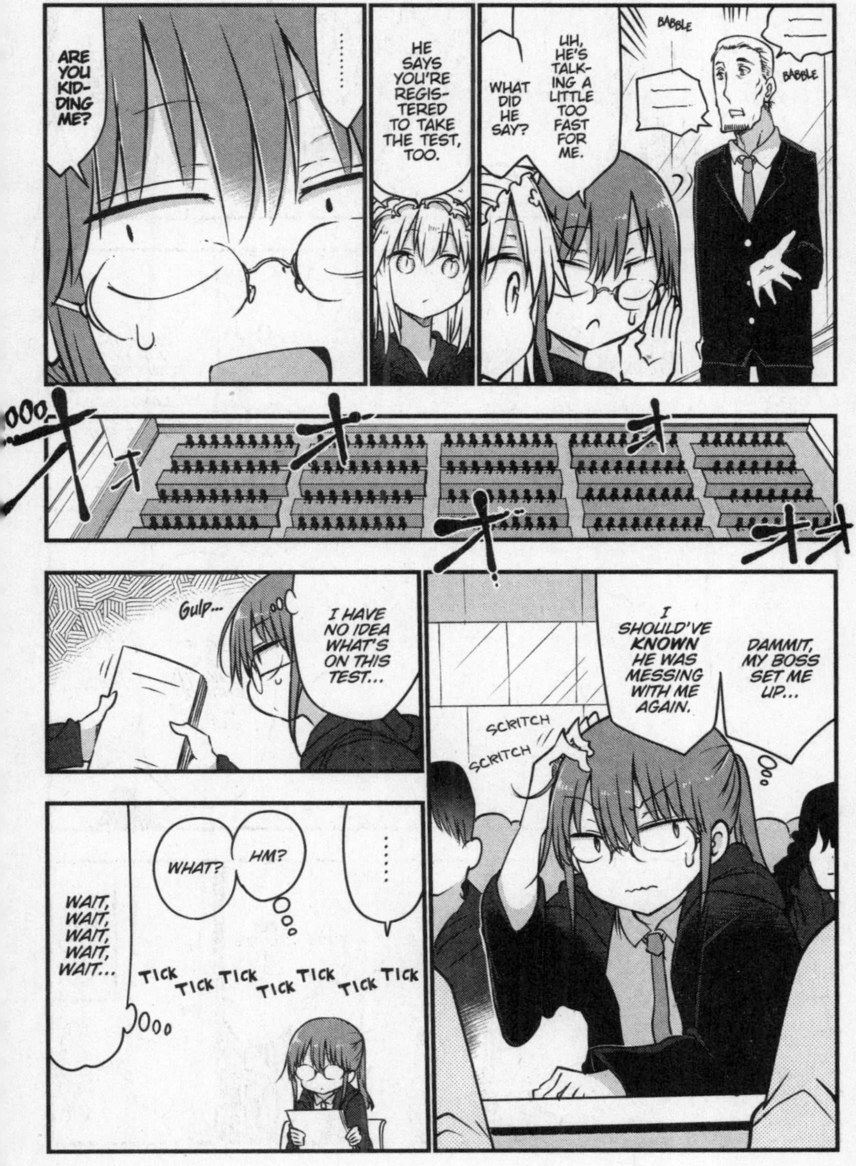
BABBLE
BABBLE
UH, HE'S TALKING A LITTLE TOO FAST FOR ME.
WHAT DID HE SAY?
HE SAYS YOU'RE REGISTERED TO TAKE THE TEST, TOO.
......
ARE YOU KIDDING ME?
OOO-
DAMMIT, MY BOSS SET ME UP...
I SHOULD'VE KNOWN HE WAS MESSING WITH ME AGAIN.
SCRITCH
SCRITCH
I HAVE NO IDEA WHAT'S ON THIS TEST...
Gulp...
......
HM?
WHAT?
WAIT, WAIT, WAIT, WAIT, WAIT...
TICK TICK TICK TICK TICK TICK TICK

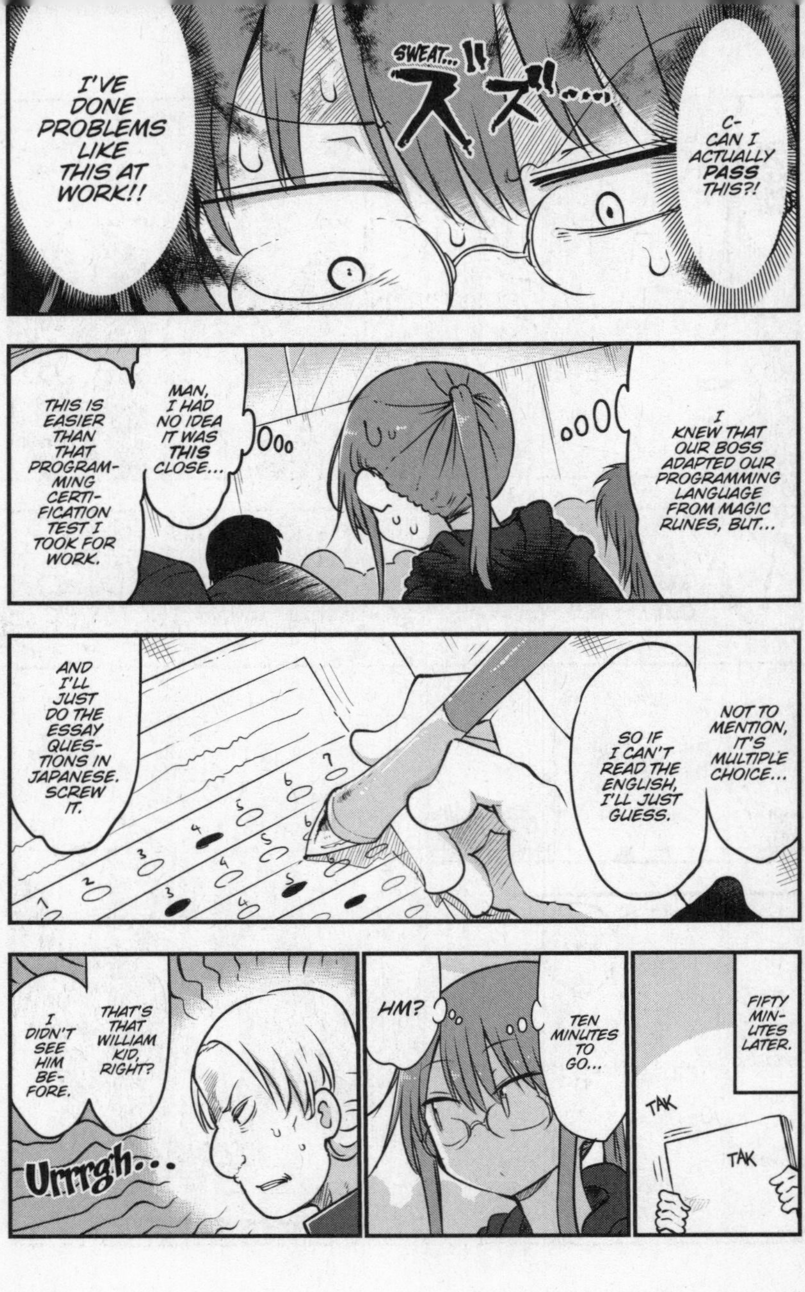
C-CAN I ACTUALLY PASS THIS?!
SWEAT...!!
スズ!…
I'VE DONE PROBLEMS LIKE THIS AT WORK!!
I KNEW THAT OUR BOSS ADAPTED OUR PROGRAMMING LANGUAGE FROM MAGIC RUNES, BUT...
MAN, I HAD NO IDEA IT WAS THIS CLOSE...
THIS IS EASIER THAN THAT PROGRAMMING CERTIFICATION TEST I TOOK FOR WORK.
NOT TO MENTION, IT'S MULTIPLE CHOICE...
SO IF I CAN'T READ THE ENGLISH, I'LL JUST GUESS.
AND I'LL JUST DO THE ESSAY QUESTIONS IN JAPANESE. SCREW IT.
FIFTY MINUTES LATER.
TAK
TAK
TEN MINUTES TO GO...
HM?
THAT'S THAT WILLIAM KID, RIGHT?
I DIDN'T SEE HIM BEFORE.
Urrrgh...

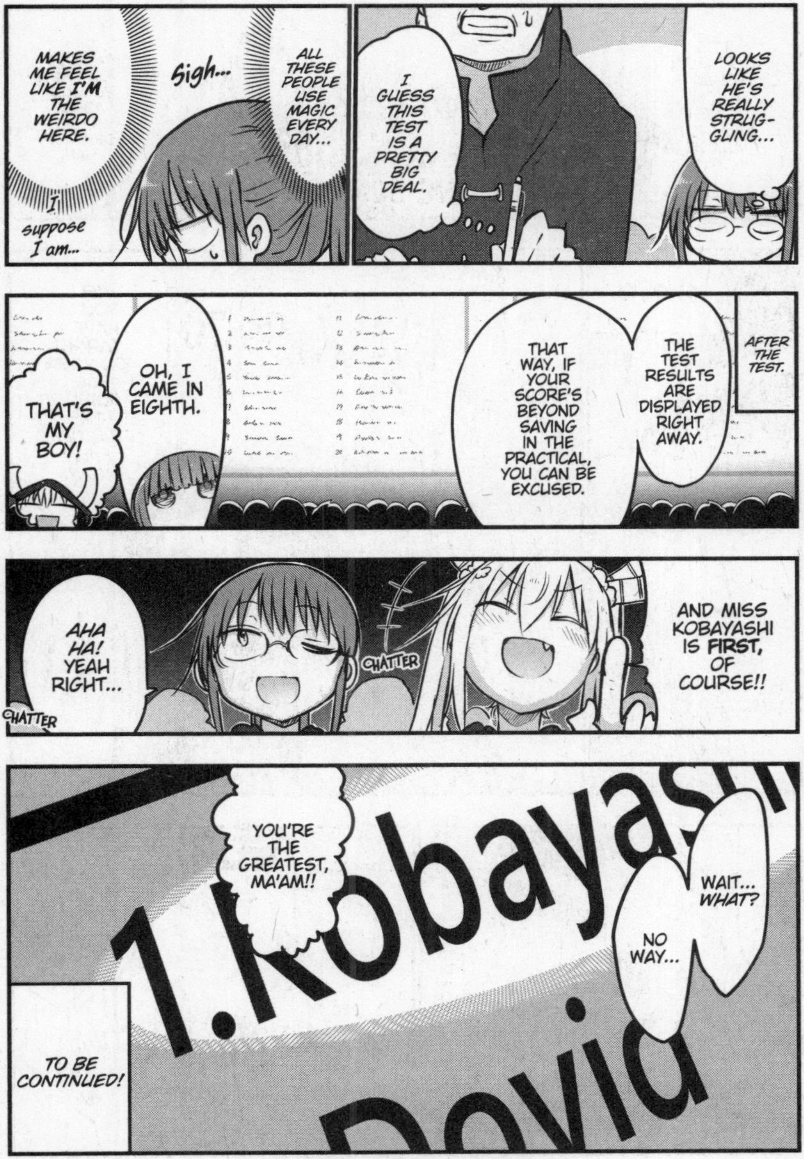
LOOKS LIKE HE'S REALLY STRUG-GLING...
I GUESS THIS TEST IS A PRETTY BIG DEAL.
ALL THESE PEOPLE USE MAGIC EVERY DAY...
Sigh...
MAKES ME FEEL LIKE I'M THE WEIRDO HERE.
I suppose I am...
AFTER THE TEST.
THE TEST RESULTS ARE DISPLAYED RIGHT AWAY.
THAT WAY, IF YOUR SCORE'S BEYOND SAVING IN THE PRACTICAL, YOU CAN BE EXCUSED.
OH, I CAME IN EIGHTH.
THAT'S MY BOY!
AND MISS KOBAYASHI IS FIRST, OF COURSE!!
CHATTER
AHA HA! YEAH RIGHT...
CHATTER
WAIT... WHAT?
NO WAY...
1.Kobayash
David
YOU'RE THE GREATEST, MA'AM!!
TO BE CONTINUED!

CHAPTER 65/END

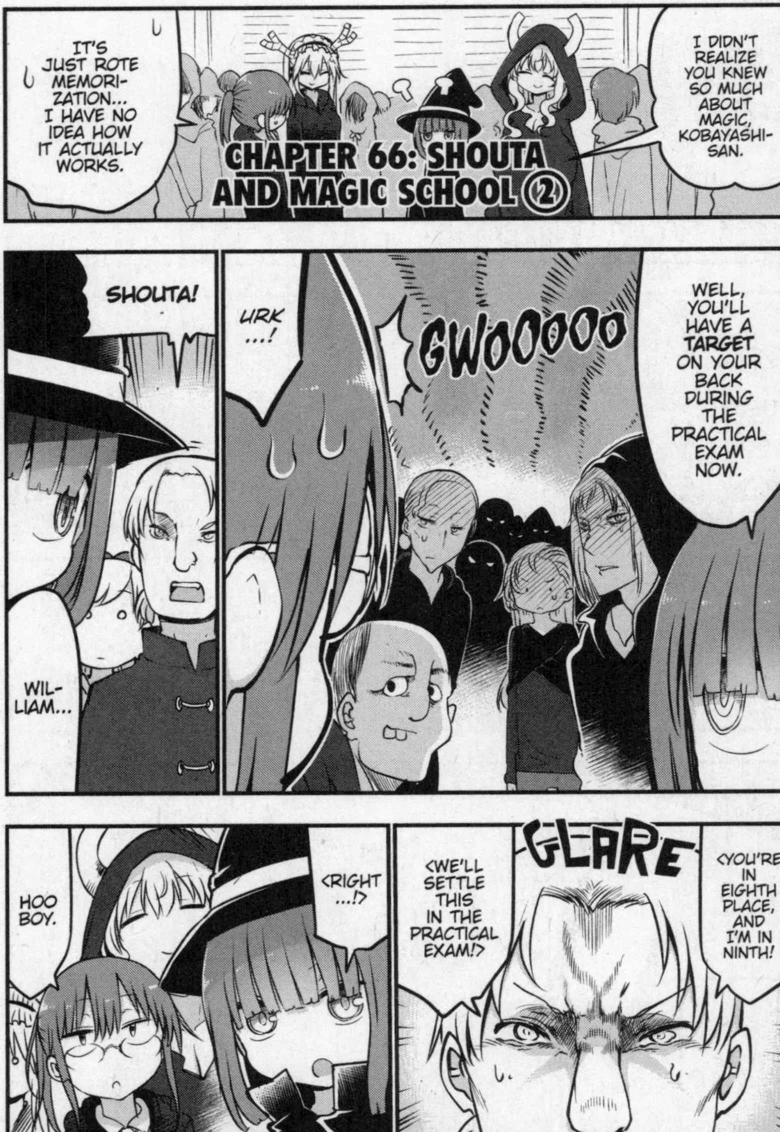
I DIDN'T REALIZE YOU KNEW SO MUCH ABOUT MAGIC, KOBAYASHI-SAN.
CHAPTER 66: SHOUTA AND MAGIC SCHOOL ②
IT'S JUST ROTE MEMORIZATION... I HAVE NO IDEA HOW IT ACTUALLY WORKS.
WELL, YOU'LL HAVE A TARGET ON YOUR BACK DURING THE PRACTICAL EXAM NOW.
GWOOOOO
URK ...!
SHOUTA!
WIL-LIAM...
<YOU'RE IN EIGHTH PLACE, AND I'M IN NINTH!
GLARE
<WE'LL SETTLE THIS IN THE PRACTICAL EXAM!>
<RIGHT ...!>
HOO BOY.

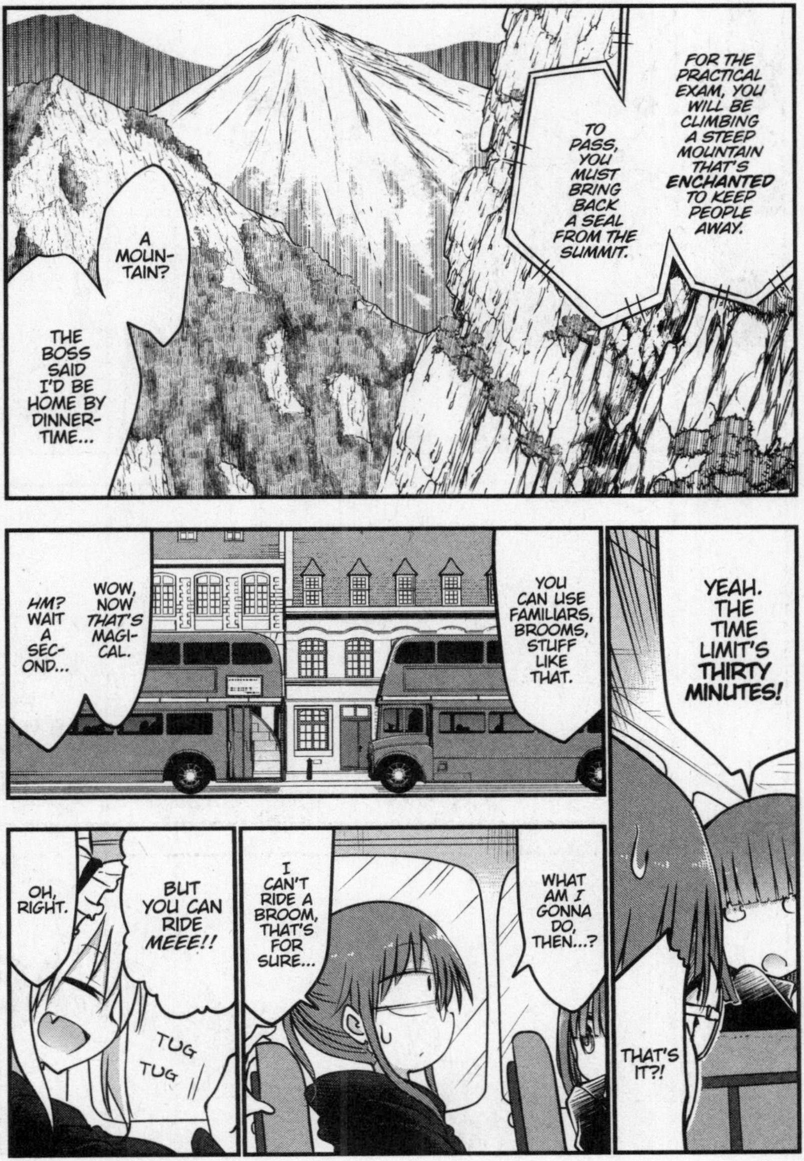
FOR THE PRACTICAL EXAM, YOU WILL BE CLIMBING A STEEP MOUNTAIN THAT'S ENCHANTED TO KEEP PEOPLE AWAY.
TO PASS, YOU MUST BRING BACK A SEAL FROM THE SUMMIT.
A MOUNTAIN?
THE BOSS SAID I'D BE HOME BY DINNER-TIME...
YEAH. THE TIME LIMIT'S THIRTY MINUTES!
THAT'S IT?!
YOU CAN USE FAMILIARS, BROOMS, STUFF LIKE THAT.
WOW, NOW THAT'S MAGICAL.
HM? WAIT A SEC-OND...
WHAT AM I GONNA DO, THEN...?
I CAN'T RIDE A BROOM, THAT'S FOR SURE...
BUT YOU CAN RIDE MEEE!!
OH, RIGHT.
TUG
TUG

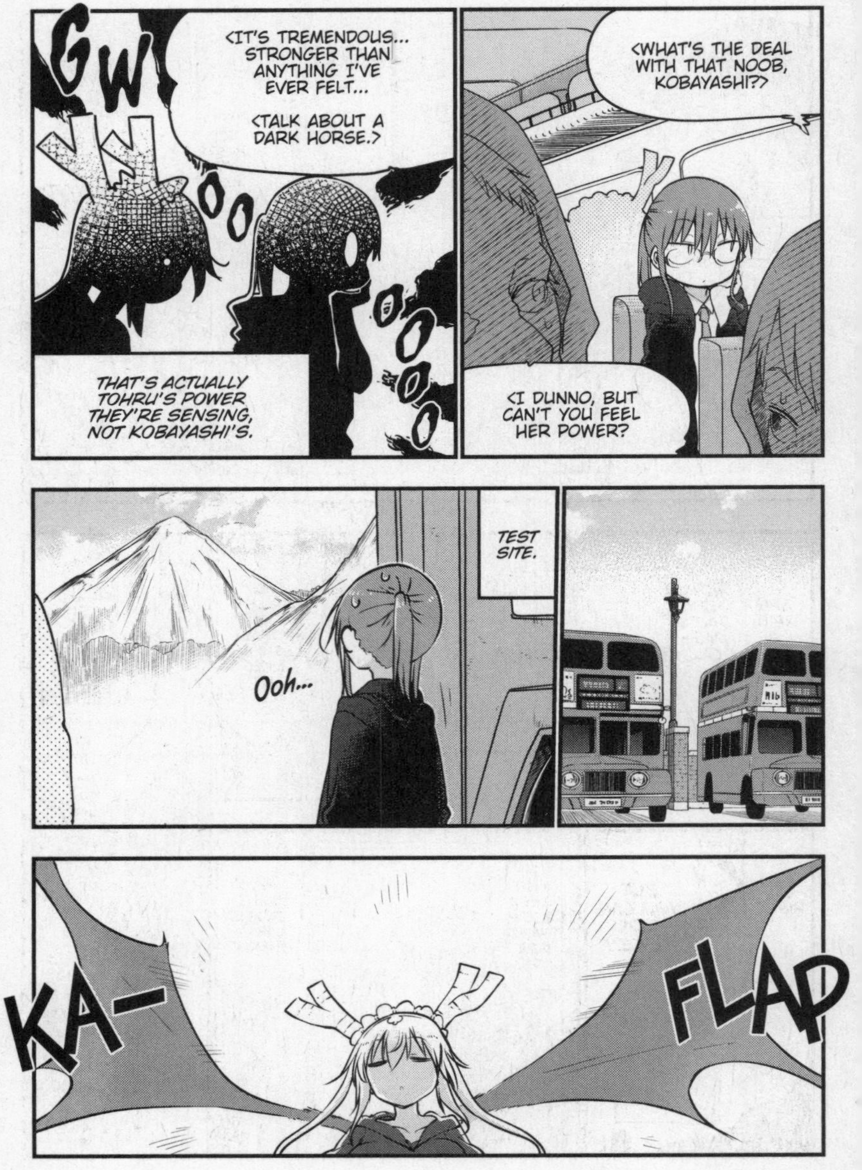
<WHAT'S THE DEAL WITH THAT NOOB, KOBAYASHI?>
<I DUNNO, BUT CAN'T YOU FEEL HER POWER?
GWOOOOOO
<IT'S TREMENDOUS... STRONGER THAN ANYTHING I'VE EVER FELT...
<TALK ABOUT A DARK HORSE.>
THAT'S ACTUALLY TOHRU'S POWER THEY'RE SENSING, NOT KOBAYASHI'S.
TEST SITE.
Ooh...
KA-FLAP

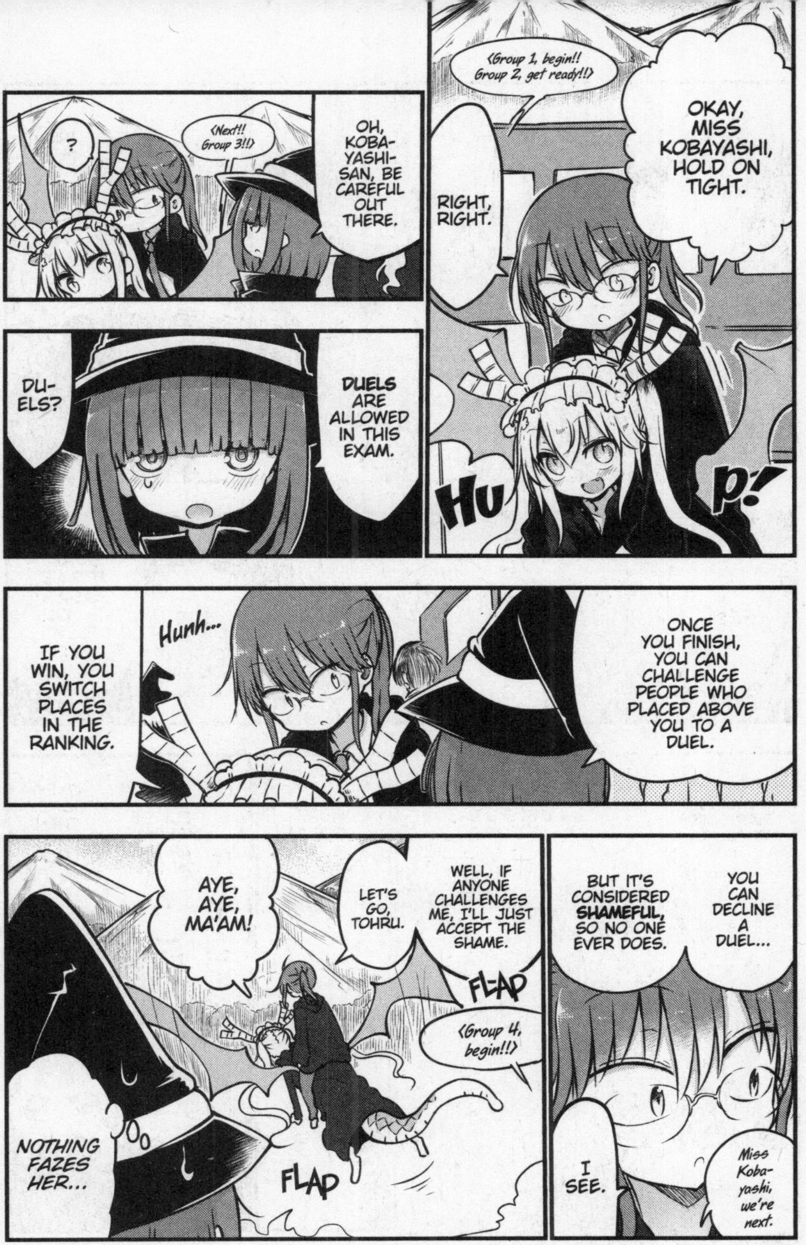
‹Group 1, begin!! Group 2, get ready!!›
OKAY, MISS KOBAYASHI, HOLD ON TIGHT.
RIGHT, RIGHT.
HUP!
OH, KOBA-YASHI-SAN, BE CAREFUL OUT THERE.
‹Next!! Group 3!!›
?
DUELS ARE ALLOWED IN THIS EXAM.
DU-ELS?
ONCE YOU FINISH, YOU CAN CHALLENGE PEOPLE WHO PLACED ABOVE YOU TO A DUEL.
Hunh...
IF YOU WIN, YOU SWITCH PLACES IN THE RANKING.
YOU CAN DECLINE A DUEL...
BUT IT'S CONSIDERED SHAMEFUL, SO NO ONE EVER DOES.
I SEE.
Miss Kobayashi, we're next.
WELL, IF ANYONE CHALLENGES ME, I'LL JUST ACCEPT THE SHAME.
LET'S GO, TOHRU.
AYE, AYE, MA'AM!
FLAP
‹Group 4, begin!!›
NOTHING FAZES HER...
FLAP

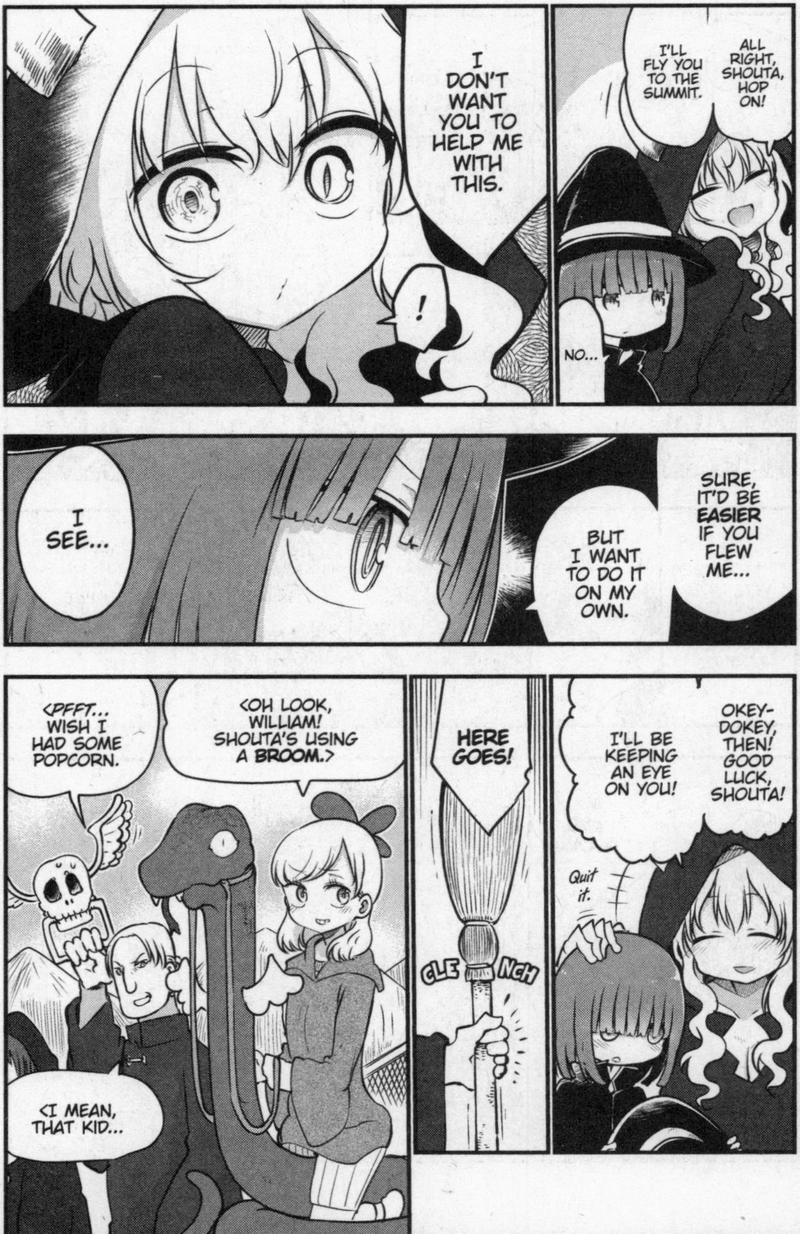
ALL RIGHT, SHOUTA, HOP ON!
I'LL FLY YOU TO THE SUMMIT.
NO...
I DON'T WANT YOU TO HELP ME WITH THIS.
!
SURE, IT'D BE **EASIER** IF YOU FLEW ME...
BUT I WANT TO DO IT ON MY OWN.
I SEE...
OKEY-DOKEY, THEN! GOOD LUCK, SHOUTA!
I'LL BE KEEPING AN EYE ON YOU!
Quit it.
HERE GOES!
CLENCH
<OH LOOK, WILLIAM! SHOUTA'S USING A **BROOM.**>
<PFFT... WISH I HAD SOME POPCORN.
<I MEAN, THAT KID...

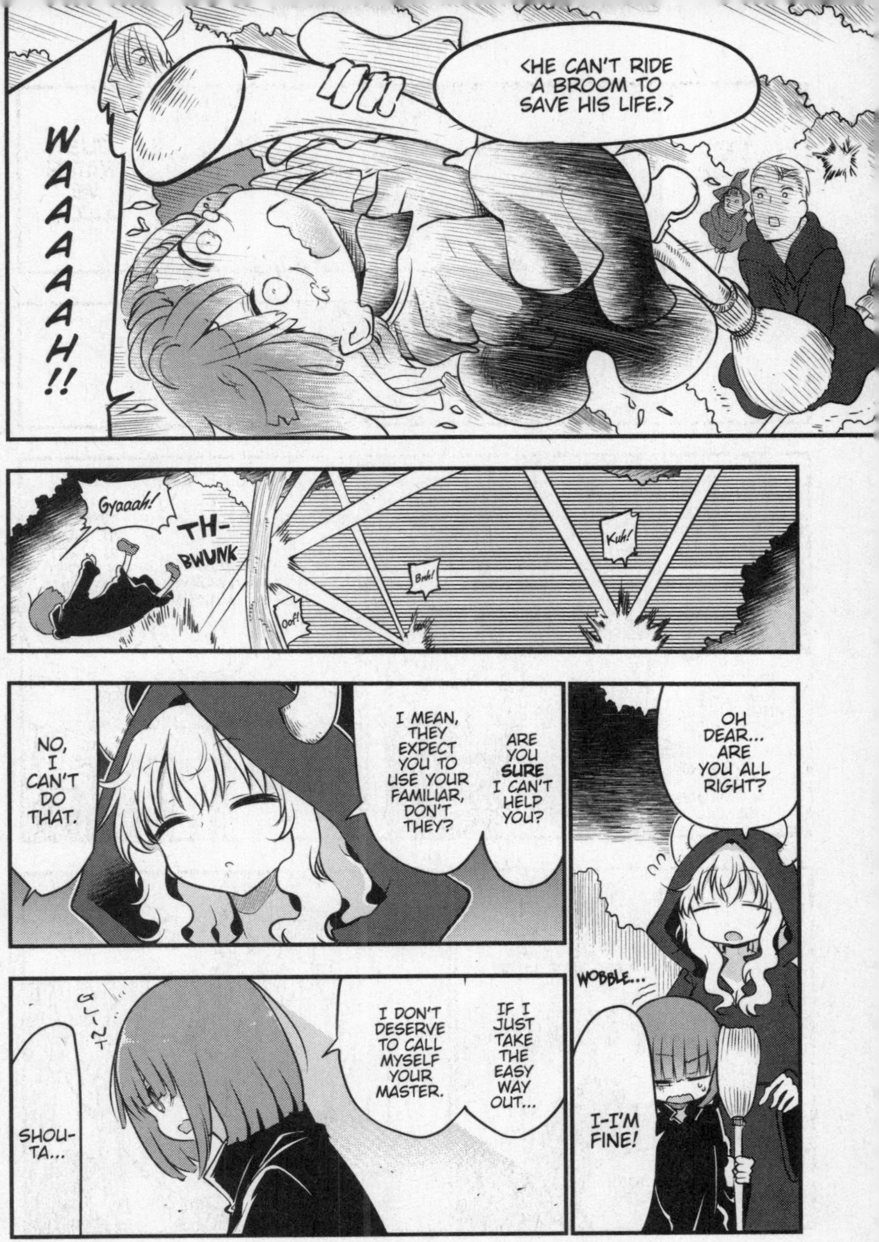
<HE CAN'T RIDE A BROOM TO SAVE HIS LIFE.>
WAAAAAAAH!!
Kuh!
Bnh!
Oof!
Gyaaah!
TH-BWUNK
OH DEAR... ARE YOU ALL RIGHT?
WOBBLE...
I-I'M FINE!
ARE YOU SURE I CAN'T HELP YOU?
I MEAN, THEY EXPECT YOU TO USE YOUR FAMILIAR, DON'T THEY?
NO, I CAN'T DO THAT.
IF I JUST TAKE THE EASY WAY OUT...
I DON'T DESERVE TO CALL MYSELF YOUR MASTER.
GLINT
SHOUTA...

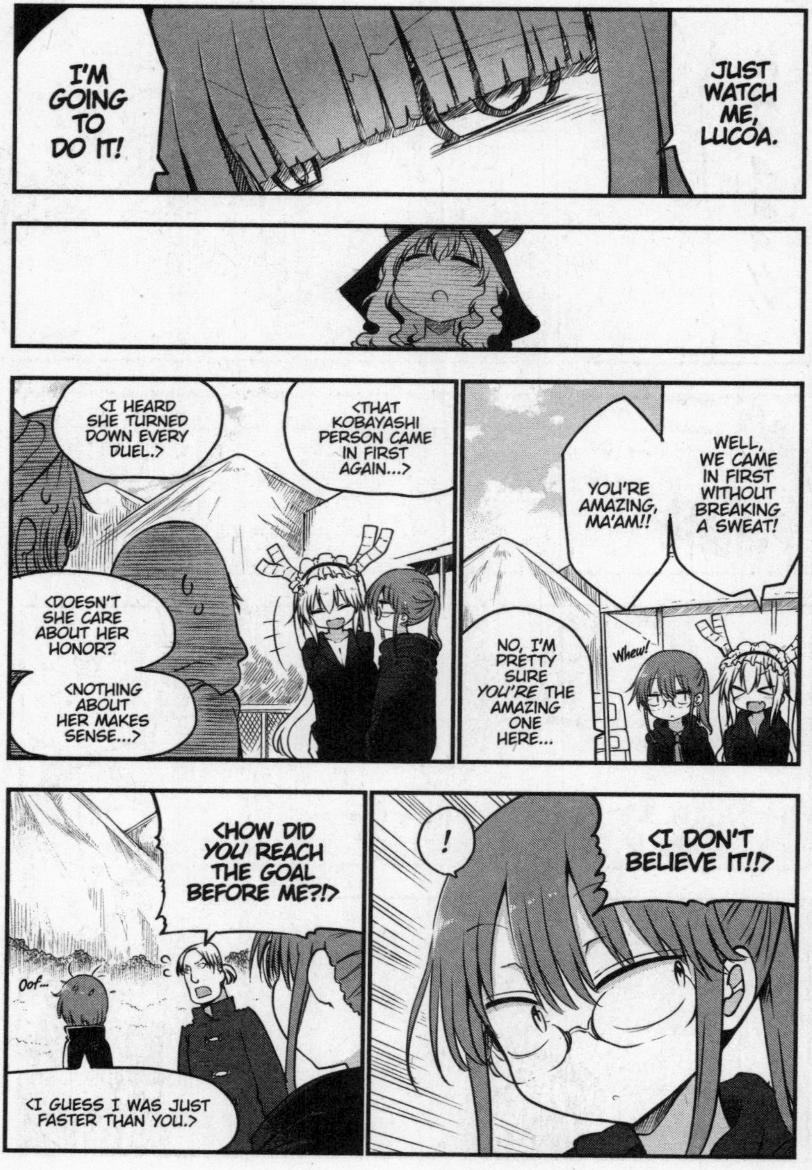
JUST WATCH ME, LUCOA.
I'M GOING TO DO IT!
WELL, WE CAME IN FIRST WITHOUT BREAKING A SWEAT!
YOU'RE AMAZING, MA'AM!!
Whew!
NO, I'M PRETTY SURE *YOU'RE* THE AMAZING ONE HERE...
<THAT KOBAYASHI PERSON CAME IN FIRST AGAIN...>
<I HEARD SHE TURNED DOWN EVERY DUEL.>
<DOESN'T SHE CARE ABOUT HER HONOR?
<NOTHING ABOUT HER MAKES SENSE...>
<I DON'T BELIEVE IT!!>
!
<HOW DID *YOU* REACH THE GOAL BEFORE ME?!>
Oof...
<I GUESS I WAS JUST FASTER THAN YOU.>

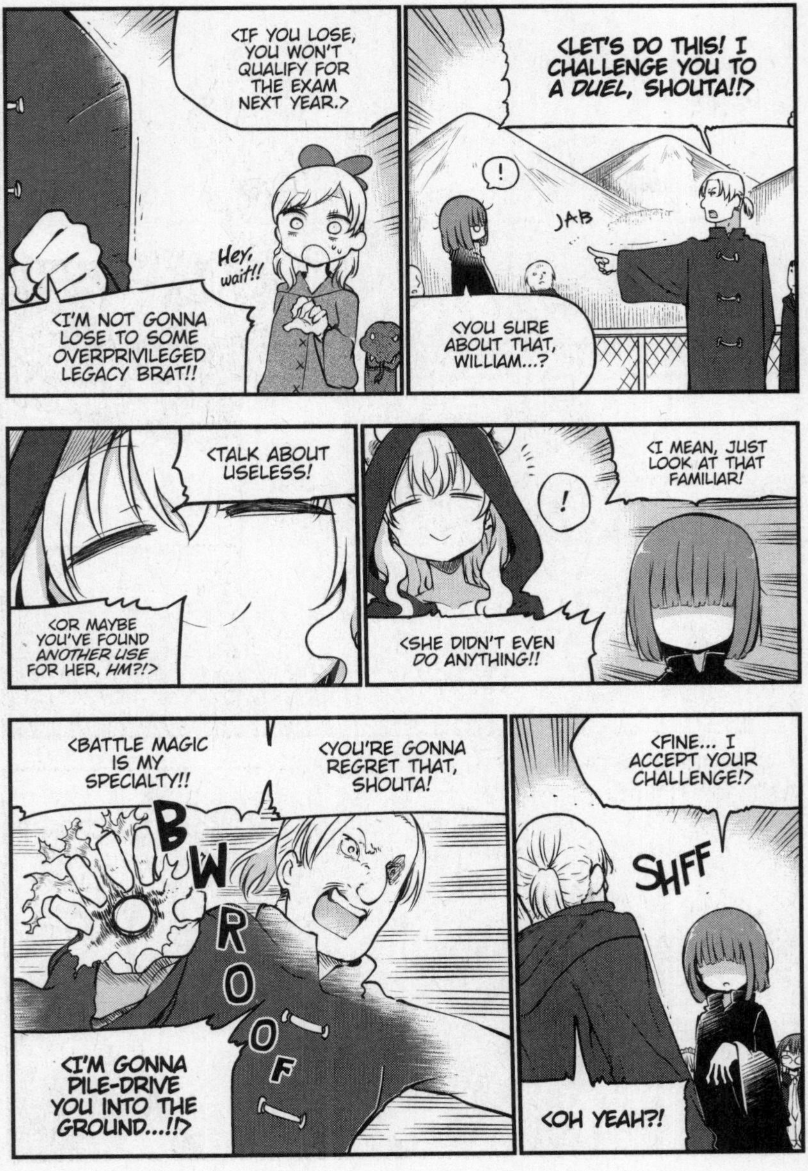
<LET'S DO THIS! I CHALLENGE YOU TO A *DUEL*, SHOUTA!!>
!
JAB
<YOU SURE ABOUT THAT, WILLIAM...?
<IF YOU LOSE, YOU WON'T QUALIFY FOR THE EXAM NEXT YEAR.>
Hey, wait!!
<I'M NOT GONNA LOSE TO SOME OVERPRIVILEGED LEGACY BRAT!!
<I MEAN, JUST LOOK AT THAT FAMILIAR!
!
<SHE DIDN'T EVEN *DO* ANYTHING!!
<TALK ABOUT USELESS!
<OR MAYBE YOU'VE FOUND *ANOTHER USE* FOR HER, *HM?!*>
<FINE... I ACCEPT YOUR CHALLENGE!>
SHFF
<OH YEAH?!
<YOU'RE GONNA REGRET THAT, SHOUTA!
<BATTLE MAGIC IS MY SPECIALTY!!
BWROOF
<I'M GONNA PILE-DRIVE YOU INTO THE GROUND...!!>

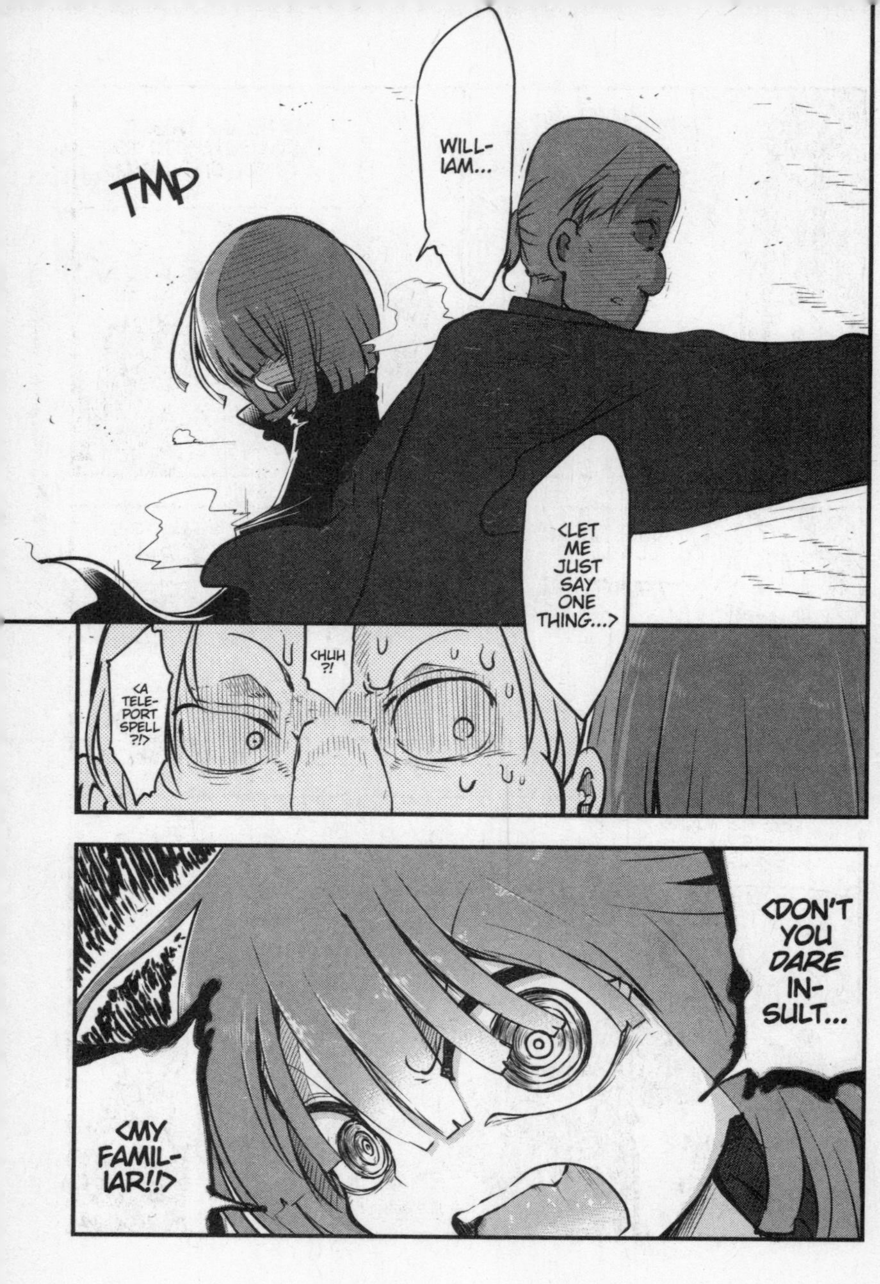
WILL-IAM...
TMP
<LET ME JUST SAY ONE THING...>
<HUH?!
<A TELE-PORT SPELL?!>
<DON'T YOU DARE IN-SULT...
<MY FAMIL-IAR!!>

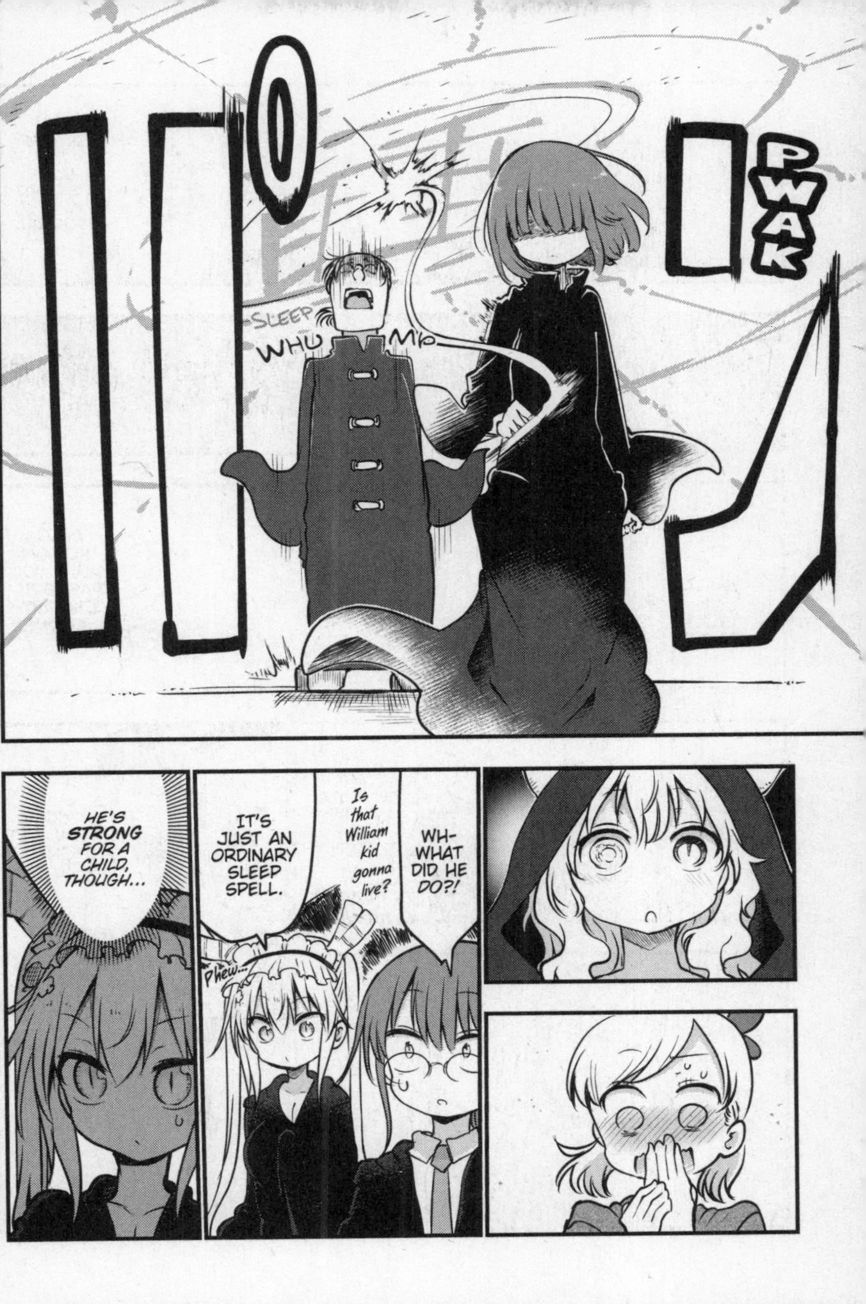
PWAK
SLEEP
WHUMP
WH-WHAT DID HE DO?!
Is that William kid gonna live?
IT'S JUST AN ORDINARY SLEEP SPELL.
Phew...
HE'S STRONG FOR A CHILD, THOUGH...

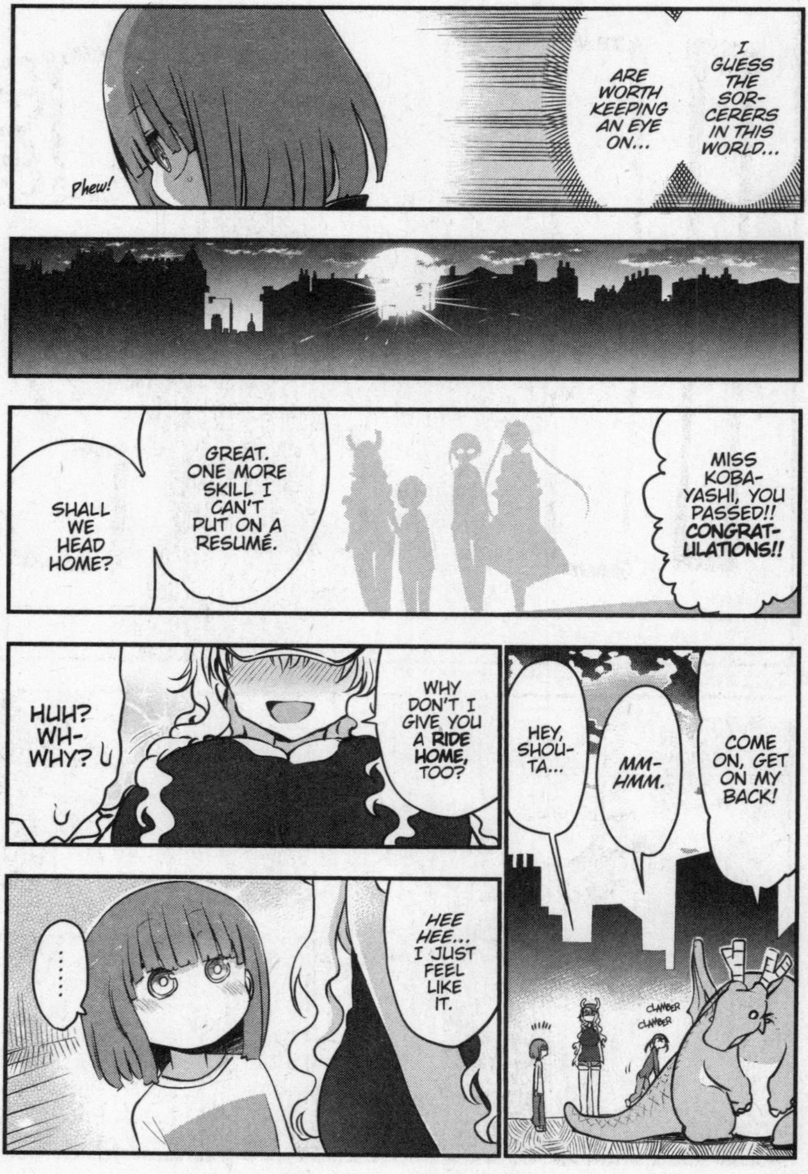
I GUESS THE SOR-CERERS IN THIS WORLD...
ARE WORTH KEEPING AN EYE ON...
Phew!
MISS KOBA-YASHI, YOU PASSED!! CONGRAT-ULATIONS!!
GREAT. ONE MORE SKILL I CAN'T PUT ON A RESUMÉ.
SHALL WE HEAD HOME?
COME ON, GET ON MY BACK!
MM-HMM.
HEY, SHOU-TA...
CLAMBER CLAMBER
WHY DON'T I GIVE YOU A RIDE HOME, TOO?
HUH? WH-WHY?
HEE HEE... I JUST FEEL LIKE IT.
......

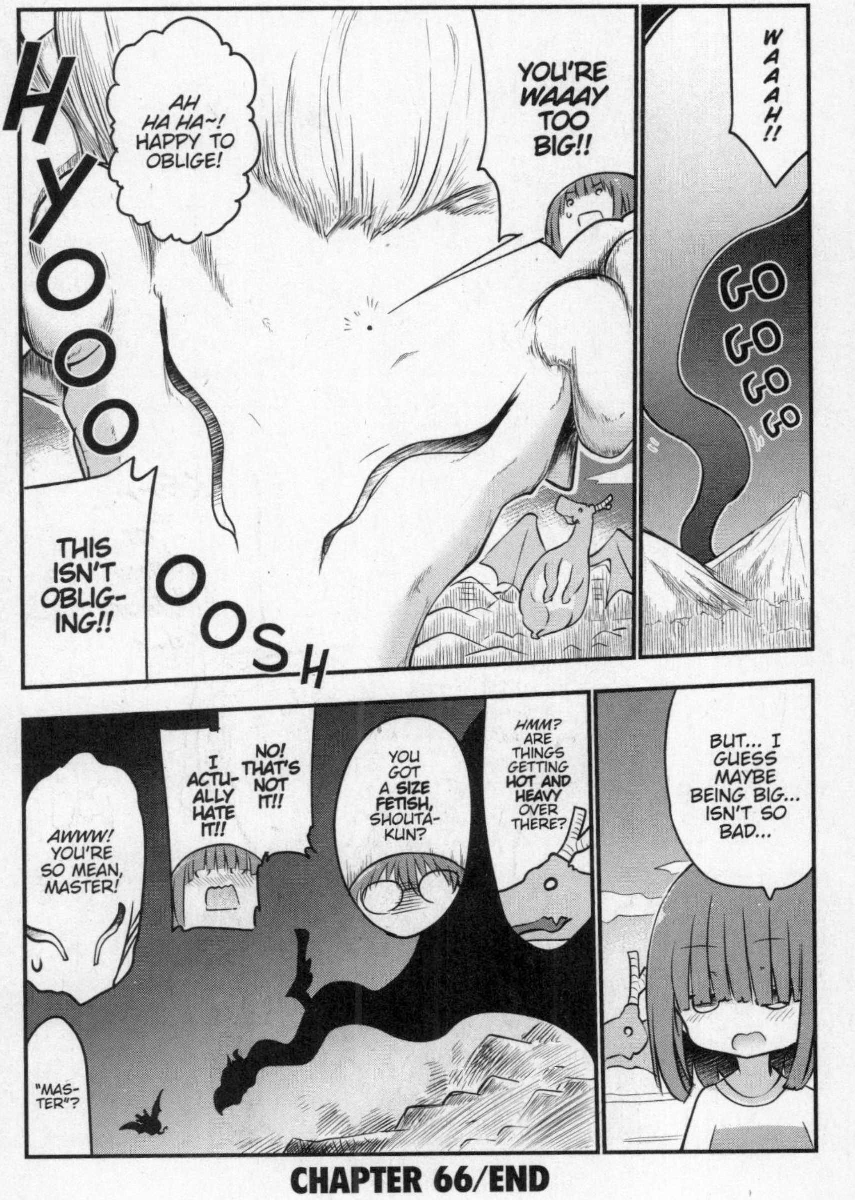
WAAAAH!!
GO GO GO GO GO GO
YOU'RE WAAAY TOO BIG!!
AH HA HA~! HAPPY TO OBLIGE!
HYOOOOOOSH
THIS ISN'T OBLIG-ING!!
BUT... I GUESS MAYBE BEING BIG... ISN'T SO BAD...
HMM? ARE THINGS GETTING HOT AND HEAVY OVER THERE?
YOU GOT A SIZE FETISH, SHOUTA-KUN?
NO! THAT'S NOT IT!!
I ACTU-ALLY HATE IT!!
AWWW! YOU'RE SO MEAN, MASTER!
"MAS-TER"?

CHAPTER 66/END

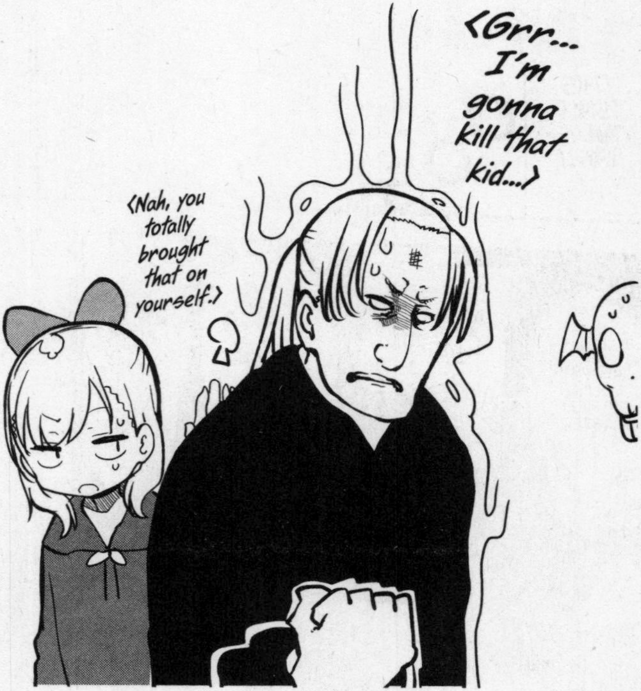
<Grr... I'm gonna kill that kid...>
<Nah, you totally brought that on yourself.>

Miss Kobayashi's
Dragon Maid

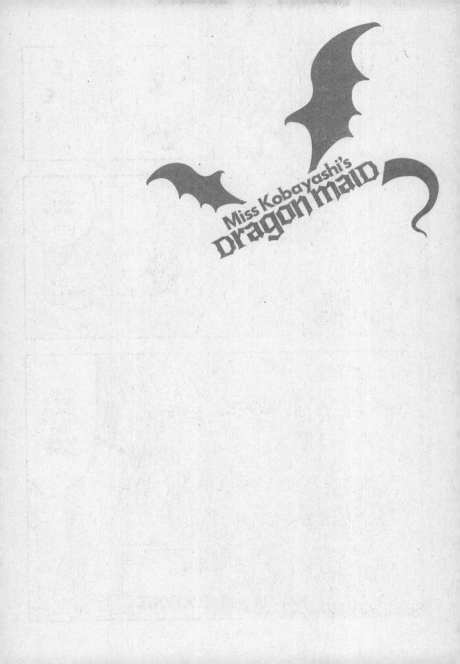

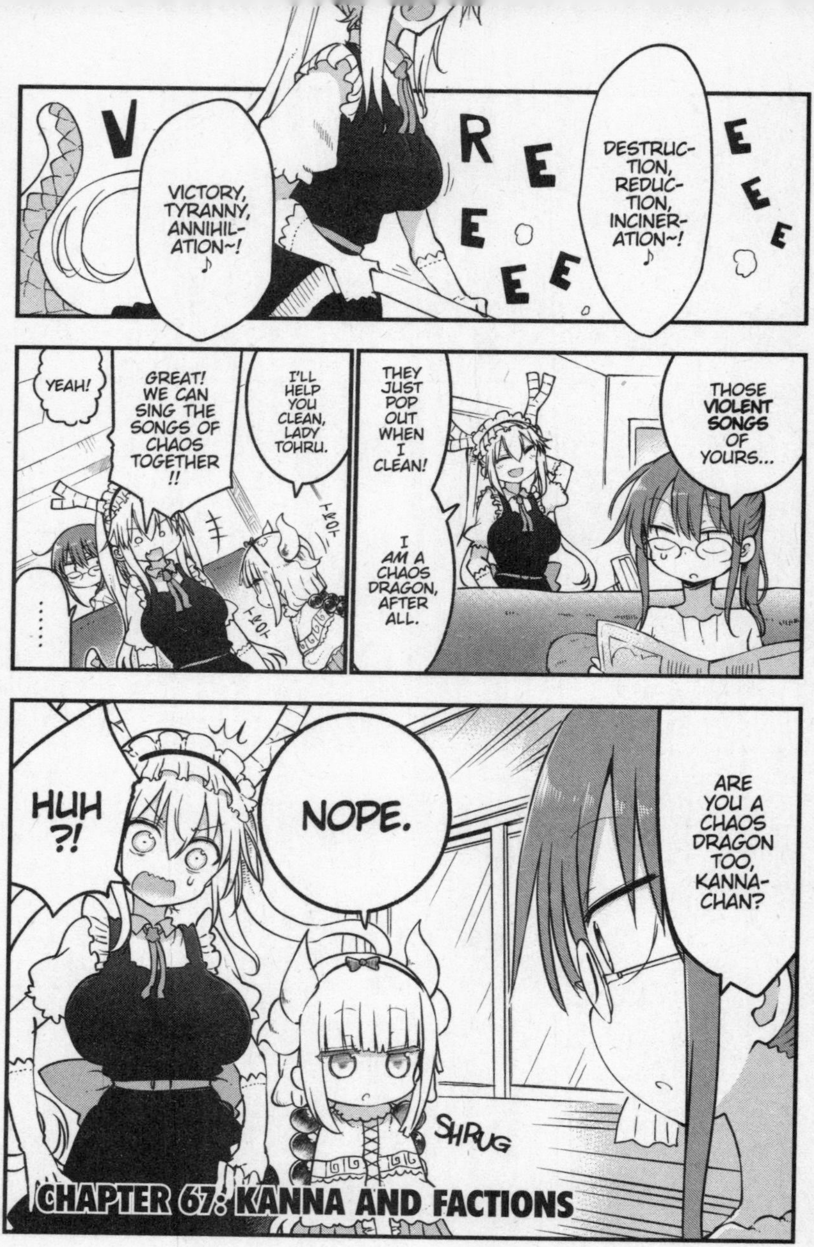
DESTRUCTION, REDUCTION, INCINERATION~! ♪
VICTORY, TYRANNY, ANNIHILATION~! ♪
VREEEEEEE
THOSE VIOLENT SONGS OF YOURS...
THEY JUST POP OUT WHEN I CLEAN!
I AM A CHAOS DRAGON, AFTER ALL.
I'LL HELP YOU CLEAN, LADY TOHRU.
TROT
TROT
GREAT! WE CAN SING THE SONGS OF CHAOS TOGETHER!!
YEAH!
......
ARE YOU A CHAOS DRAGON TOO, KANNA-CHAN?
NOPE.
HUH?!
SHRUG
CHAPTER 67: KANNA AND FACTIONS

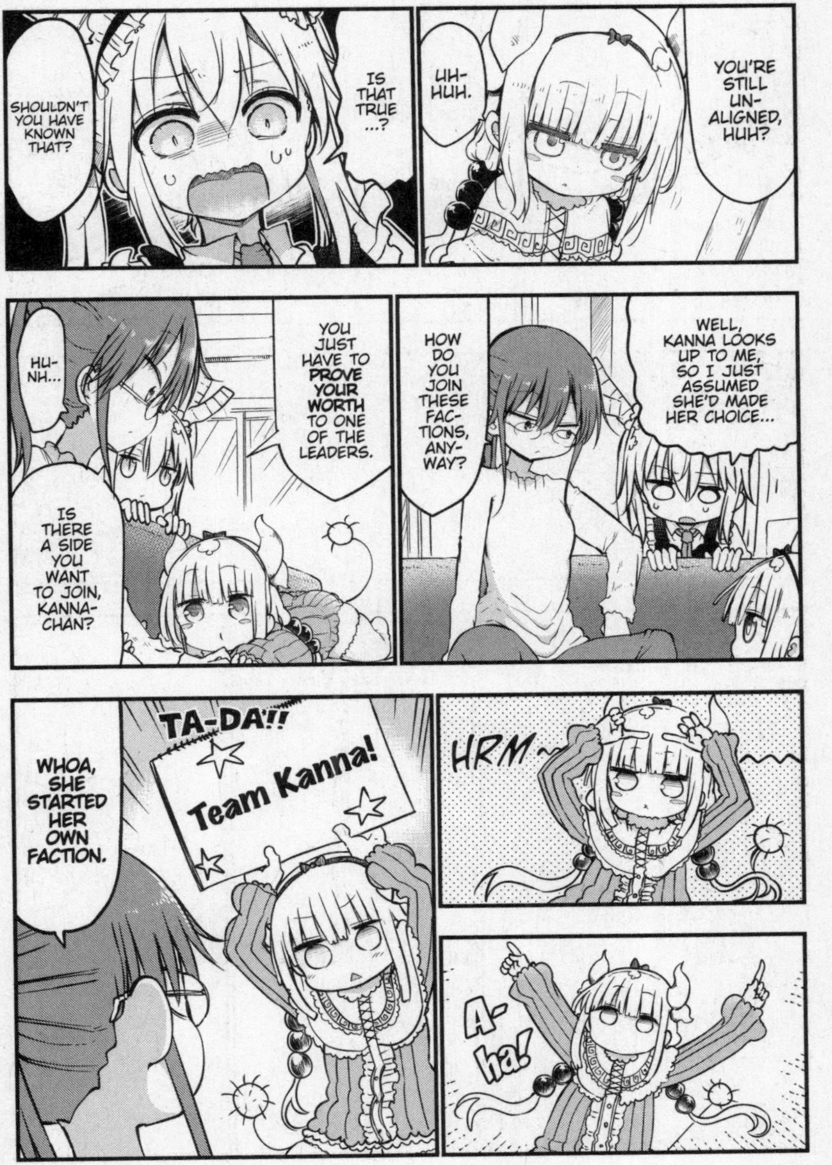
YOU'RE STILL UN-ALIGNED, HUH?
UH-HUH.
IS THAT TRUE ...?
SHOULDN'T YOU HAVE KNOWN THAT?
WELL, KANNA LOOKS UP TO ME, SO I JUST ASSUMED SHE'D MADE HER CHOICE...
HOW DO YOU JOIN THESE FACTIONS, ANYWAY?
YOU JUST HAVE TO PROVE YOUR WORTH TO ONE OF THE LEADERS.
HU-NH...
IS THERE A SIDE YOU WANT TO JOIN, KANNA-CHAN?
HRM~
A-ha!
TA-DA!!
Team Kanna!
WHOA, SHE STARTED HER OWN FACTION.

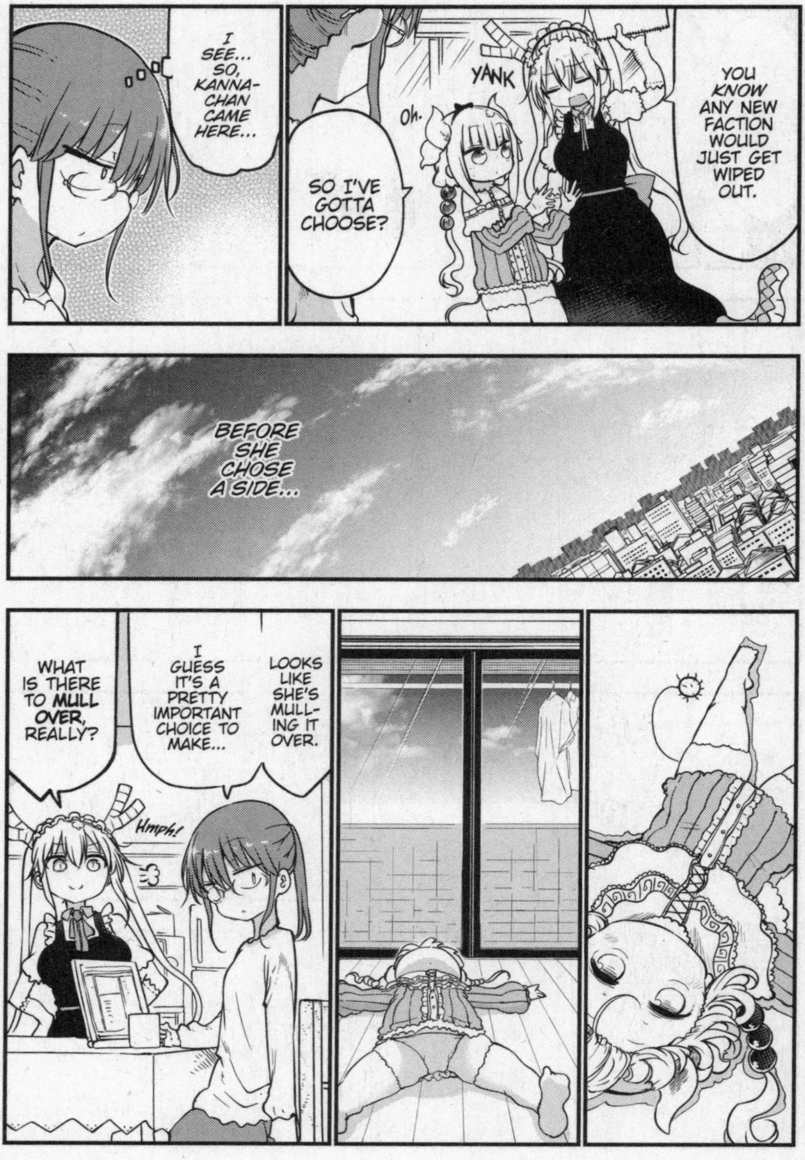
YOU KNOW ANY NEW FACTION WOULD JUST GET WIPED OUT.
YANK
Oh.
SO I'VE GOTTA CHOOSE?
I SEE... SO, KANNA-CHAN CAME HERE...
BEFORE SHE CHOSE A SIDE...
LOOKS LIKE SHE'S MULLING IT OVER.
I GUESS IT'S A PRETTY IMPORTANT CHOICE TO MAKE...
WHAT IS THERE TO MULL OVER, REALLY?
Hmph!

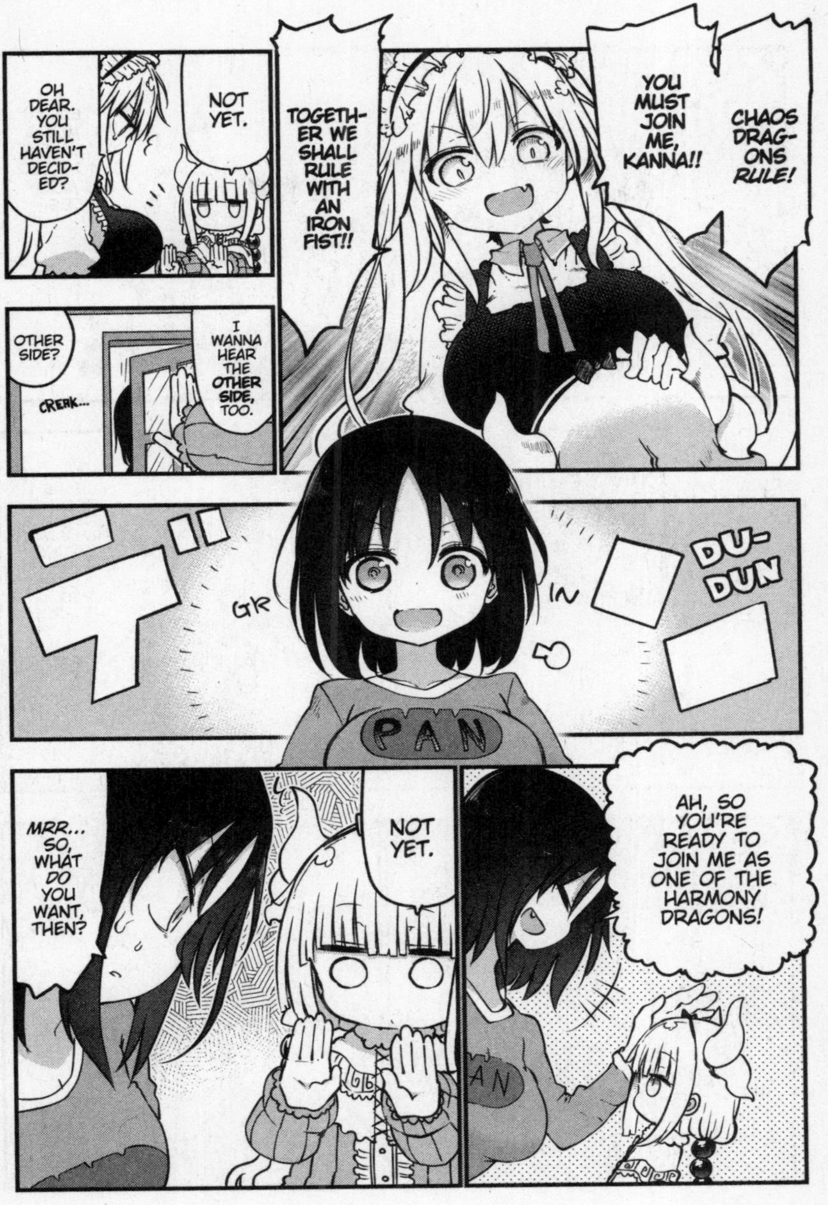
CHAOS DRAG-ONS RULE!
YOU MUST JOIN ME, KANNA!!
TOGETH-ER WE SHALL RULE WITH AN IRON FIST!!
NOT YET.
OH DEAR. YOU STILL HAVEN'T DECID-ED?
I WANNA HEAR THE OTHER SIDE, TOO.
OTHER SIDE?
CREAK...
DU-DUN
GR IN
PAN
AH, SO YOU'RE READY TO JOIN ME AS ONE OF THE HARMONY DRAGONS!
NOT YET.
MRR... SO, WHAT DO YOU WANT, THEN?

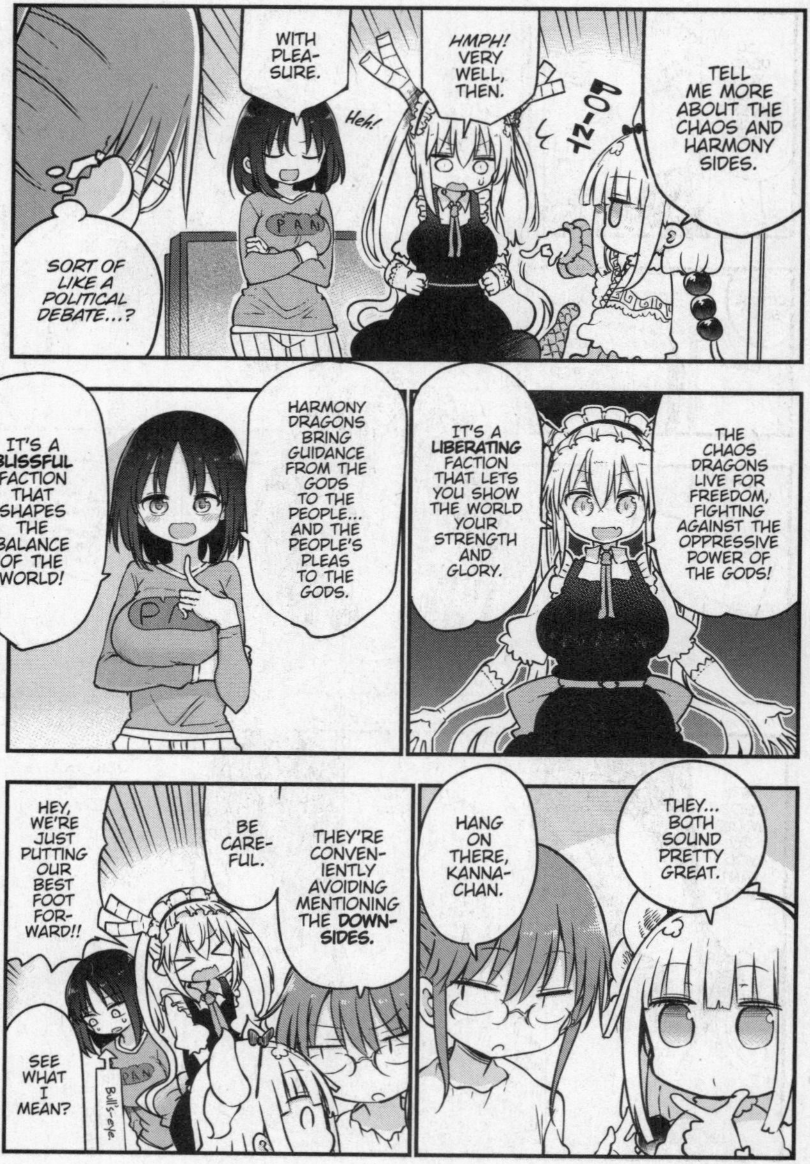
TELL ME MORE ABOUT THE CHAOS AND HARMONY SIDES.
POINT
HMPH! VERY WELL, THEN.
WITH PLEA-SURE.
Heh!
SORT OF LIKE A POLITICAL DEBATE...?
THE CHAOS DRAGONS LIVE FOR FREEDOM, FIGHTING AGAINST THE OPPRESSIVE POWER OF THE GODS!
IT'S A **LIBERATING** FACTION THAT LETS YOU SHOW THE WORLD YOUR STRENGTH AND GLORY.
HARMONY DRAGONS BRING GUIDANCE FROM THE GODS TO THE PEOPLE... AND THE PEOPLE'S PLEAS TO THE GODS.
IT'S A **BLISSFUL** FACTION THAT SHAPES THE BALANCE OF THE WORLD!
THEY... BOTH SOUND PRETTY GREAT.
HANG ON THERE, KANNA-CHAN.
BE CARE-FUL.
THEY'RE CONVEN-IENTLY AVOIDING MENTIONING THE **DOWN-SIDES.**
HEY, WE'RE JUST PUTTING OUR BEST FOOT FOR-WARD!!
Bull's-eye.
SEE WHAT I MEAN?

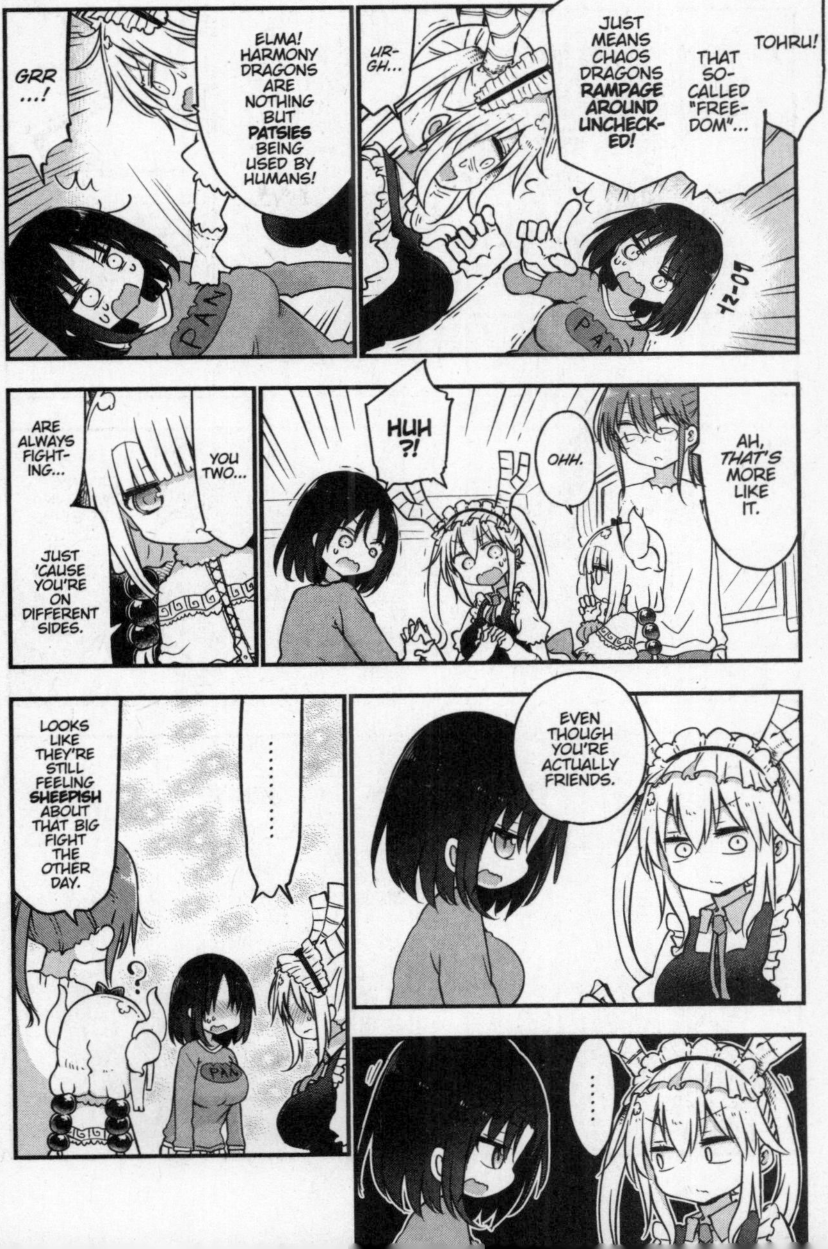
TOHRU!
THAT SO-CALLED "FREEDOM"...
JUST MEANS CHAOS DRAGONS RAMPAGE AROUND UNCHECKED!
URGH...
ELMA! HARMONY DRAGONS ARE NOTHING BUT PATSIES BEING USED BY HUMANS!
GRR...!
AH, THAT'S MORE LIKE IT.
OHH.
HUH?!
YOU TWO...
ARE ALWAYS FIGHTING...
JUST 'CAUSE YOU'RE ON DIFFERENT SIDES.
EVEN THOUGH YOU'RE ACTUALLY FRIENDS.
......
......
LOOKS LIKE THEY'RE STILL FEELING SHEEPISH ABOUT THAT BIG FIGHT THE OTHER DAY.
?

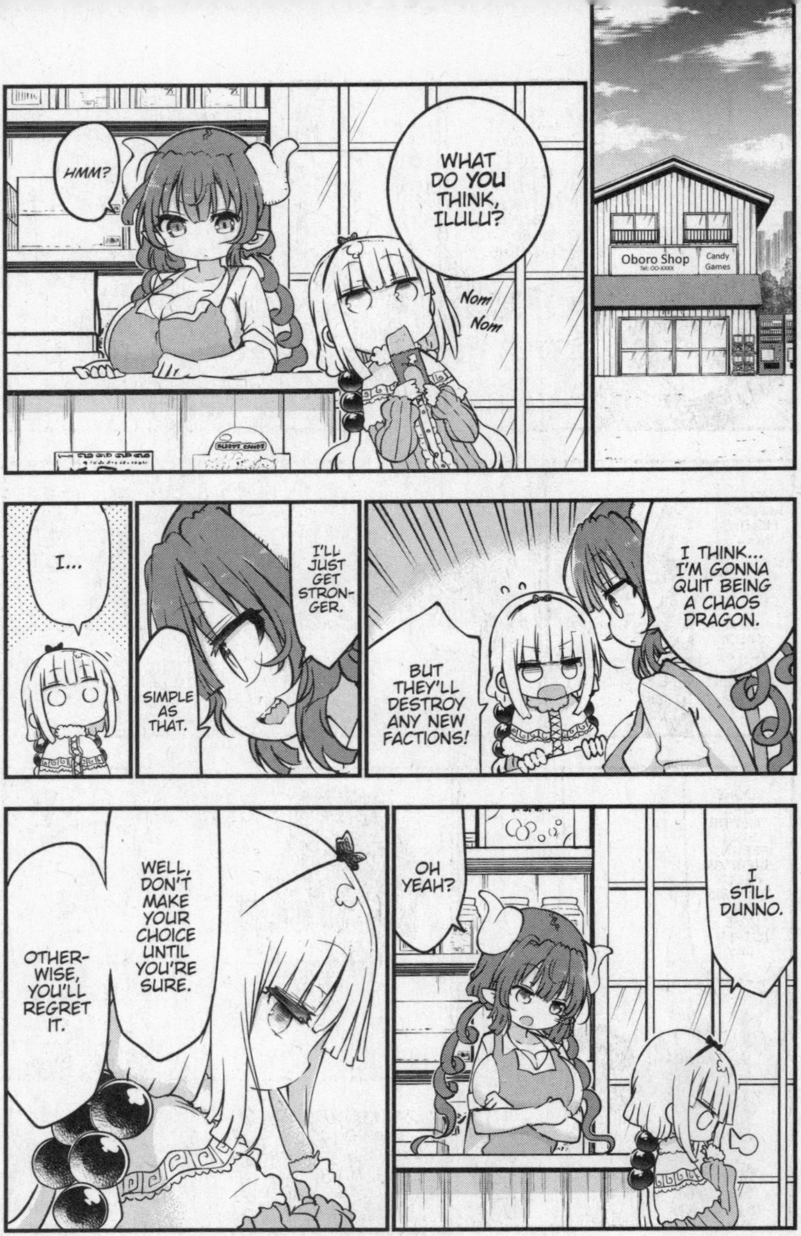
Oboro Shop
Tel: OO-XXXX
Candy Games
WHAT DO YOU THINK, ILULU?
Nom Nom
HMM?
I THINK... I'M GONNA QUIT BEING A CHAOS DRAGON.
BUT THEY'LL DESTROY ANY NEW FACTIONS!
I'LL JUST GET STRONGER.
SIMPLE AS THAT.
I...
I STILL DUNNO.
OH YEAH?
WELL, DON'T MAKE YOUR CHOICE UNTIL YOU'RE SURE.
OTHER-WISE, YOU'LL REGRET IT.

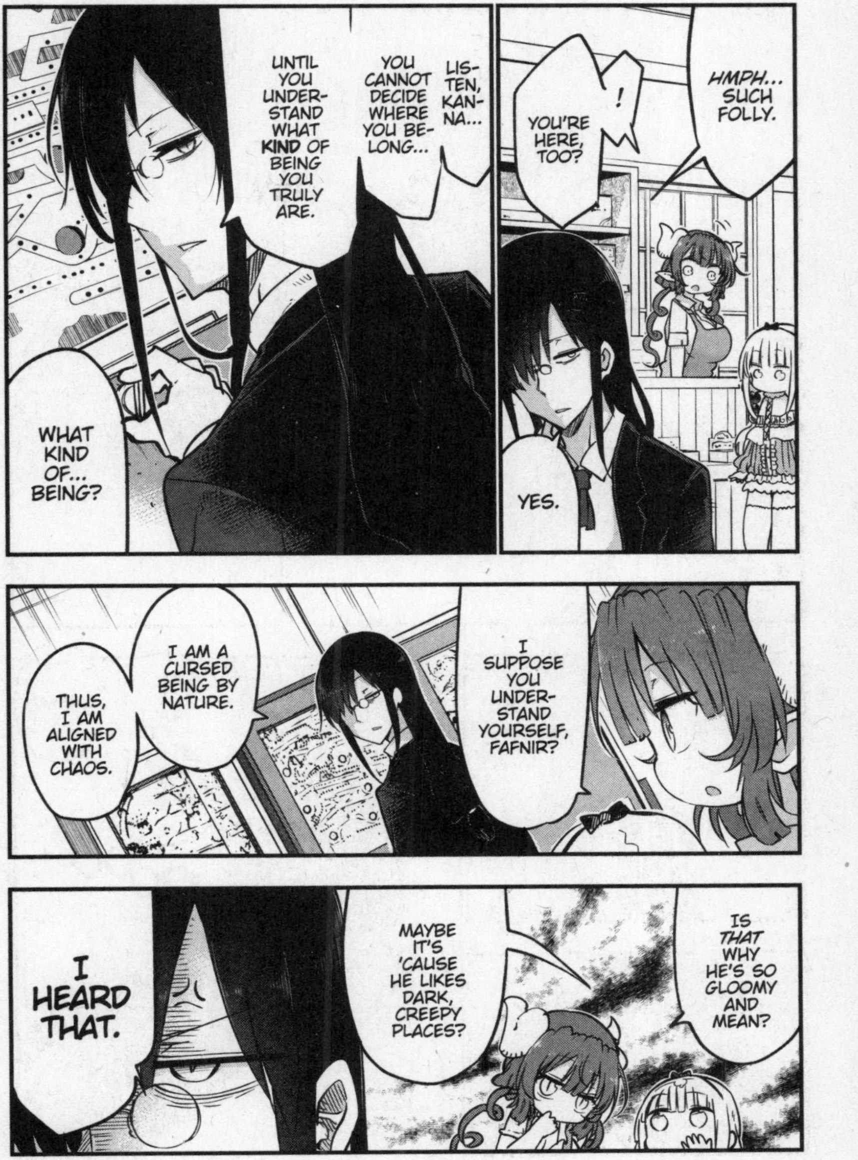
HMPH... SUCH FOLLY.
!
YOU'RE HERE, TOO?
YES.
LISTEN, KANNA...
YOU CANNOT DECIDE WHERE YOU BELONG...
UNTIL YOU UNDERSTAND WHAT KIND OF BEING YOU TRULY ARE.
WHAT KIND OF... BEING?
I SUPPOSE YOU UNDERSTAND YOURSELF, FAFNIR?
I AM A CURSED BEING BY NATURE.
THUS, I AM ALIGNED WITH CHAOS.
IS THAT WHY HE'S SO GLOOMY AND MEAN?
MAYBE IT'S 'CAUSE HE LIKES DARK, CREEPY PLACES?
I HEARD THAT.

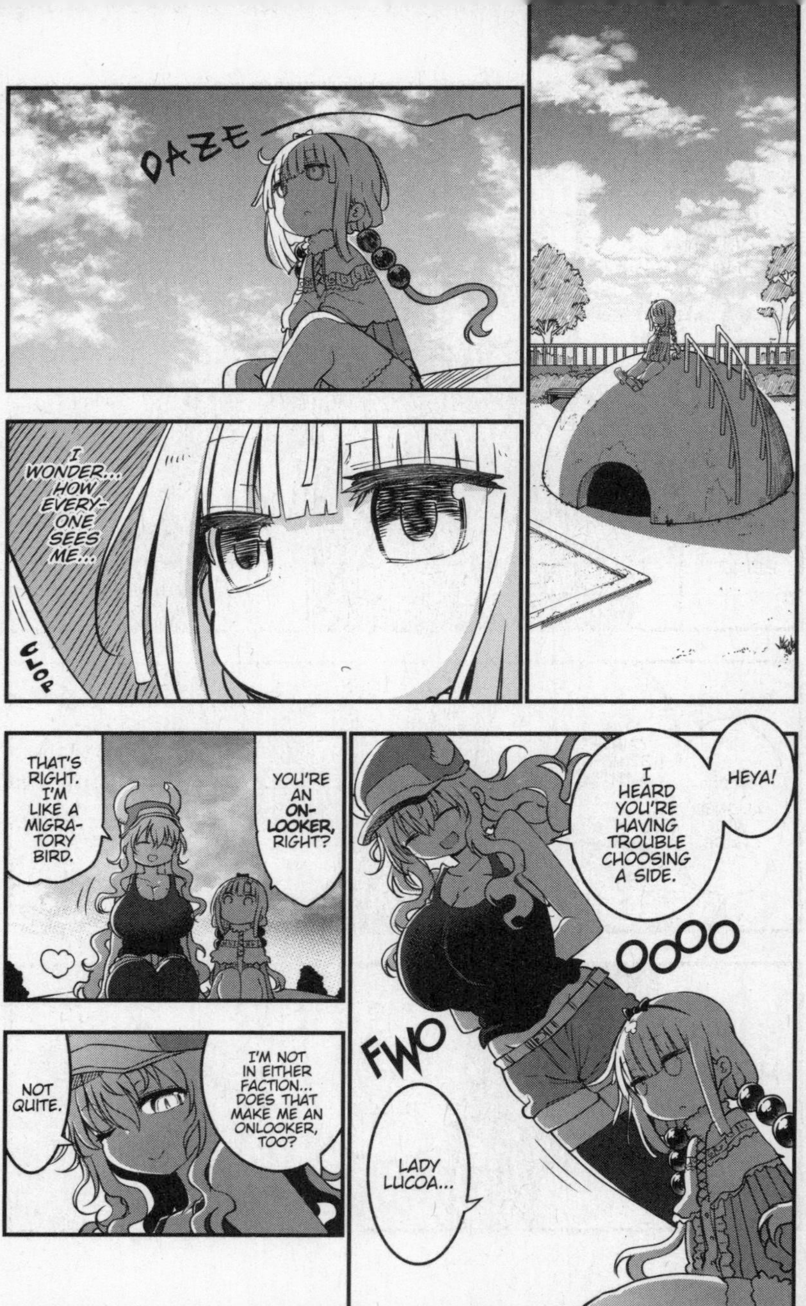
DAZE
I WONDER... HOW EVERY-ONE SEES ME...
CLOP
HEYA!
I HEARD YOU'RE HAVING TROUBLE CHOOSING A SIDE.
OOOO
FWO
LADY LUCOA...
YOU'RE AN ON-LOOKER, RIGHT?
THAT'S RIGHT. I'M LIKE A MIGRA-TORY BIRD.
I'M NOT IN EITHER FACTION... DOES THAT MAKE ME AN ONLOOKER, TOO?
NOT QUITE.

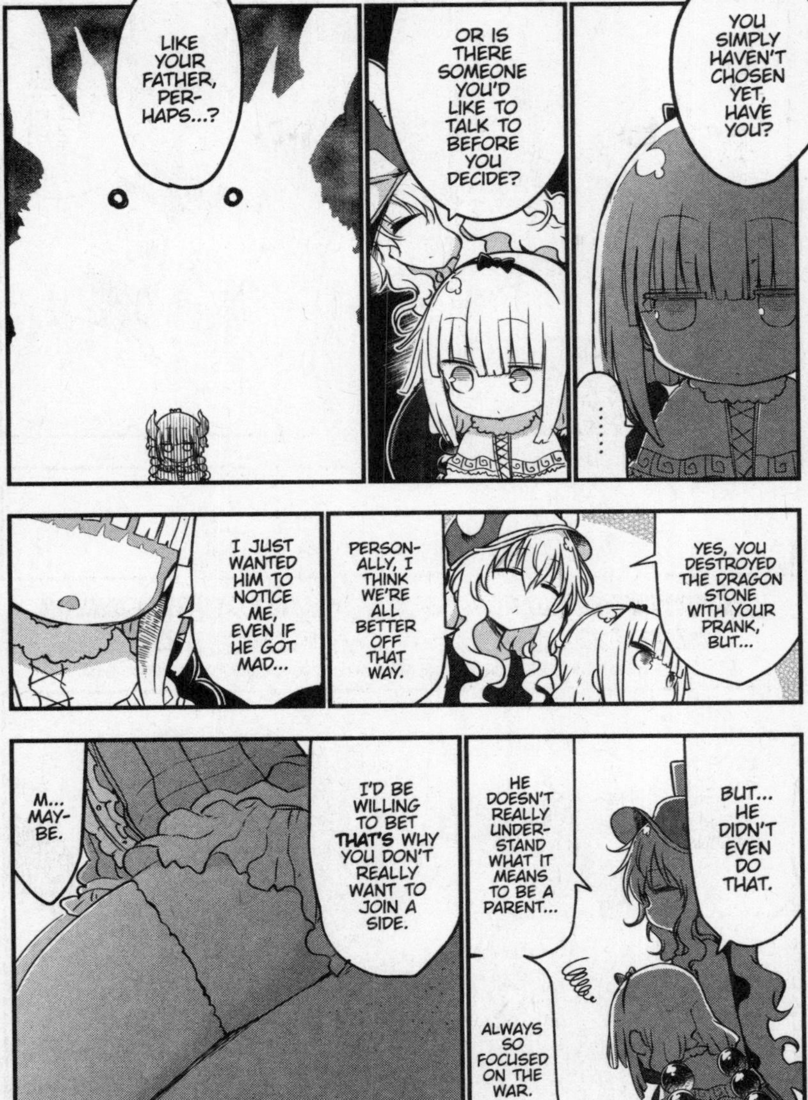
YOU SIMPLY HAVEN'T CHOSEN YET, HAVE YOU?
......
OR IS THERE SOMEONE YOU'D LIKE TO TALK TO BEFORE YOU DECIDE?
LIKE YOUR FATHER, PER-HAPS...?
YES, YOU DESTROYED THE DRAGON STONE WITH YOUR PRANK, BUT...
PERSON-ALLY, I THINK WE'RE ALL BETTER OFF THAT WAY.
I JUST WANTED HIM TO NOTICE ME, EVEN IF HE GOT MAD...
BUT... HE DIDN'T EVEN DO THAT.
HE DOESN'T REALLY UNDER-STAND WHAT IT MEANS TO BE A PARENT...
ALWAYS SO FOCUSED ON THE WAR.
I'D BE WILLING TO BET **THAT'S** WHY YOU DON'T REALLY WANT TO JOIN A SIDE.
M... MAY-BE.

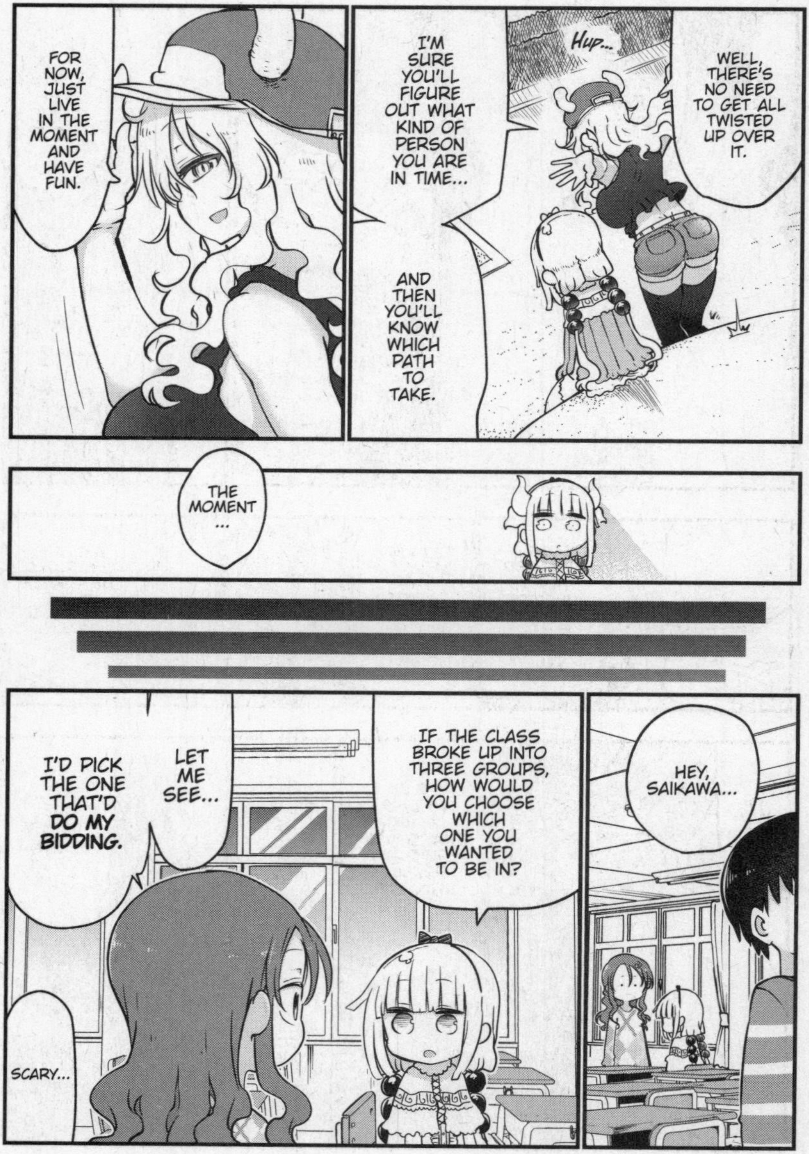
WELL, THERE'S NO NEED TO GET ALL TWISTED UP OVER IT.
Hup...
I'M SURE YOU'LL FIGURE OUT WHAT KIND OF PERSON YOU ARE IN TIME...
AND THEN YOU'LL KNOW WHICH PATH TO TAKE.
FOR NOW, JUST LIVE IN THE MOMENT AND HAVE FUN.
THE MOMENT ...
HEY, SAIKAWA...
IF THE CLASS BROKE UP INTO THREE GROUPS, HOW WOULD YOU CHOOSE WHICH ONE YOU WANTED TO BE IN?
LET ME SEE...
I'D PICK THE ONE THAT'D DO MY BIDDING.
SCARY...

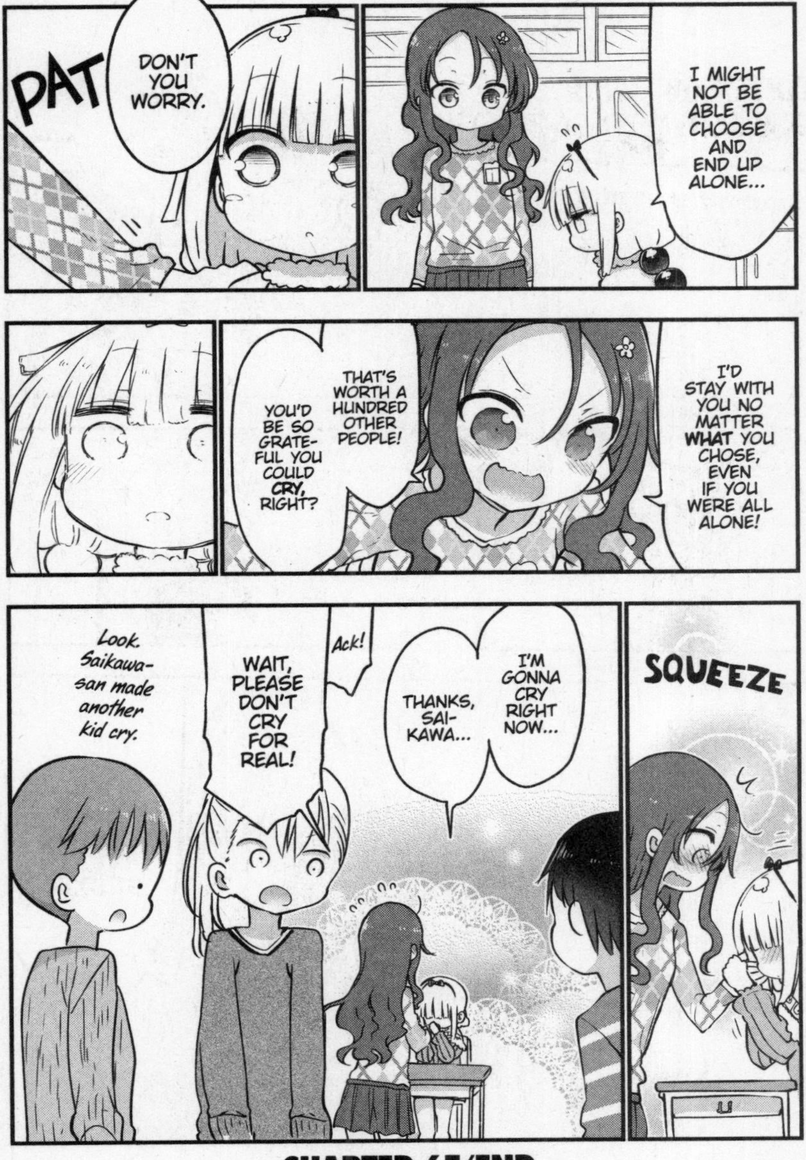
I MIGHT NOT BE ABLE TO CHOOSE AND END UP ALONE...
PAT
DON'T YOU WORRY.
I'D STAY WITH YOU NO MATTER **WHAT** YOU CHOSE, EVEN IF YOU WERE ALL ALONE!
THAT'S WORTH A HUNDRED OTHER PEOPLE!
YOU'D BE SO GRATE-FUL YOU COULD **CRY**, RIGHT?
SQUEEZE
I'M GONNA CRY RIGHT NOW...
THANKS, SAI-KAWA...
Ack!
WAIT, PLEASE DON'T CRY FOR REAL!
Look. Saikawa-san made another kid cry.

CHAPTER 67/END

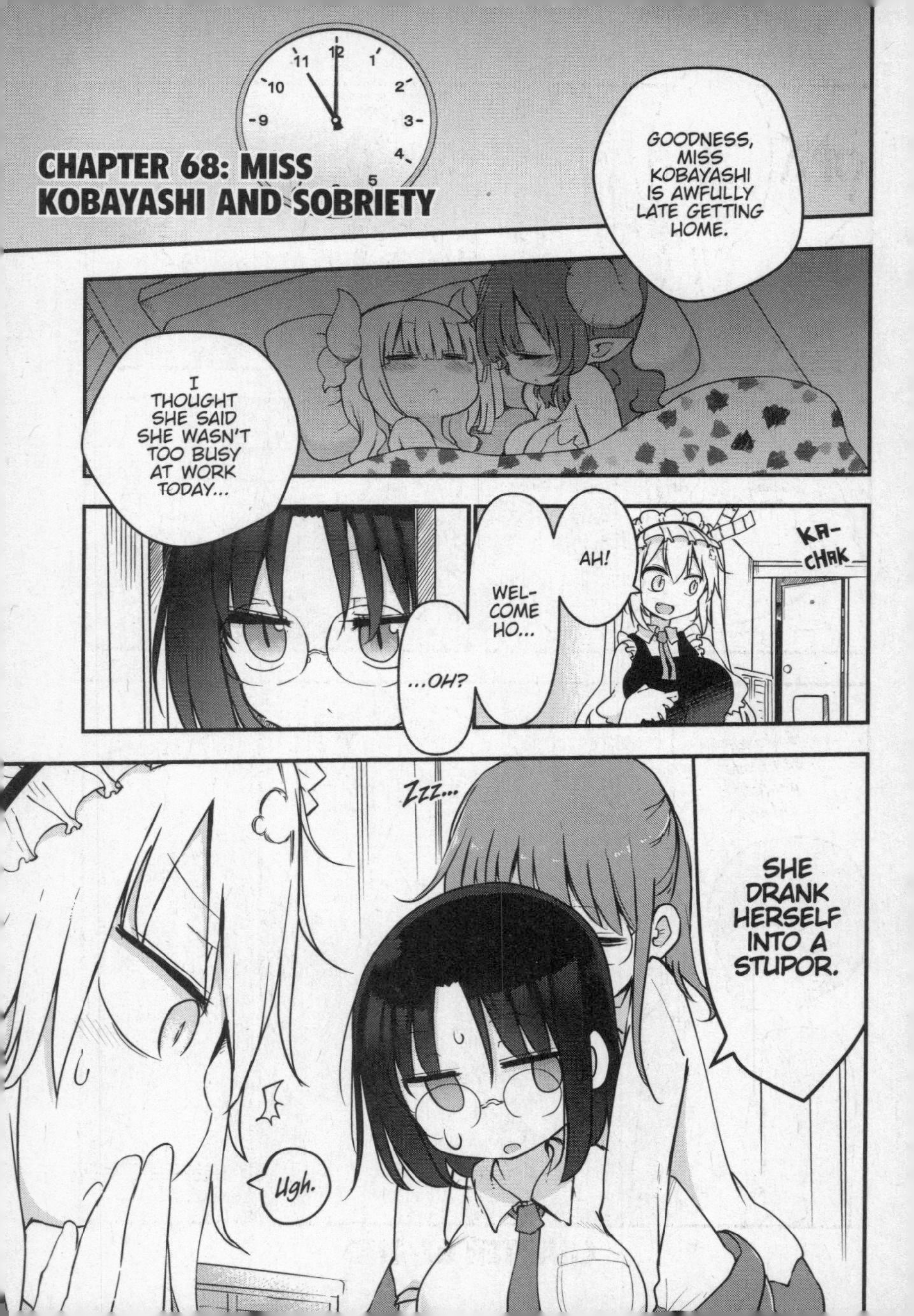
CHAPTER 68: MISS KOBAYASHI AND SOBRIETY
GOODNESS, MISS KOBAYASHI IS AWFULLY LATE GETTING HOME.
I THOUGHT SHE SAID SHE WASN'T TOO BUSY AT WORK TODAY...
KA-CHAK
AH!
WEL-COME HO...
...OH?
SHE DRANK HERSELF INTO A STUPOR.
ZZZ...
Ugh.

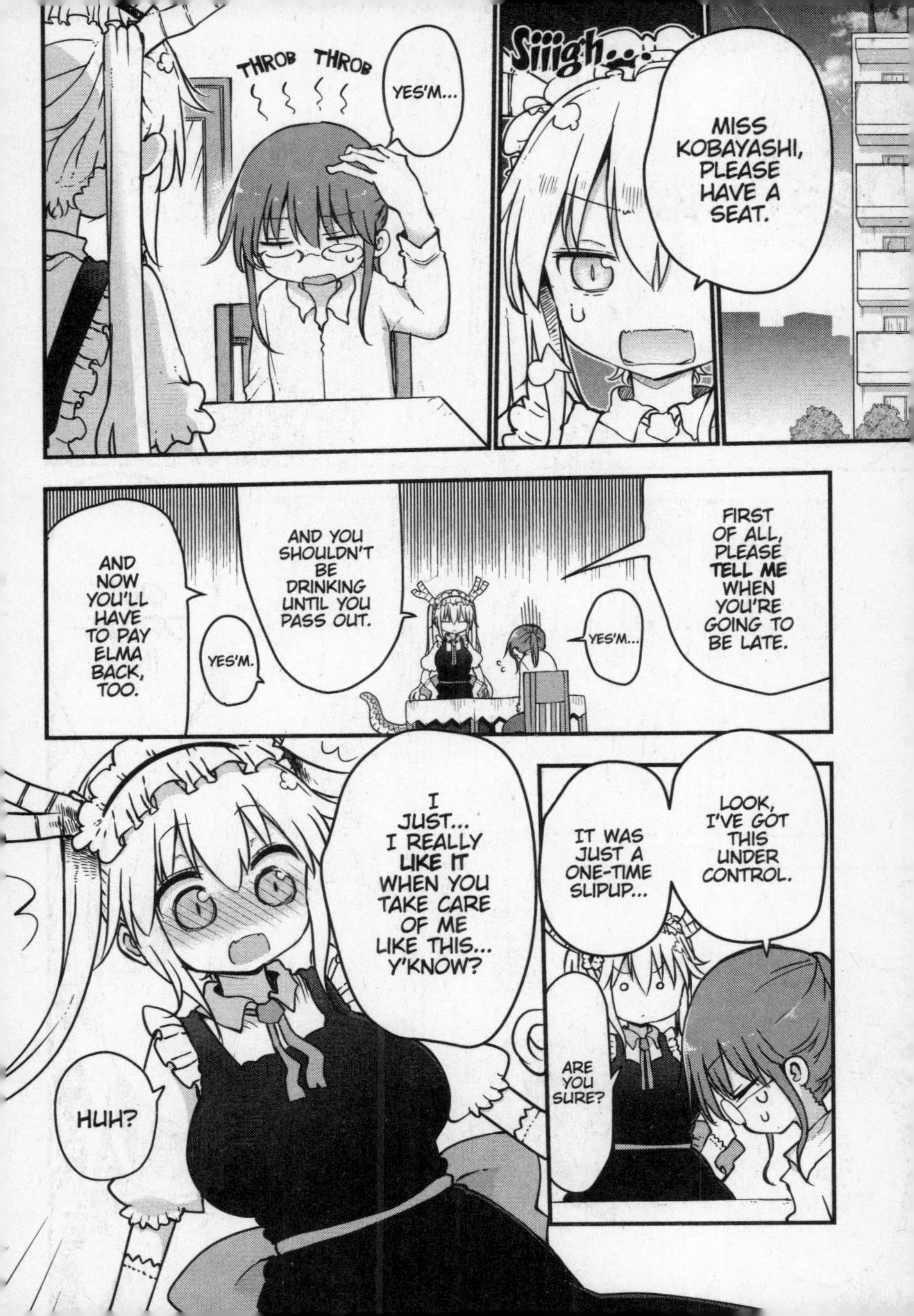
Siiigh...
MISS KOBAYASHI, PLEASE HAVE A SEAT.
THROB THROB
YES'M...
FIRST OF ALL, PLEASE TELL ME WHEN YOU'RE GOING TO BE LATE.
YES'M...
AND YOU SHOULDN'T BE DRINKING UNTIL YOU PASS OUT.
YES'M.
AND NOW YOU'LL HAVE TO PAY ELMA BACK, TOO.
LOOK, I'VE GOT THIS UNDER CONTROL.
IT WAS JUST A ONE-TIME SLIPUP...
ARE YOU SURE?
I JUST... I REALLY LIKE IT WHEN YOU TAKE CARE OF ME LIKE THIS... Y'KNOW?
HUH?

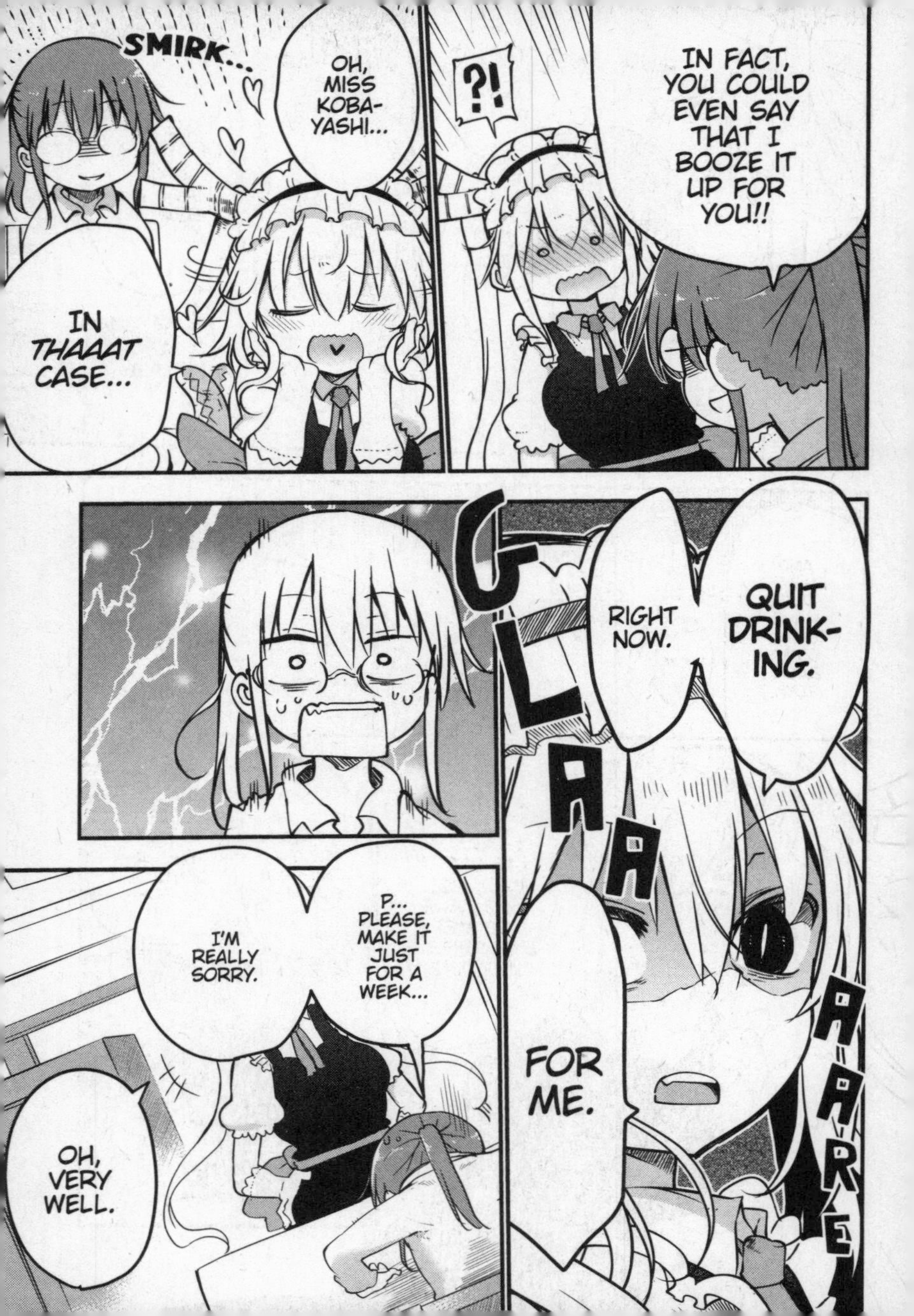
IN FACT, YOU COULD EVEN SAY THAT I BOOZE IT UP FOR YOU!!
?!
OH, MISS KOBA-YASHI...
SMIRK...
IN THAAAT CASE...
QUIT DRINKING.
RIGHT NOW.
GLAAAARE
FOR ME.
P... PLEASE, MAKE IT JUST FOR A WEEK...
I'M REALLY SORRY.
OH, VERY WELL.

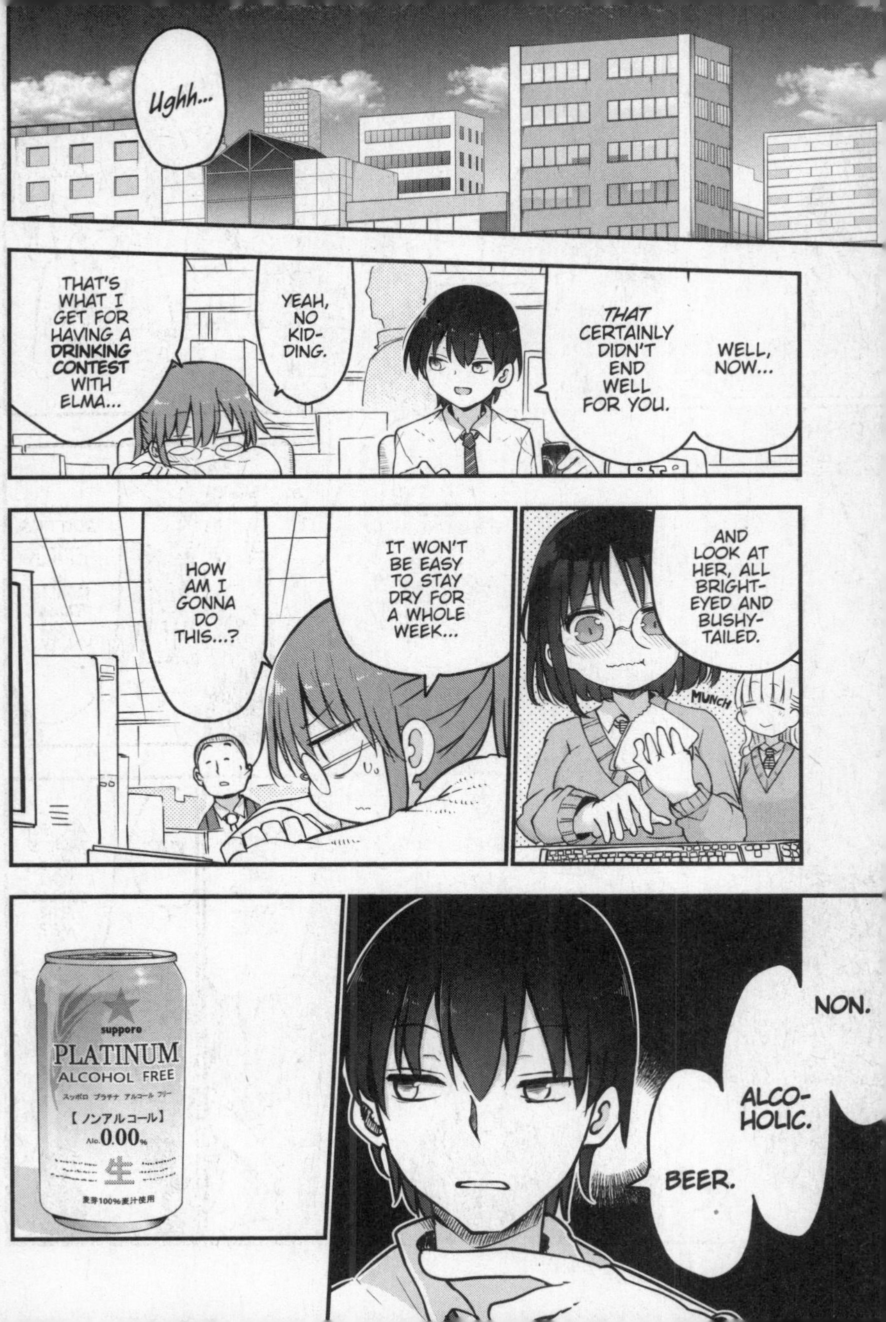
Ughh...
WELL, NOW...
THAT CERTAINLY DIDN'T END WELL FOR YOU.
YEAH, NO KID-DING.
THAT'S WHAT I GET FOR HAVING A DRINKING CONTEST WITH ELMA...
AND LOOK AT HER, ALL BRIGHT-EYED AND BUSHY-TAILED.
MUNCH
IT WON'T BE EASY TO STAY DRY FOR A WHOLE WEEK...
HOW AM I GONNA DO THIS...?
NON.
ALCO-HOLIC.
BEER.
sapporo
PLATINUM
ALCOHOL FREE
スッポロ プラチナ アルコール フリー
【ノンアルコール】
Alc. 0.00%
生
麦芽100%麦汁使用

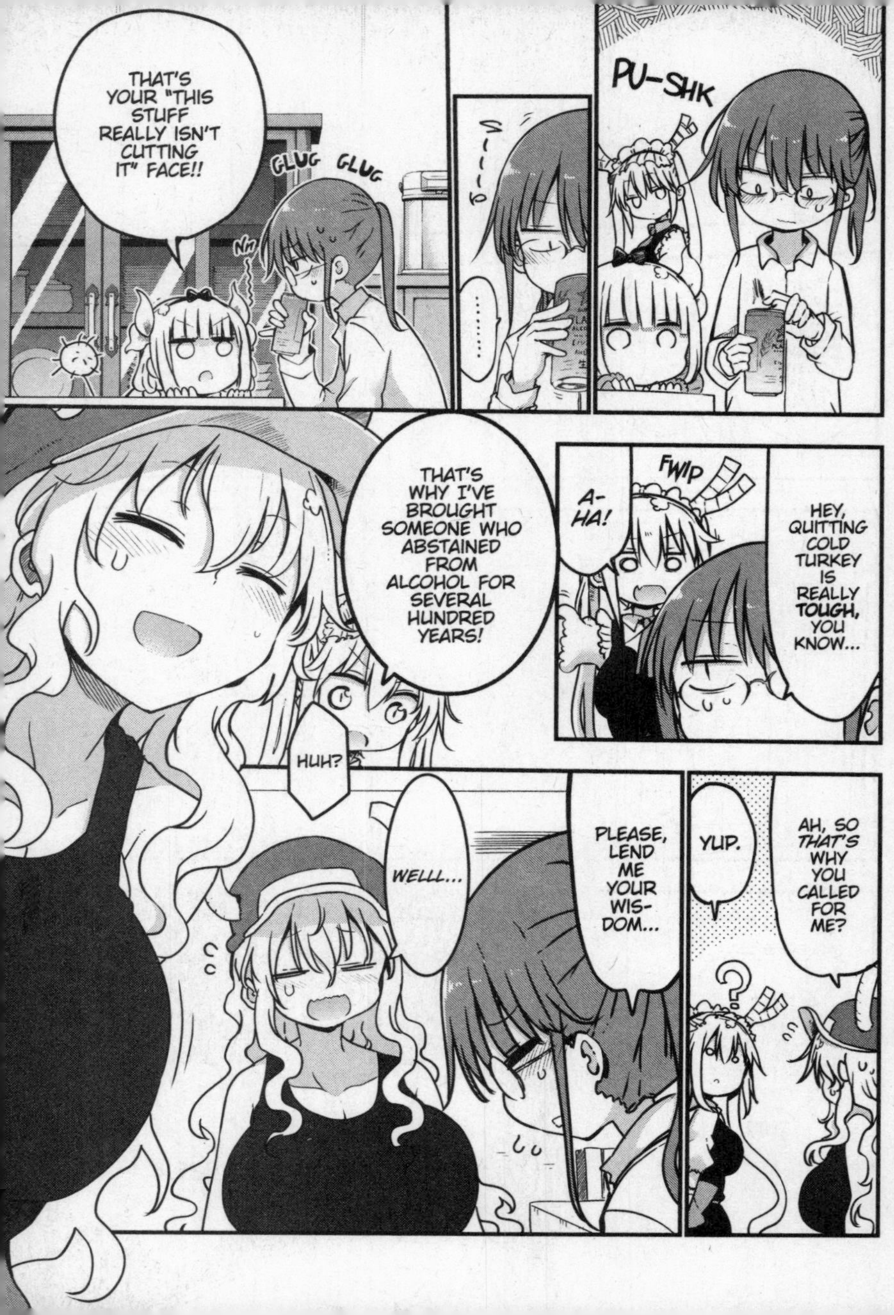

PU-SHK
......
THAT'S YOUR "THIS STUFF REALLY ISN'T CUTTING IT" FACE!!
GLUG GLUG
FWIP
HEY, QUITTING COLD TURKEY IS REALLY TOUGH, YOU KNOW...
A-HA!
THAT'S WHY I'VE BROUGHT SOMEONE WHO ABSTAINED FROM ALCOHOL FOR SEVERAL HUNDRED YEARS!
HUH?
AH, SO THAT'S WHY YOU CALLED FOR ME?
YUP.
PLEASE, LEND ME YOUR WIS-DOM...
WELLL...

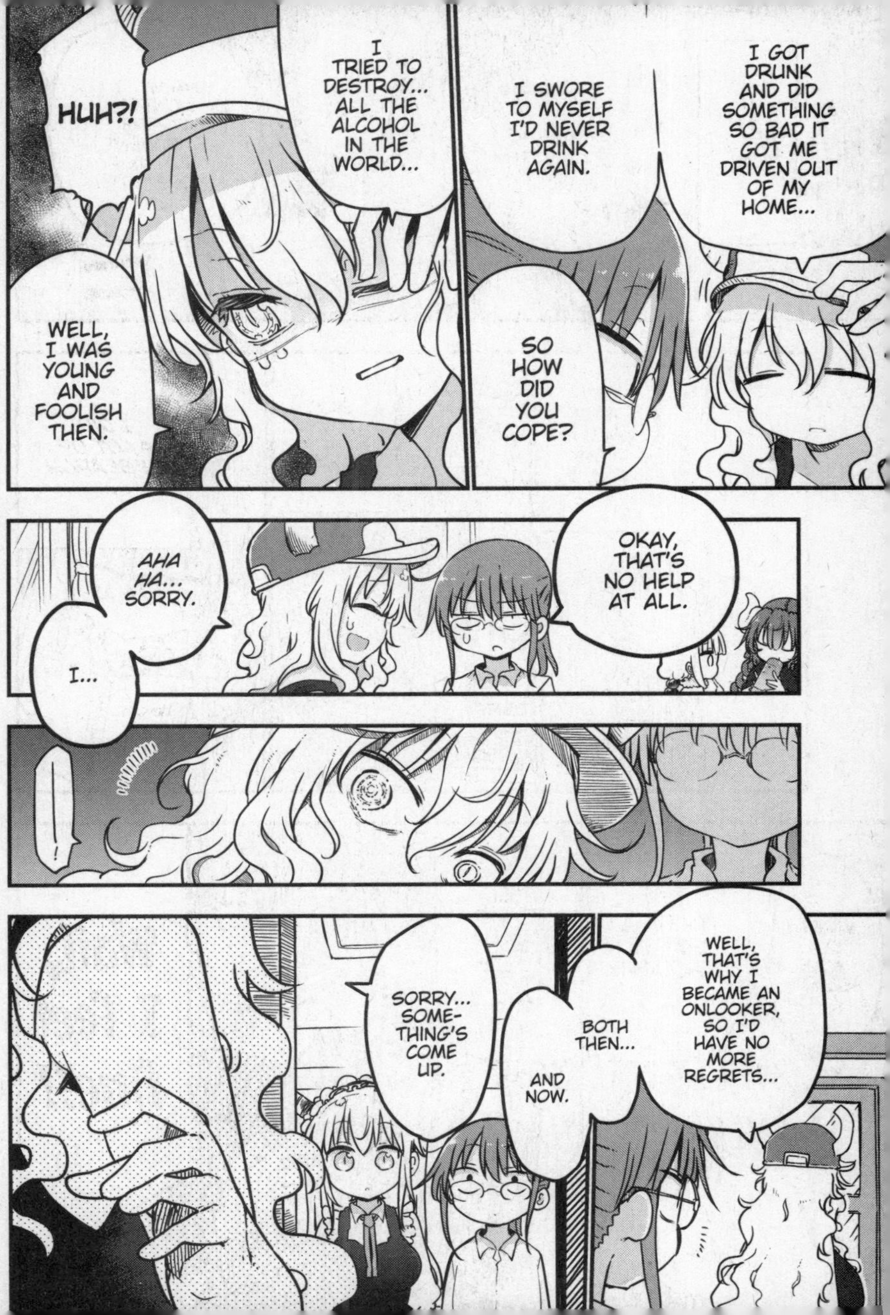
I GOT DRUNK AND DID SOMETHING SO BAD IT GOT ME DRIVEN OUT OF MY HOME...
I SWORE TO MYSELF I'D NEVER DRINK AGAIN.
SO HOW DID YOU COPE?
I TRIED TO DESTROY... ALL THE ALCOHOL IN THE WORLD...
HUH?!
WELL, I WAS YOUNG AND FOOLISH THEN.
OKAY, THAT'S NO HELP AT ALL.
AHA HA... SORRY.
I...
!
WELL, THAT'S WHY I BECAME AN ONLOOKER, SO I'D HAVE NO MORE REGRETS...
BOTH THEN...
AND NOW.
SORRY... SOME-THING'S COME UP.

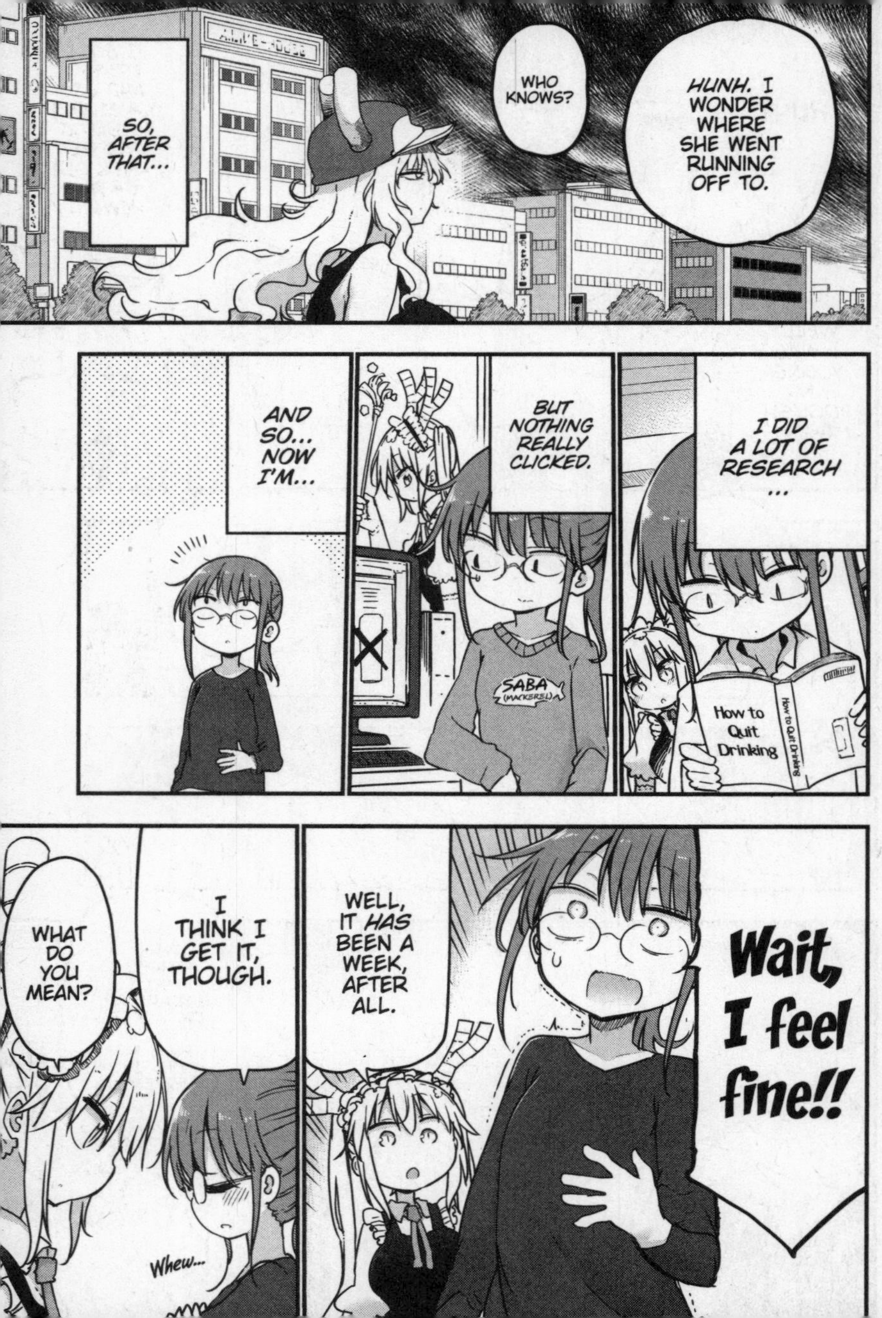
HUNH. I WONDER WHERE SHE WENT RUNNING OFF TO.
WHO KNOWS?
SO, AFTER THAT...
I DID A LOT OF RESEARCH ...
How to Quit Drinking
How to Quit Drinking
BUT NOTHING REALLY CLICKED.
SABA (MACKEREL)
AND SO... NOW I'M...
Wait, I feel fine!!
WELL, IT HAS BEEN A WEEK, AFTER ALL.
I THINK I GET IT, THOUGH.
WHAT DO YOU MEAN?
Whew...

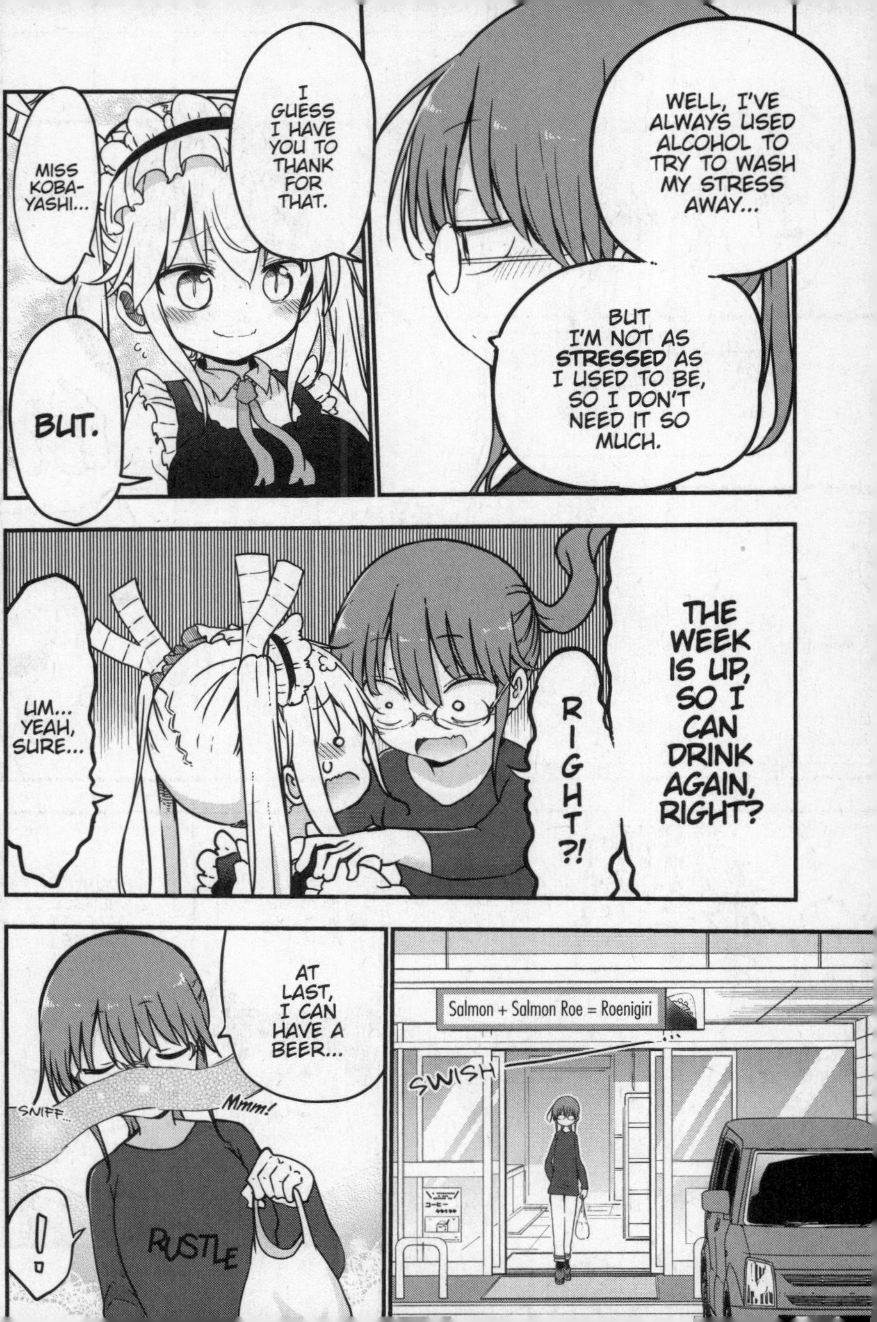
WELL, I'VE ALWAYS USED ALCOHOL TO TRY TO WASH MY STRESS AWAY...
BUT I'M NOT AS STRESSED AS I USED TO BE, SO I DON'T NEED IT SO MUCH.
I GUESS I HAVE YOU TO THANK FOR THAT.
MISS KOBA-YASHI...
BUT.
THE WEEK IS UP, SO I CAN DRINK AGAIN, RIGHT?
RIGHT?!
UM... YEAH, SURE...
Salmon + Salmon Roe = Roenigiri
SWISH
...
AT LAST, I CAN HAVE A BEER...
Mmm!
SNIFF...
!
RUSTLE

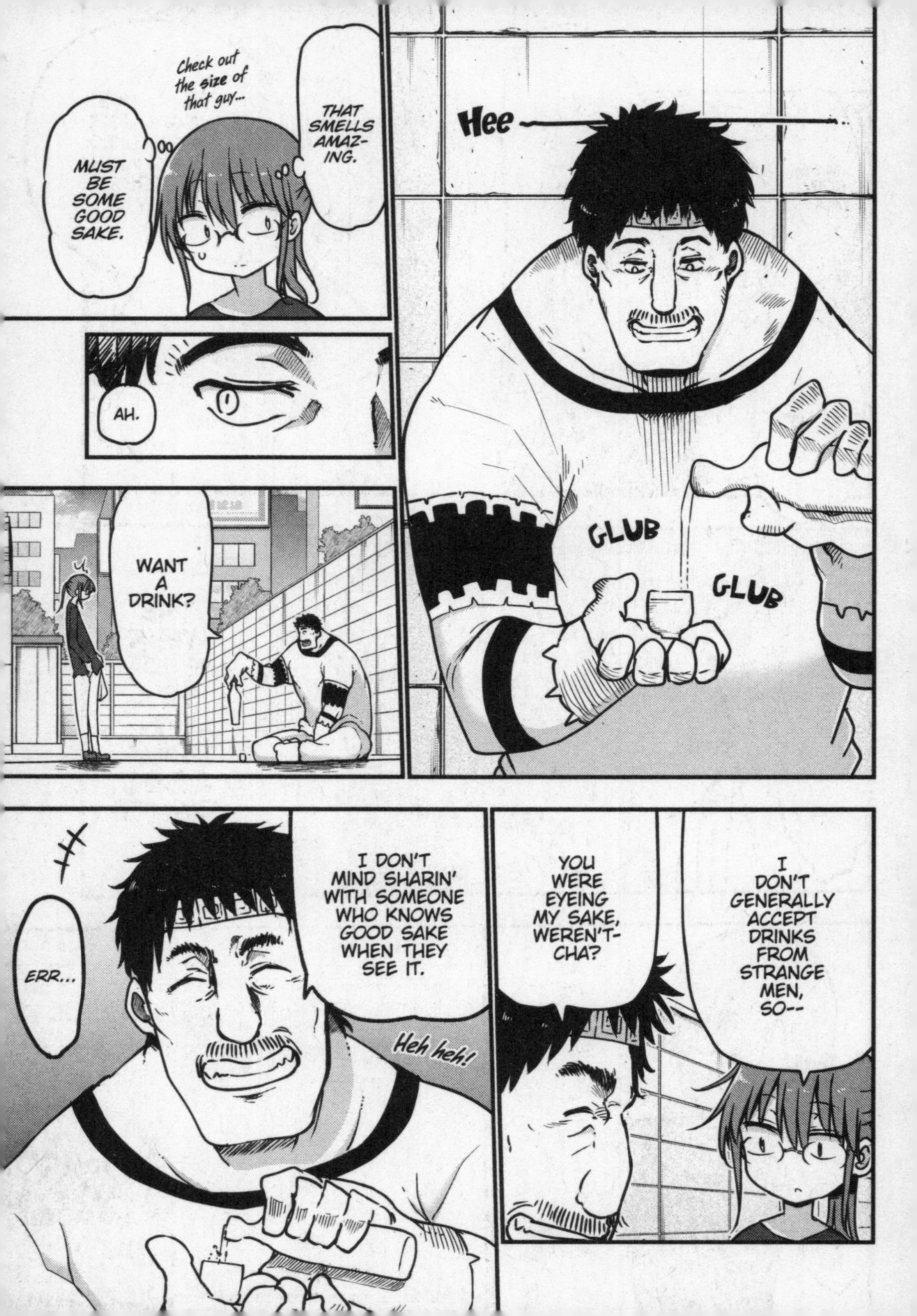

Hee——..
GLUB
GLUB
THAT SMELLS AMAZING.
Check out the size of that guy...
MUST BE SOME GOOD SAKE.
AH.
WANT A DRINK?
I DON'T GENERALLY ACCEPT DRINKS FROM STRANGE MEN, SO--
YOU WERE EYEING MY SAKE, WEREN'T-CHA?
I DON'T MIND SHARIN' WITH SOMEONE WHO KNOWS GOOD SAKE WHEN THEY SEE IT.
Heh heh!
ERR...

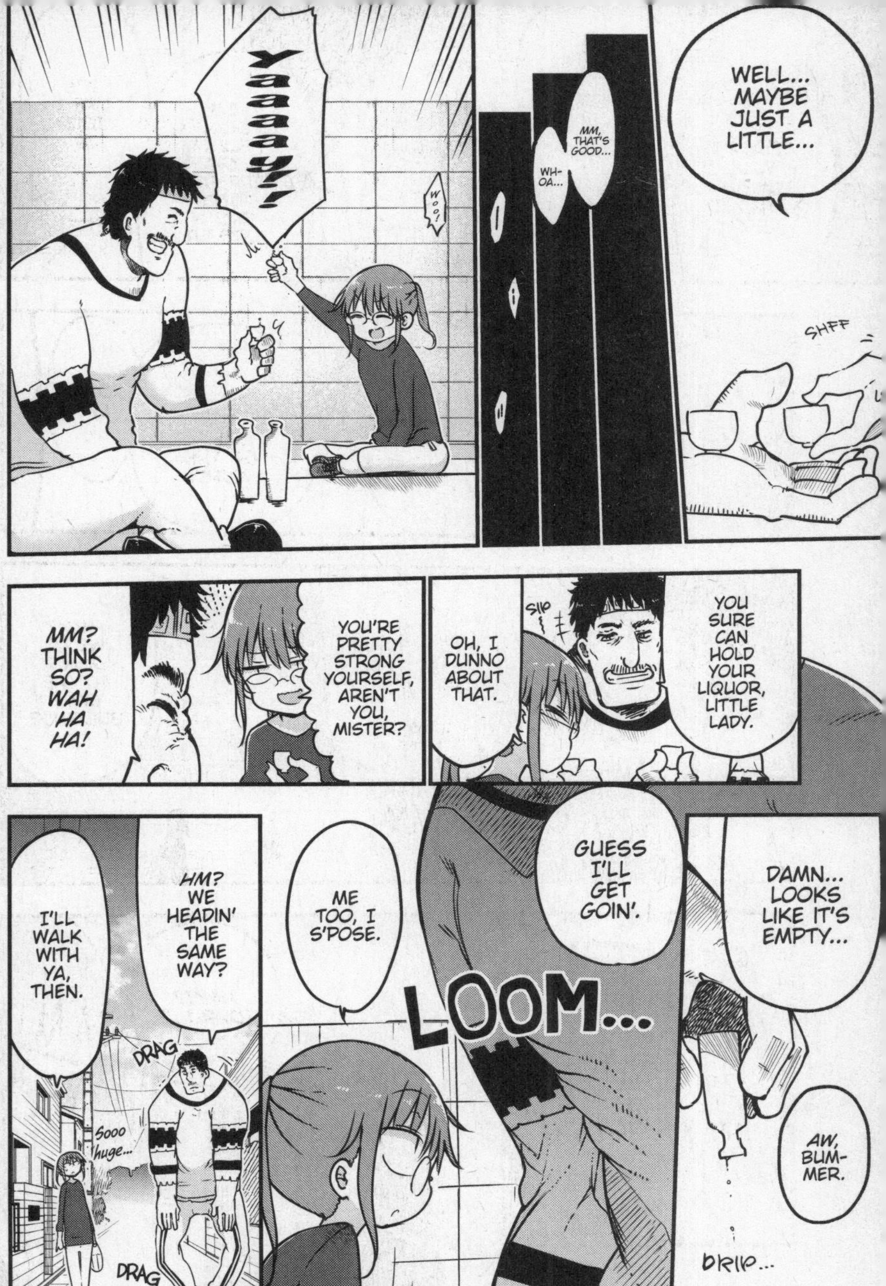
WELL... MAYBE JUST A LITTLE...
SHFF
MM, THAT'S GOOD...
WH-OA...
Yaaaay!!
Woo!
YOU SURE CAN HOLD YOUR LIQUOR, LITTLE LADY.
SIP
OH, I DUNNO ABOUT THAT.
YOU'RE PRETTY STRONG YOURSELF, AREN'T YOU, MISTER?
MM? THINK SO? WAH HA HA!
DAMN... LOOKS LIKE IT'S EMPTY...
AW, BUMMER.
DRIP...
GUESS I'LL GET GOIN'.
LOOM...
ME TOO, I S'POSE.
HM? WE HEADIN' THE SAME WAY?
I'LL WALK WITH YA, THEN.
DRAG
Sooo huge...
DRAG

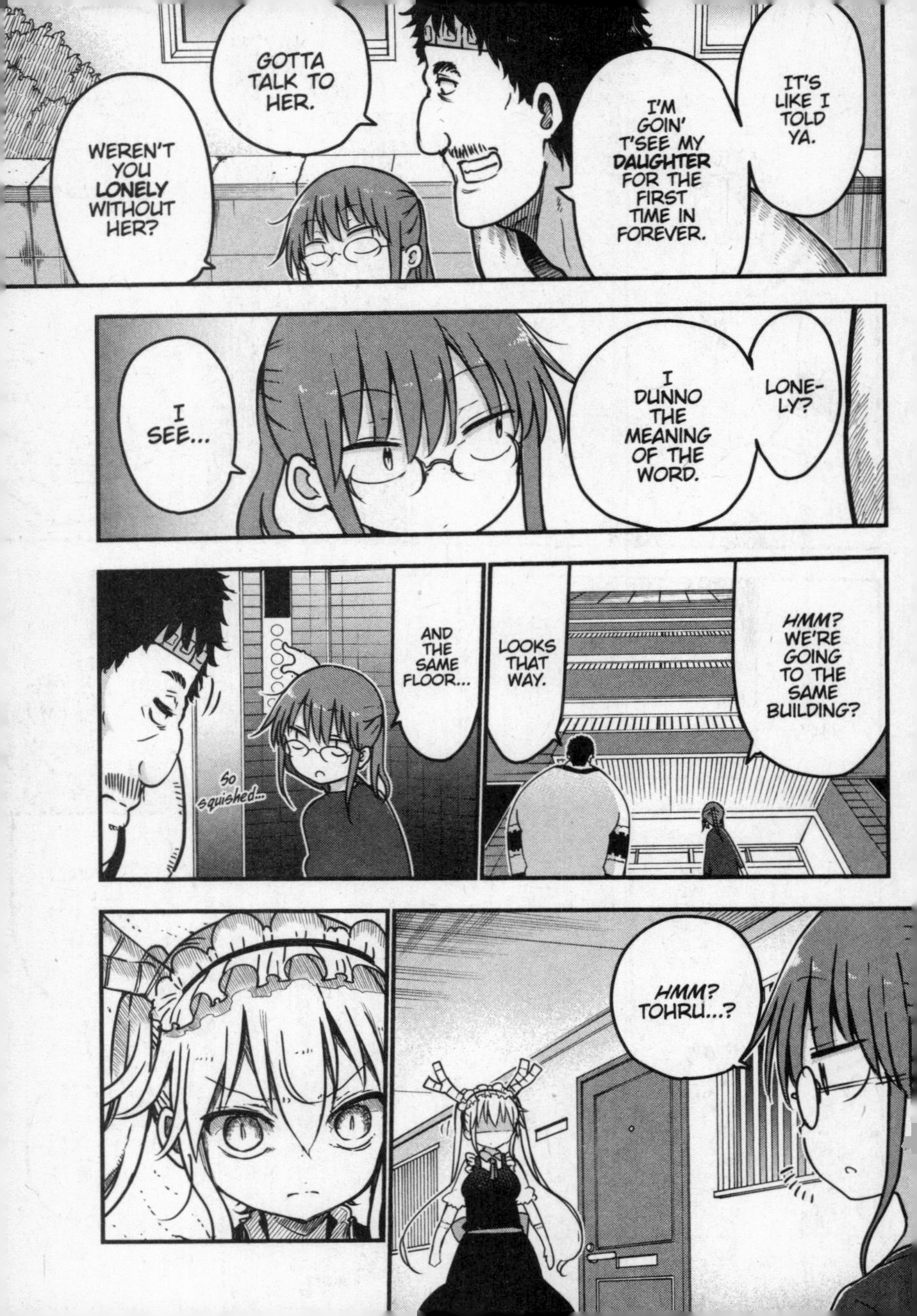
IT'S LIKE I TOLD YA.
I'M GOIN' T'SEE MY DAUGHTER FOR THE FIRST TIME IN FOREVER.
GOTTA TALK TO HER.
WEREN'T YOU LONELY WITHOUT HER?
LONE-LY?
I DUNNO THE MEANING OF THE WORD.
I SEE...
HMM? WE'RE GOING TO THE SAME BUILDING?
LOOKS THAT WAY.
AND THE SAME FLOOR...
So squished...
HMM? TOHRU...?

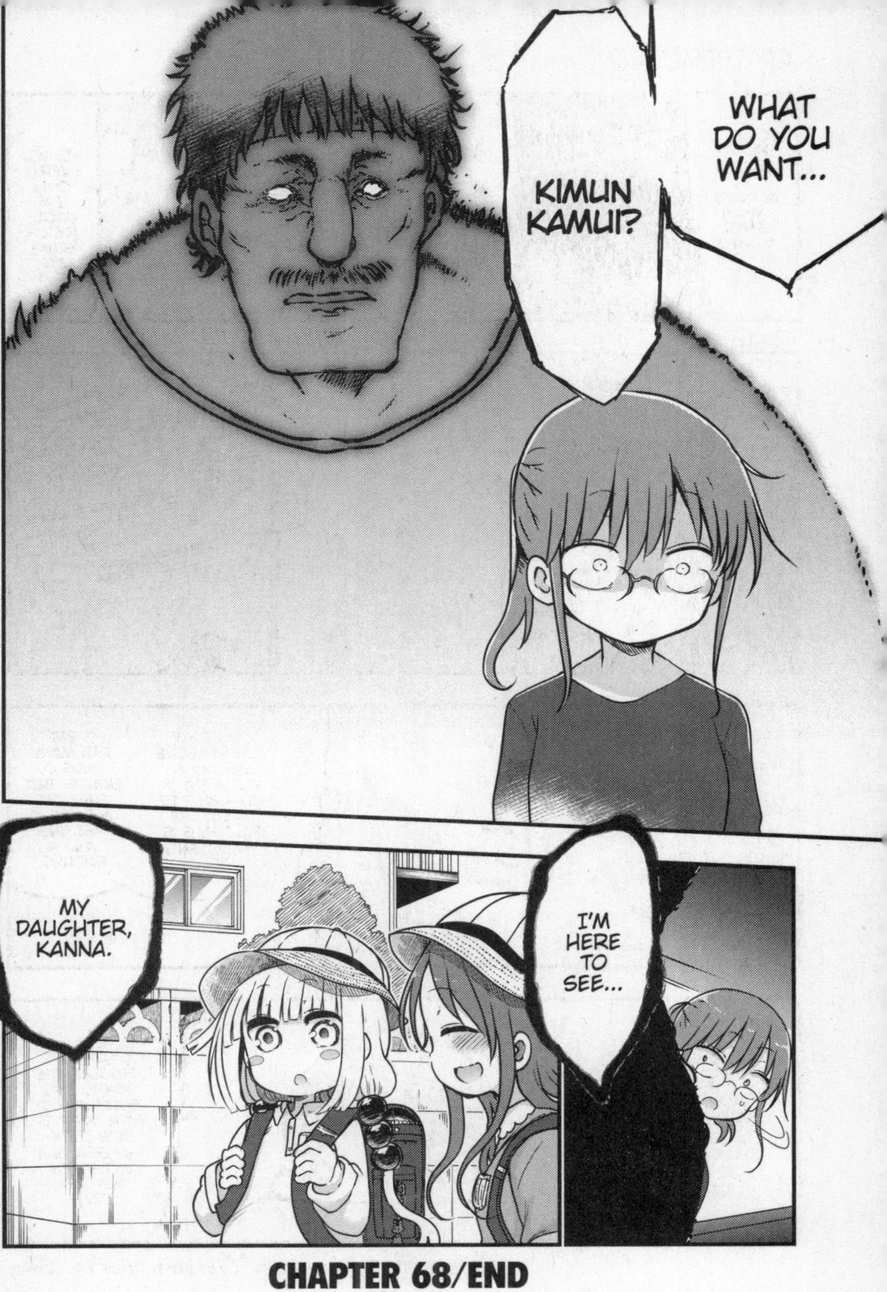
WHAT DO YOU WANT...
KIMUN KAMUI?
I'M HERE TO SEE...
MY DAUGHTER, KANNA.

CHAPTER 68/END

AFTERWORD

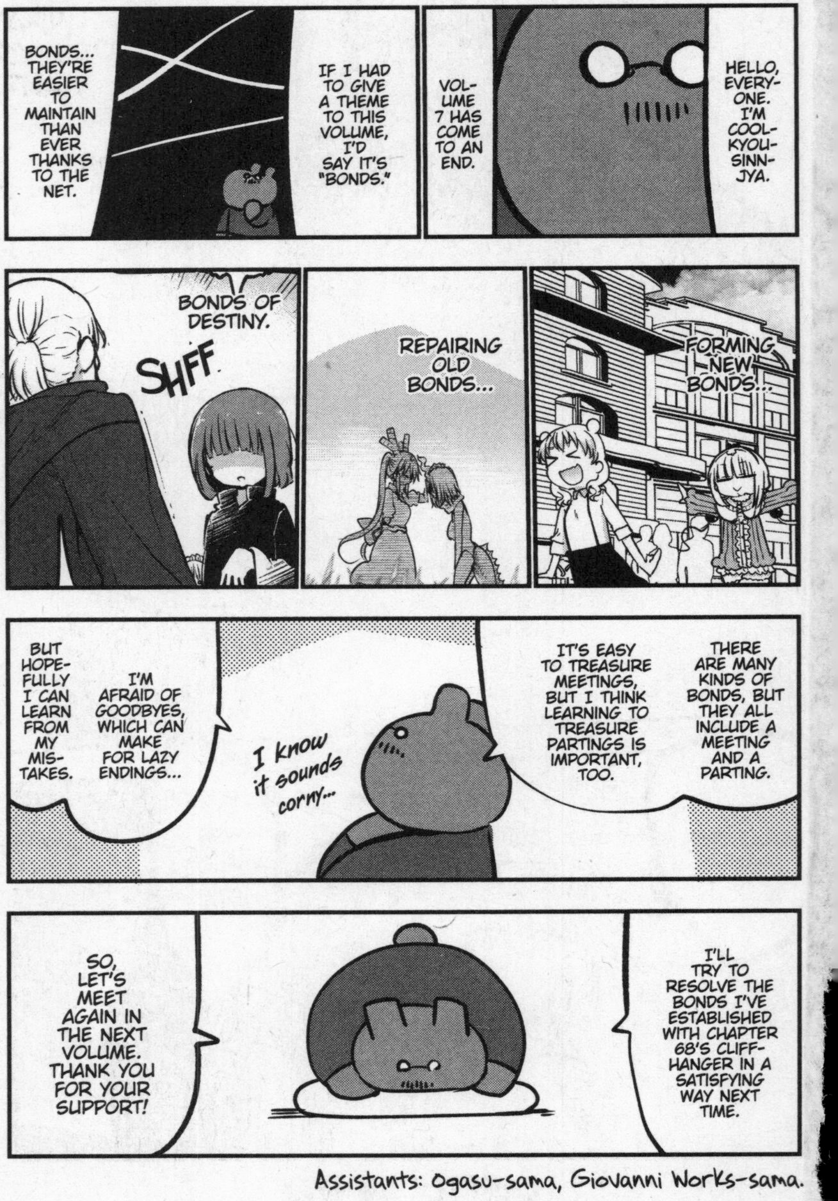
HELLO, EVERYONE. I'M COOL-KYOU-SINNJYA.
VOLUME 7 HAS COME TO AN END.
IF I HAD TO GIVE A THEME TO THIS VOLUME, I'D SAY IT'S "BONDS."
BONDS... THEY'RE EASIER TO MAINTAIN THAN EVER THANKS TO THE NET.
FORMING NEW BONDS...
REPAIRING OLD BONDS...
BONDS OF DESTINY.
SHFF
THERE ARE MANY KINDS OF BONDS, BUT THEY ALL INCLUDE A MEETING AND A PARTING.
IT'S EASY TO TREASURE MEETINGS, BUT I THINK LEARNING TO TREASURE PARTINGS IS IMPORTANT, TOO.
I know it sounds corny...
I'M AFRAID OF GOODBYES, WHICH CAN MAKE FOR LAZY ENDINGS...
BUT HOPEFULLY I CAN LEARN FROM MY MISTAKES.
I'LL TRY TO RESOLVE THE BONDS I'VE ESTABLISHED WITH CHAPTER 68'S CLIFFHANGER IN A SATISFYING WAY NEXT TIME.
SO, LET'S MEET AGAIN IN THE NEXT VOLUME. THANK YOU FOR YOUR SUPPORT!

Assistants: Ogasu-sama, Giovanni Works-sama.

SEVEN SEAS ENTERTAINMENT PRESENTS

Miss Kobayashi's Dragon Maid

VOL. 7

story and art by coolkyousinnjya

TRANSLATION
Jenny McKeon

ADAPTATION
Shanti Whitesides

LETTERING
Jennifer Skarupa

LOGO DESIGN
KC Fabellon

COVER DESIGN
Nicky Lim

PROOFREADING
Brett Hallahan

ASSISTANT EDITOR
Jenn Grunigen

PRODUCTION ASSISTANT
CK Russell

PRODUCTION MANAGER
Lissa Pattillo

EDITOR-IN-CHIEF
Adam Arnold

PUBLISHER
Jason DeAngelis

First published in Japan in 2018 by Futabasha Publishers Ltd., Tokyo.
English version published by Seven Seas Entertainment, LLC.
Under license from Futabasha Publishers Ltd.

ISBN: 978-1-626928-98-5

Printed in Canada

First Printing: November 2018

10 9 8 7 6 5 4 3 2 1

READING DIRECTIONS

This book reads from ***right to left***, Japanese style. If this is your first time reading manga, you start reading from the top right panel on each page and take it from there. If you get lost, just follow the numbered diagram here. It may seem backwards at first, but you'll get the hang of it! Have fun!!

1
2
3
4
5
6
7
8
9

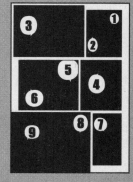